The New Designer

The MIT Press   Cambridge, Massachusetts   London, England

The New Designer

REJECTING MYTHS, EMBRACING CHANGE

Manuel Lima

The MIT Press would like to thank the anonymous peer reviewers who provided comments on drafts of this book. The generous work of academic experts is essential for establishing the authority and quality of our publications. We acknowledge with gratitude the contributions of these otherwise uncredited readers.

This book was set in Tasman and Solano by the MIT Press. Printed and bound in the United States of America.

Library of Congress Cataloging-in-Publication Data

Names: Lima, Manuel, 1978- author.
Title: The new designer : rejecting myths, embracing change / Manuel Lima.
Description: Cambridge, Massachusetts ; London, England : The MIT Press, [2023] | Includes bibliographical references and index.
Identifiers: LCCN 2022021526 (print) | LCCN 2022021527 (ebook) | ISBN 9780262047630 (hardcover) | ISBN 9780262373012 (epub) | ISBN 9780262373029 (pdf)
Subjects: LCSH: Industrial design—Vocational guidance. | Design—Philosophy. | Design—Vocational guidance. | Designers—Psychology.
Classification: LCC TS171.4 .L56 2023 (print) | LCC TS171.4 (ebook) | DDC 124—dc23/eng/20220809
LC record available at https://lccn.loc.gov/2022021526
LC ebook record available at https://lccn.loc.gov/2022021527

10 9 8 7 6 5 4 3 2 1

To Chloe and Camila, who have always taught me to embrace change with open arms.

Contents

Preface

Today it has become necessary to demolish the myth of the "star" artist who only produces masterpieces for a small group of ultra-intelligent people. It must be understood that as long as art stands aside from the problems of life it will only interest a very few people. Culture today is becoming a mass affair, and the artist must step down from his pedestal and be prepared to make a sign for a butcher's shop (if he knows how to do it). The artist must cast off the last rags of romanticism and become active as a man among men, well up in present-day techniques, materials and working methods. Without losing his innate aesthetic sense he must be able to respond with humility and competence to the demands his neighbors may make of him.

—Bruno Munari[1]

I was sixteen when I read this passage from Bruno Munari in his seminal work *Design as Art* (1966). The words have been awake in my brain ever since. This pragmatic, utilitarian, and pluralistic view of the design discipline, so often regarded as artsy or superficial, was immensely powerful and evocative. This book, with passages like this, was one of the reasons I decided to pursue a design career.

Later, as an undergraduate industrial design student, I learned that design can be shallow at times, but it also can be a great force for good, able to improve the human condition with a singular solution. My very first project at college was an enlightening one. We were to imagine an apocalyptic scenario where most human technology had been destroyed or deemed unusable. We were then asked to create a survival tool from the trash. I ended up creating a fishing rod with a mix of natural ingredients and man-made scraps. Other solutions, all better than mine, included water purifiers, carriers, and weapons. While somewhat disappointed with my creation, over time I came to appreciate the underlying lesson. The exercise made devastation a more concrete and tactile possibility, something that could well happen if we weren't careful enough. It also conveyed that design was not a luxury but a practice fundamental to our survival and continuation as a species. Although revealing, this first project turned out to be a solitary moment of reflection in a subsequent fast-paced and deadline-oriented curriculum.

Looking back at this formative period in my design education, I recall learning about many influential disciplines, such as ergonomics, material engineering, and design criticism. However, to this day, I haven't come to terms with the absence of a fundamental subject—ethics. If this educational gap was perplexing in the mid-1990s, it's even more so nowadays, when design has pervaded every daily experience. After all, people today interact with a myriad of digital products, tools, and applications that help determine what they read, watch, share, purchase, and consume and, as a result, influence how they process information and react to their surrounding environment. The reach of design has never been greater. While this is a positive accomplishment for a discipline eager for recognition, it also brings an acute layer of responsibility. I remember thinking to myself many times when confronted with friends who were studying domains with deep deontological roots, such as law or medicine, "Why don't designers, as the primary shapers of our material culture, have to take a single class on ethics and their responsibility for their actions?"

Another important gap in my undergraduate curriculum was psychology. Classes in this field also were missing from my graduate program at Parsons School of Design in New York City and from the countless design programs around the world where I participated in talks, seminars, and workshops. How someone can teach designers today without delving into cognitive, social, and behavioral psychology and its underlying subjects like perception, memory, attention, information processing is puzzling to me. We design primarily for our fellow humans—not always (and we examine this later in the book) but quite often. Therefore, understanding the workings of the human brain—our numerous biases and triggers, attitudes and behaviors—is of greatest importance to any creative professional. The entrenched roots of most design programs in art schools can in part explain this noticeable oversight and a detachment from relevant fields of knowledge. However, this dismissal of the brain sciences is no longer acceptable.

During my career I noticed another gap. I saw talented designers who lacked the ability to communicate and sell their ideas—getting lost in their lengthy justifications, being paralyzed by complexity, at times finding problems where they didn't exist, and losing the ability to see the big picture. I have witnessed designers being overly attached to their initial perfect idea to a point where it didn't matter anymore. Sometimes their lack of self-awareness and willingness to learn from others meant they became isolated islands and burned out as a result. In all these cases, there was no shortage of talent. These were highly creative and intelligent individuals with a solid understanding of their craft. So what could explain such outcome? In all these situations, the causes have to do with what sociologists call *soft skills*, a set of noncognitive abilities such as personality traits, attitudes, and character, as well as communication and social skills—in short, human skills. These unspoken faculties—which, like ethics and psychology, are often overlooked in design programs around the globe—can play a critical role in the workplace and be an ultimate determinant of success.

This book is meant to fill these gaps by providing a series of approaches—derived from ethics, psychology, economics, ecology, and countless other domains of knowledge—that help designers reflect on their practice and unshackle themselves from the hidden forces shaping design today. These forces are no more than ingrained ideas, sometimes even stereotypical fallacies, that are out of touch with contemporary challenges and continue blinding designers from seeing what truly matters—in other words, design myths. If design wants to become a force for good, we must abandon such myths. We must be open to a deep introspection of what design is and what it ought to be. This is the goal of the book—to debunk deep-rooted design mythologies, shed light on our modern-day sightlessness and moral failing, and provide a frame of reference for developing a thriving, conscientious, and ethical design practice. Ultimately, this will lead designers to realize a much-coveted positive impact in the world.

Many designers today, particularly young ones, are eager for meaningful impact. That is a good thing. Yet many don't know how to achieve that impact. They don't even know what impact means. While you might think of impact as having a beneficial effect on something external to you—your fellow humans, other species, or the environment at large—impact can also be a personal, inward-looking pursuit. External impact is in a way more obvious. One might argue that the primary reason we exist is to help others less fortunate than we are and leave our planet better off for future generations. That's certainly something I strive for. Yet impact is not just external. We spend too much time locked in our own heads and as such are the primary catalysts of our happiness, fulfillment, and well-being. You might have the most incredible idea that will exert the type of influence you want to see in the world, yet you need to develop the right skills to bring it to fruition. You need to make yourself better first. For us to become more ethical and conscientious designers, for society and our planet, we must make sure we become more knowledgeable, self-reliant, and fulfilled individuals.

The nine design myths discussed in this book are organized into three major areas of impact—*personal* (chapters 1–3), *societal* (chapters 4–6), and *environmental* (chapters 7–9), with a final chapter 10 on what all of this means to the *designer of the future*. In chapters 1 to 3 in the personal impact part, a range of cognitive biases and soft skills are covered as we navigate into multiple areas of psychology and debunk some deeply ingrained ideas that are stopping designers from reaching their fullest impact as creative professionals. This is where we ask readers to question themselves, and as the common adage tells us, to put on their mask first before helping others. While ethics is embedded in various chapters throughout the book, this subject is explored more closely in chapters 4 to 6 as we expand on designers' moral obligation to the well-being of their fellow humans and society at large, particularly at a time when technological disruption poses a major threat to our existence. In chapters 7 to 9, we delve into ecology and systems theory, among other related topics, as we explain design's responsibility in the face of a looming ecological suicide and discuss the need for an earth-centered design methodology. Like technological disruption, ecological collapse is a critical existential thread we face as a species, and where design can and should do more. Finally, chapter 10 reviews many of the unprecedented challenges the designer of the future will have to overcome and provides a list of high-level principles and considerations on how to start embracing change.

While this book has been written for all creative types, you might notice an emphasis on digital design. Not only is this a domain I know well—as a practitioner, lecturer, manager, and mentor—but it also has the biggest slice of the professional market. About 30 percent of designers who graduate each year begin working in an area of digital design—user experience (UX), user interface (UI), product, interaction, and data. Perhaps not coincidentally, it is also the best-paid design job. Moreover, it's the discipline with the broadest reach and impact today. Because it is behind the digital tools and products used by billions of people around the world, it carries a substantial footprint and calls for accountability in how we address social and environmental concerns. The goal of this book is to help you, regardless of your specific design title, reflect deeply on your responsibilities as a creative professional in today's ever-changing world. You might even revisit it occasionally throughout your career to remind yourself why you decided to become a designer in the first place.

Personal Impact

You have to get bad
in order to get good.
—Paula Scher[1]

Do not seek praise.
Seek criticism.
—Paul Arden[2]

1

Design is perfection

Around 1.76 million years ago, before they could articulate a single word, our prehistoric ancestors already showed a deep appreciation for perfection. Among the various artifacts they built were a set of pear-shaped stone utensils known today as Acheulean tools. Crafted by *Homo erectus* across Africa, Europe, and West Asia, these stone specimens display a remarkable workmanship and symmetrical oval shape. While no one can say for sure, the ones that exhibit some signs of damage are thought to have had multiuse cutting properties as hand axes. But some are pristine, as if they were carefully shaped from a single piece of flint just yesterday. Because many such Acheulean tools are too large for proper use as hand tools and show no signs of wear and tear on their edges, American professor of philosophy Denis Dutton suggests that these were objects of delight, perhaps the earliest works of art. As he argues in *The Art Instinct: Beauty, Pleasure, and Human Evolution*, these artifacts were contemplated for their elegant form and "virtuoso craftsmanship," a prized skill that would have given experts a high status among their peers and a likely reproductive advantage.

Surrounded by natural shapes that evoke excellence and precision, our ancestors were likely absorbed by the elaborate arrangements found in nature. Their fascination was not accidental. We are hardwired to look for patterns amid apparent disarray. So we derive pleasure from carefully examining intricate forms, details, and configurations. It was only a matter of time before inspiration led to emulation. Over millennia, humans continued to pursue virtuoso craftmanship in all sorts of tools, objects, and buildings, often imitating elegant formulas found in nature. "All art is but imitation of nature,"[3] wrote the Roman Stoic philosopher Lucius Annaeus Seneca about our intrinsic desire to mimic it. We can see our pursuit for perfection in the symmetrical layout and proportions of famous sites like Stonehenge, the Egyptian pyramids, the Greek Parthenon, the Roman colosseum, and the ancient cities of Uruk, Persepolis, Angkor Wat, and Teotihuacán. The quest for quality and flawlessness is such a universal pursuit that one can argue it is an inherent human aspiration.

Such yearning for perfection is still present and very much alive in modern-day design. Our discipline is filled with great quotes equating designers to godlike saviors of the mundane world with their magic wand of perfection. When French writer and poet Antoine de Saint-Exupéry wrote in *Wind, Sand and Stars* (1949) that "perfection is finally attained not when there is no longer anything to add, but when there is no longer anything to take away,"[4] little did he know his words would be revered by generations of designers and eventually make their way into the modern manifestation of popularity—cups, t-shirts, posters, and screensavers. Italian designer Massimo Vignelli vividly depicted design as a war for perfection when he wrote: "The life of a designer is a life of fight. Fight against the ugliness. Just like a doctor fights against disease."[5] Other quotations allude to the importance of paying attention to the details as a testament of excellence. This is best expressed by the statement that "God is in the details," attributed to German American architect Ludwig Mies van der Rohe, and later by the observation of the American industrial design duo Charles Eames and Ray Eames that "The details are not the details. They make the product."[6]

Some of these quotes remind us that in the past, the act of creation was often reserved for divinity. After all, it is the aspiration for the idealized form that defines creativity. As American journalist Bill Moyers put it, "creativity is piercing the mundane to find the marvelous."[7] This is an admirable pursuit but one that is unattainable for many. Creativity can be a meandering, messy process that doesn't always end well. It is far from the glamorized idea associated with the divine. And designers are not gods. We are human beings trying to live the best lives we can amid uncertainty and self-doubt. Even if designers don't feel overwhelmed by the accomplishments of the past or the unrealistic hopes of their peers, they can feel the pain of falling short of their own perfectionist ideals. While inspiring, many of these famous design quotes can reveal how far we are from where we ought to be. They can be reminders of disappointments and triggers for self-evaluation, particularly at a time when designers have an inflated sense of mission but not a lot of power to change things. This can lead to unhappiness and a deeply rooted fear of failure and rejection.

As primary shapers of culture, designers have long carried the torch for perfection, sometimes with undeniable conceit and other times at a great personal cost. Underachievement can be stressful, particularly for a perfectionist, who often measures success by comparison to others. "Good design is all about making other designers feel like idiots because that idea wasn't theirs," joked American designer Frank Chimero.[8] Designers crave validation and originality, and at the same time, they sometimes resent others' achievements. Perfection appears to be the only way out of this mental trap.

Anything short of it will not suffice. Yet underneath most seemingly brilliant ideas are plenty of failed ones. And while many designers are open about their mistakes, such openness usually comes only after achieving success. There is still a social stigma about failure. Also, failure is not pleasant when you're going through it. Feeling like an idiot is not fun. You don't want to share or boast about how miserable you are. With enough detachment, one can look at failure in a more positive light and see more clearly the path that led to success.

Far beyond the confines of design, unmet expectations are a widespread issue in modern society, causing a great amount of concealed pain. In the past, social classes were rigidly self-imposed. If you happened to be poor in medieval Europe, it was simply your condition. It was God's will. No one was to blame for your circumstances, let alone yourself. Over time, the West progressively adopted the idea of meritocracy, where one's status in society is dependent on skill and merit instead of wealth, class, or family ties. While a good idea in principle, true meritocracy is an unachievable illusion. Yet the most worrying aspect of the ingrained idea of meritocracy, as author and philosopher Alain de Botton argues in *Status Anxiety*, is that in a society where everyone has seemingly the same opportunities and an equal chance in the game of life, rewards are plentiful for those who succeed, and yet failure can be as painful as ever for those who don't. If success is within everyone's reach, then you have only yourself to blame if you can't achieve it. Perhaps you can blame your lack of ambition, grit, persistence, perfectionism, or any other trait advanced by the modern-day entrepreneurial spirit. Failing to achieve high status has become a much heavier burden to bear. "To the injury of poverty," says de Botton, "a meritocratic system now added the insult of shame."[9]

"Shame is an epidemic in our culture," said American author and researcher Brené Brown in a TED talk watched by over sixteen million people.[10] It is certainly the cause of anxiety for countless people around the world. Yet you might still be led to believe that a healthy dose of perfectionism can be positive—that it can be an important driver of excellence, performance, and determination.

However, social scientists are realizing that the downsides of such a pursuit likely outweigh any beneficial upside. And shame and anxiety are not the only worrying outcomes. Even subtle perfectionist tendencies have been associated with mental disorders, such as depression, obsessive-compulsive disorder, social alienation, eating disorder, and self-harm. The most disastrous of all is suicide. A 2017 study that looked at fifty years of research and over eleven thousand patients concluded that "self-generated and socially based pressures to be perfect" can make people "prone to suicide ideation and attempts."[11] The fact that perfectionists, by their nature, are less likely than others to seek help only aggravates the problem.

Research has uncovered two primary dimensions of perfectionism—*excellence seeking* and *failure avoidance*.[12] While both can be detrimental to the self and assail designers with equal weight, we will look more attentively at failure avoidance and its subtle, yet pervasive consequence—perfection paralysis. Instead of taking a step forward, designers will often remain still—frozen, worried that the work is not good enough or that they will lose the respect of others if they fall short of perfection.[13] And as is shown in the remainder of the chapter, inertia can become your worst opponent. Not only does it affect your confidence and self-esteem, but it can dramatically curtail your design impact. As Jacqueline Novogratz, founder and CEO of Acumen, wrote, "Too many who yearn to make a difference become paralyzed by the fear of leaping without having worked out every detail. Yet the decision we face is not to chart the perfect way forward; it is simply to embark on a journey."[14]

1. Fail fast and adapt

In 2017, American engineer Mark Rober did an experiment with his YouTube followers. He invited people to learn a simple programming language by assembling code blocks in order to move a car through a maze, and fifty thousand people ended up playing the puzzle. Two versions of the game were presented, and they were seen by two groups of people. In one version, players who failed were asked to try again, and in the other version, players who failed were told they had lost five points of their original two hundred points. The outcome was interesting. Not only was the success rate much higher for those who were not penalized (16 percent), but they also tried more. As he explained, "Those who didn't see failing under a negative light, nearly had two and a half times more attempts to solve the puzzle."[15] Over time, they learned more and eventually found the solution. Success, after all, has a lot to do with how people react to failure and rejection. While self-blame is normal, it can easily lead to a downward spiral. However, if failure is looked at as a lesson, something that can be assimilated and applied in the future, it can boost self-confidence and expertise. In the words of American designer Paula Scher, "It's through mistakes that you actually can grow. You have to get bad in order to get good."[16]

Errors and dead ends are part of any creative process. They are meant to happen and can be a good thing. Being wrong makes you diverge and adopt new strategies. This should be an important realization for any designer. Often, getting it wrong can be a creative catalyst. Whenever new designers join my team, I like to give them a small project with a short timeline. It won't be the most challenging effort of their lives, but it will provide an important lesson. They will learn that the best way to overcome perfection paralysis is to fail fast, to get it out of their system quickly. If they fail, they can learn from it and adjust as needed. As Steven Johnson writes, "Being right keeps you in place. Being wrong forces you to explore."[17] Failure brings the attention back to the problem. It can help designers recognize its multifaceted nature, the inner nuts and bolts of the challenge at hand. It also helps them understand that success might take more than one attempt. After all, finding the right answer takes time. It is an evolving, iterative process.

Most designers are surrounded by finalized ideas. Most of the things we see around us, particularly well-crafted ones, took long production cycles and were validated and perfected countless times. They didn't just appear out of thin air. This is the case for both natural organisms and man-made objects. But we see only the end result. We don't see the cemetery of failed attempts. Out of those completed ideas, many were born out of failure. Over the long history of science and technology, there have been numerous accidental discoveries, sometimes based on chance and other times on mistakes. Getting it wrong can often lead to getting it right. We wouldn't have Post-it notes today if a 3M technician in the late 1960s hadn't failed to create a strong adhesive, producing instead a lightly sticky one that could be easily peeled from surfaces. Play-Doh was accidentally invented in the 1950s while someone was attempting to create a wallpaper cleaner. In order to get to a final idea, you must be willing to fail, adjust, and adapt.

Often, I'm asked in interviews for the kind of trait I'm looking for in a specific designer role. My answer, almost always, is adaptability. Adaptable people are problem-solvers at heart. They are not stuck in their own minds or their own ways of doing things. They are open to change and frequently seek it. They tend to be receptive to feedback in order to grow and improve. They embody the type of growth mindset described by Stanford psychology professor Carol Dweck as an eagerness to learn at all costs, as opposed to a fixed mindset that sees one's ability as immutable.[18] They also know they can't change everything all at once. Being adaptive is critical in dealing with ambiguity. And which workplace does not have its share of uncertainty? Have you ever been in a role where goals are crystal clear and boundaries are well-defined? Would you even want to? Life is complicated, and companies tend to mirror this complexity. Projects are abandoned, priorities change, and resources are shifted. And most of these changes are out of your control. Being able to overcome this in an effective manner is one of the most critical and sought-after qualities in a modern-day designer.

Being adaptive means you are also well suited to react when things go wrong. You can circumvent and learn from mistakes. It is not an easy skill to master. Sometimes we have to fight against our inner demons. It is hard to look a mistake in the face. Many of us have been there ourselves or know "people whose rigidity serves to protect a certain inner fragility," writes American journalist Kathryn Schulz, people "who cannot bend precisely because they are at risk of breaking."[19]

It's hard to be vulnerable, but being wrong will help you focus on the right, not the desired, solution. With time, you start seeing the merits of failing, developing an appetite for learning, and abandoning unattainable pursuits. Resourcefulness becomes a creative achievement on its own. As investigative reporter David Epstein mentions in *Range: Why Generalists Triumph in a Specialized World*, "Approach your own personal voyage and projects like Michelangelo approached a block of marble, willing to learn and adjust as you go, and even to abandon a previous goal and change directions entirely should the need arise."[20]

2. Create many instead of one

Brilliant ideas can be the worst. As soon as you come up with one, you want to protect it. You become sensitive to criticism and suspicious of others. You can experience this tendency for self-preservation even in a brainstorming session. You can try to be unbiased and to treat your own brilliant idea with detachment, as if it is someone else's. But from the moment you utter it, it's now officially yours. It is now in everyone's ears. And even in a safe environment that is conducive to exchanging ideas with no judgment, brainstorming is still a considerable test of your social skills and personal restraint. Brainstorming sessions are a kind of a social experiment for adults that can test how well they have embraced the "sharing is caring" motto they learned as children. They can be effective at times but can also surface numerous self-preserving biases that make the exchange painful.

When you come up with a bright concept, you tend to inflate its significance. As time passes and you become more attached to it, your aim is to defend it at all costs. Confirmation bias is a common predisposition that leads people to seek information that confirms a belief or point of view and to discard contradictory evidence. In the case of design, it means ignoring all the signs and feedback against your idea and cherry-picking the few instances that appear to endorse it. This can be dangerous. Instead of changing course at the right time, you keep falling further into the trap. This happens frequently to designers. They get stuck to the initial concept and are unable to move on and think about alternatives. When challenged, they create adaptations or concessions of the original idea. They go too deep, too fast. The early, bright idea becomes an anchor on which all future judgments and decisions are dependent. It becomes a skewed lens through which they evaluate alternatives. The ability to circumvent this trap comes to most designers as they accumulate experience. And the trick is really to avoid becoming overly attached to that brilliant idea—to know when to stop and move on.

However, abandoning an idea is not easy. You might have been perfecting it, going over the details and use cases. Perhaps it even has gone through several stages of approval. Turning back or choosing another path seems like a daunting and laborious prospect, not to mention possibly embarrassing. There is simply too much on the line. And the worst of all is that your mind is holding you hostage, showing you all the reasons you shouldn't let go. You could be the victim of several biases, such as the sunk-cost fallacy (preference for continuing a project after a significant investment has been made), loss-aversion bias (preference for not losing over winning), or even status quo bias (preference for keeping things as they are). Falling a victim to these common mind tricks means you could be missing out on better and more viable options and stopping yourself from reaching your full potential. Your tunnel vision pursuit for quality and perfection could get you further away from it. As American psychologist Adam Grant recognizes in his book *Originals: How Non-Conformists Move the World*, "Many people fail to achieve originality because they generate a few ideas and then obsess about refining them to perfection."[21] This sounds like many designers I know. If you are looking for a genius spark of originality, you would make a better bet on quantity.

Think about a large project you were tasked in the past. You might have been filled with self-doubt at first, paralyzed by fear, or overwhelmed by the sheer scale of it. Insecurity will likely be there until the end. Yet by setting the work in motion and keeping up with the momentum, you can make it seem possible and reachable. Every step builds confidence. For one, you actually move closer to your goal, but you also develop a sense of achievement, no matter how small, for each step you take forward. If you stop for too long, you might go back to square one. As Albert Einstein once wrote to his son: "Life is like riding a bicycle. To keep your balance, you must keep moving."[22] Movement is key. It pushes you forward and reveals what you might not yet see. When you're stuck in a familiarity trap, holding onto what you know well or the only idea you had, it is time to move on. For a creative problem-solver, moving means coming up with more ideas— prioritizing quantity over quality, valuing abundance over scarcity, striving for progress instead of perfection. In the words of American poet civil rights activist Maya Angelou, "You can't use up creativity. The more you use, the more you have."[23]

Pablo Picasso was an exceptionally prolific artist. During his seventy-eight-year career, he produced approximately 147,800 pieces—100,000 graphic prints, 34,000 illustrations, 13,500 paint-ings, and 300 sculptures and ceramics.[24] He was not just a productive artist but one of the most versatile creators of all time, developing and exploring multiple styles, from cubism to surrealism, over a wide variety of mediums, from collage to constructive sculpture. In 1934, in an allusion to his incessant adaptation, Picasso remarked, "It is as though I have never been able to build up a painting myself. I begin with an idea and then it becomes something else."[25] I have kept this quotation close to me for many years, taping it on many walls as its paper corners have torn. It reminds me of the importance of departure, of making a first step in a creative journey. It expresses the notion that true change comes only with motion. Picasso was an embodiment of this approach, able to endlessly transform himself with every step forward.

To come up with more ideas, you don't necessarily have to abandon your original one. You can simply put it on hold. It's always worth keeping an archive of dormant ideas that you can reassess occasionally. Put them on the back burner, and let them sit. I have a list of projects I would like to pursue and topics I would like to write about that I revisit frequently. At any particular time, the context might not be right, the conditions might be unfavorable, or the idea might not have matured yet. It could be missing something. There is value in distancing yourself for a while, particularly if you're feeling blocked. When you come back to it, you might see things differently. "When you procrastinate, you're more likely to let your mind wander," says Grant. "That gives you a better chance of stumbling onto the unusual and spotting unexpected patterns."[26] You might associate procrastination with laziness, but it can be the biggest catalyst for creativity and problem-solving.

Another great example of productive procrastination comes from the American painter Jackson Pollock, who is known for never quite finishing his pieces. He was a great enthusiast of the "continuous dynamic" technique, which mimics the cyclical routine of nature by building multiple layers over time on a canvas. He would leave a painting for a time, sometimes several weeks, and occasionally revisit it to add a few things or contemplate it, only to leave again. Pollock is far from being an exception. Some of the most original individuals were also the biggest procrastinators. Leonardo da Vinci worked on and off on the *Mona Lisa* for sixteen years and spent another fifteen developing ideas for his *Last Supper*.[27] And from the early days of Charles Darwin's research on a theory of evolution to the day he published his landmark work *On the Origin of Species* in 1859, roughly twenty years went by. A common misconception is that he was afraid of the public's reaction to his work. But in a 2007 study, British historian of science John van Wyhe speculates that

Darwin was simply busy, working on ten other books and occasionally revising his ideas and substantiating them with more evidence.[28] As American screenwriter Aaron Sorkin put it, when asked about his occasional delays: "You call it procrastinating. I call it thinking."[29]

3. Embrace discomfort

A desire for perfection is rooted in fear—fear of failing, fear of losing your status or your income, and sometimes fear of negative judgment by your peers. At its most extreme, a fear of being unsuccessful can become immobilizing. People can prefer to stay put rather than do anything at all. Nothing will ever meet their high standards. For designers, this is an undesired outcome. Yet it is an ancient technique the mind uses to avoid risks and keep safe. As an evolutionary strategy, it conserves energy and avoids strain. Therefore, most of us often fall back on what is familiar to us—perhaps an idea that was relevant in the past, a presentation technique that once worked, a document that was well crafted. Familiarity is tight with comfort. But such comfort is simply a restraining crutch. "The more we consciously dwell on a problem that requires an innovative solution," says Bulgarian writer and critic Maria Popova, "the more likely we are to corner ourselves into the nooks of the familiar, entrenched in habitual patterns of thought that lead where they always have."[30]

Perfection paralysis can be the result of many other related fears. There's the fear of not knowing enough, which can inevitably lead people to doubt their own competence and skills. This sort of negative thinking trick of the mind normally accompanies impostor syndrome—a widespread phenomenon that assaults most of us at least once in our lives. Most times, a lack of confidence is merely the projection of someone else onto your mind—someone else who is not you. And if you are experiencing impostor syndrome, you probably know more than you think. As it turns out, people with low ability tend to overestimate their aptitude, while people of high competence tend to underestimate their capability. This is known as the Dunning–Kruger effect.[31] Many perfectionists also judge accomplishment through the validation they receive from others. Hence, it's no surprise that the fear of rejection can feel very palpable at times— fear of disapproval by coworkers, managers, clients, competitors, or the general public; fear that a solution won't be well received or might become a source of scorn.

Of all the fears related to perfectionism, the most paralyzing of all is the fear of being exposed and being vulnerable. For some, voicing an idea is already a major accomplishment. Insecurity can be a crippling factor. One strategy I embrace as a practitioner, manager, and teacher is to share work in progress as often as possible. In such a setting, common excuses such as "it's too early to share" or "it's not done yet" are normally frowned upon. Making this a routine practice that is noted on the calendar is also important. It might take time for some to get into the habit, particularly for those who are new to the team. But frequency matters. It conveys we care about this practice as a tool for personal growth and well-being and not merely as a random, one-off exercise. It slowly reduces everyone's perfectionist tendencies and the fears that come with them. Exposing yourself to others and others to you with work that is not refined or finalized creates a platform for mutual trust. You realize no one is perfect or particularly impressive. Everyone is as limited, damaged, and flawed as you are.

Whenever you voice an idea or a point of view, it can very well become a target. This is normal and expected in some social contexts. Yet the attack is not always personal. Conflating criticism of your idea with criticism of yourself can be damaging. Confusing the rejection of a project with a rejection of you as an individual also can be damaging. You should avoid this common line of reasoning. You are not your idea. Being beaten on the outside should not hurt your spirit. In fact, it can make it stronger. As the Greek Stoic philosopher Epictetus once wrote, "Men are disturbed not by events but by their opinion about events."[32] All of us have the tendency to attach our self-worth to our work. This tendency can be more acute for creatives since we put so much of ourselves in our work. "This is shit, my work is shit, therefore I'm shit"[33] is a common extrapolation we play in our minds too often. However, as Brené Brown explains, "What I produce is part of me and a reflection of me, but it is not me."[34] It can be a lifetime pursuit to learn how to decouple ourselves from an idea or our work. It helps to put things in perspective and not take yourself too seriously, even to have a laugh at your own expense. It is really about the process and the journey.

Life is too short to limit ourselves by fear. The downside of all these fear-inducing biases is that they can lock people in a comfort zone and blind them from seeing the potential of acting on a whim and taking chances. If you want to do anything meaningful in life, you often must be uncomfortable and vulnerable. True novelty is always risky. It takes a leap of faith. You cannot be in a creative role if you are averse to risk. As the late Sir Ken Robinson once said, "If you are not prepared to be wrong, you will never come up with anything original."[35] Being vulnerable can also be an effective development cue. It allows you to see your own flaws and limitations and act on them. If you wish to become a more resilient, self-aware, and mentally healthy professional, vulnerability can be an important ally. It can also be a critical skill in social engagement and collaboration. Instead of shying away or projecting someone else that is different, allow yourself to be authentic. Let others see you for who you really are.

4. Embrace imperfection

The notion of perfection has long involved elegance, simplicity, and, ultimately, beauty. As with so many origin narratives, one of the earliest descriptions of perfection comes from Aristotle (384–322 BCE). In his seminal *Metaphysics*, Aristotle listed order, symmetry, and definiteness as the general elements of beauty.[36] Many

Western philosophers and artists, such as William Hogarth, Francis Hutcheson, and John Ruskin, reinforced this view over the ages. Within the design community, the connection between perfection and simplicity has been adopted with great fervor, to a point where they are almost indistinguishable. There is hardly a designer today who denies the role of simplicity in design. According to British American designer Sir Jonathan Ive, one of the most revered designers of this generation, true simplicity "is about bringing order to complexity."[37] Lindon Leader, the American graphic designer behind the iconic FedEx logo, said in this regard that he strives "for two things in design: simplicity and clarity."[38] The list of inspiring design quotes equating perfection with simplicity is extensive. There is only one problem. Most of them are based on wishful thinking.

Underlying contemporary minimalist design and architecture is perhaps the most famous quote of all, cited earlier— Antoine de Saint-Exupéry's comment that perfection is achieved by removing extraneous elements instead of adding. But here's the paradox: while we know that simplicity can improve legibility and understanding, numerous cognitive biases constantly drag us toward unnecessary complexity. As it turns out, we are inclined to solve our problems by adding instead of removing, whether objects, product features, or Lego pieces. In a study published by *Nature* in 2021, researchers studying how people try to solve for better objects, ideas, or situations asked them to improve the stability of an existing Lego structure, bearing in mind that each added block would cost 10 cents. As researchers uncovered, participants were "more likely to consider solutions that add features than solutions that remove them, even when removing features is more efficient"[39] and cost effective. In most cases, participants simply failed to consider subtractive approaches, as if their default mental shortcut for solving a problem was "What can we add here?"

A designer's existence can be one of anguish. Often torn between perfection and reality, we struggle over where to draw the line between consistency and variability, between predictability and novelty, between simplicity and complexity. But it is not so much a line as it is a sensitive pendulum that in the case of design frequently sways toward order, balance, and consistency. This is not always a good thing. Consistency, like simplicity, can be an ambitious overreaction. It can also be an easy way out. "You don't actually have to know anything about your users to talk about making things consistent. You only have to know about your design, which most designers are quite familiar with,"[40] argues American software designer Jared Spool. With too much consistency, you might end with an unimaginative, stale, and rigid experience that is not right for your customers. After all, humans are much more accommodating of variation and inconstancy than designers seem to think they are. In part, this is because we are all complicated, quirky, and flawed in more ways than one. Yet we keep striving for unattainable desires, fighting against our own biases and nature and pursuing an internal, painful conflict between what is and what ought to be.

Life is complex and imperfect. Every day is a struggle, a constant process of falling and rising. Acknowledging your own shortcomings and those of others is your first step in embracing imperfection. Recognizing there are transient forces and events outside your purview is also important. Like Lindon Leader, I believe in the value of clarity and simplicity, and I'm a strong proponent of the centuries-old principle of Occam's razor, which tells us that entities should not be multiplied without necessity. In equal circumstances, I always prefer the simplest and most elegant solution. However, because many outcomes are out of our control, we must develop the ability to differentiate between the things we can affect and the ones we can't. Otherwise, a creative journey can feel like an endless swim against the current. In this context, there is much to learn from Stoicism and Buddhism. While expressed in different ways, both philosophies teach us the value of letting go of things we can't influence. As professor of Buddhist studies Rupert Gethin wrote in this regard, "as long as there is attachment to things that are unstable, unreliable, changing and impermanent, there will be suffering."[41]

Another way to calm down your perfectionist tendencies is to embrace impermanence, as expressed by the important centuries-old Japanese aesthetic tradition *wabi-sabi*. With origins in Buddhism, *wabi-sabi* stands for the beauty of things that are flawed, transient, and incomplete. It acknowledges our fallibility and nature's imperfectability. In a way, it is not about creating an artificial, illusory perfection that lives outside of nature, as so many designers and architects have been led to believe for decades, but instead, recognizing the genuine essence of all that surrounds us. "*Wabi-sabi* nurtures all that is authentic by acknowledging three simple realities: nothing lasts, nothing is finished, and nothing is perfect."[42] In other words, it is about the perfect imperfectability of things. The sooner you can come to terms with this reality, the easier it will be for you to create, be vulnerable, and take chances. In addition to *wabi-sabi*, there are other Asian traditions, from mediation to visualization, that can help you bring peace to your mind, let the persistent thoughts pass by, and focus on what truly matters.

Actionable Advice

Designers are reminded daily of the torturous path toward perfection. It is an unattainable ideal that can cause feelings of apprehension, unworthiness, and low self-esteem. But there are many ways to fight against such anxiety-inducing thoughts. The first is to realize we are imperfect and constantly evolving creatures. There's no need for guilt or discouragement. It's reality. We are human. Even machines with their seeming perfection eventually wear down. The universe tends toward entropy. There's also a great degree of perfection in imperfection. Nature exudes this paradox in a marvelous way in almost every system you can think of and in almost every aspect that defines us as human beings. Perfection can be a valuable goal or aspiration but not an expectation. It is about putting a bit of yourself into what you do, being passionate about what you deliver. Perhaps it is best expressed by the Greek word *meraki*, meaning the idea of doing something with love, creativity, and soul. It's about doing our best in that pursuit, not actually reaching it. Salvador Dalí knew best when he said, "Have no fear of perfection—you'll never reach it."[43] Don't strive for unrealistic objectives and unreachable ideals. Take it one step at the time.

If you are starting a new job, try to begin with a tangible small task or project so you can feel good with the accomplishment and move on to something bigger. Set realistic goals and expectations. Concentrate on the results—what you finish or deliver. Celebrate every step along the way, no matter how small it might seem to be. If it doesn't go well, take a *wabi-sabi* approach. Appreciate its flaws and your mistakes as a means to learn and evolve. Don't overcommit to a given project, particularly one that has unforeseeable time and resource constraints. Worry about creating several options instead of variants of the same one. Don't get overly attached to a unique idea. Abandon it, or let it sit for a while. Each new idea is a step toward something better, something more considered and refined. The important thing is to keep moving. Never forget: you should fall in love with the problem, not the solution.

Look around and evaluate your context, your team, and its culture. We are social creatures who are prone to the influence of others. If you are surrounded by people who are afraid of making mistakes, taking changes, and launching an imperfect product, it's likely that over time you will start adopting the same mindset. So don't fall into that self-preserving trap. Look for a team that encourages the type of thinking you want to develop—one that is as much of a risk-taker as you are and that can focus on the right thing. And the focus starts with you. This means creating healthy boundaries and saying no when needed. Remember, every time you say yes to something, you are saying no to something else, possibly something more significant. Finally, don't forget to take care of yourself. Take a break, get away from work, and recharge. This is when the best ideas tend to emerge. You need to calm your mind, not stretch it to exhaustion. Each deep breath will seek for a new solution.

Together, ordinary people
can achieve extraordinary results.

—Becka Schoettle[1]

The only thing which will redeem
mankind is cooperation.

—Bertrand Russell[2]

2

Design is about sole genius

Given up for adoption after his birth in 1955, Steven was by most measures a difficult child. He had trouble adapting to conventional school from an early age. Frequently bored, distracted, and resisting authority, he often teased other kids and was suspended a few times. His adoptive parents, Paul and Clara, had no college degrees or fortunes. A high-school dropout from Wisconsin, Paul moved to California, where he struggled as a machinist and a used-car salesman and jumped "from one lousy job to another."[3] The couple adopted a daughter, Patricia, in 1957. In 1967, Paul, Clara, Steven, and Patricia moved from Mountain View to Los Altos, where they used all their savings to buy a three-bedroom home in a better school district.

Forty-six years later, in 2013, the house on Crist Drive was declared a historic site. As it turns out, Steven was not just a "discipline problem" but also a "brilliant little boy" who was "accustomed to being the center of attention."[4] By now, you might have realized Steven was in fact Steve Jobs, the charismatic leader and cofounder of Apple Inc. The house his parents bought, now a landmark, was where Apple Computer Company was founded.

Today, Steve Jobs represents brilliance. A pioneer of the personal computer age, Jobs redefined the way we interact with computers, reshaped how we consume music, and reimagined how we use mobile phones. He is one of the greatest innovators of our time, who touched and transformed multiple industries, always with a great attention to detail, beauty, and quality. Many say he was a visionary—a personification of the entrepreneurial spirit who was able to persevere and thrive against all odds. He was one of "these rare individuals from the thousands who try to create their own companies but are defeated by the market, competition, bad luck and an unwillingness to do whatever it takes to win."[5] Millions of people dream about creating their own company, and for the ones who do, the rewards don't come easily. In 2019, the failure rate of startups was close to 90 percent. Research says that roughly 20 percent of startups fail in the first year, 50 percent in the fifth year, and by their tenth anniversary, fewer than a third have survived.[6] To prosper in such an environment takes considerable force of character, determination, and imagination. It takes a brilliant mind. It can take a modern hero like Steve Jobs.

We love heroes. Every generation has a preferred set. In the past, they could have been painters or scientists, but today they are more likely to be entrepreneurs or startup founders. They can become superhuman characters and creative spirits who fill our collective imagination. The hero is one of the oldest narratives and is imbedded in most forms of myth and folklore around the world, in every stage of human written history. It shows a universal appreciation for the single individual—the leader, genius, explorer, or courageous savior—who is able to overcome all hurdles and in the process grow as a person, triumph over evil, or save the community. From an evolutionary standpoint, heroism could underpin intelligence, reproductive advantage, and genetic variation, while potentially being responsible for a "protective or restorative effect"[7] in the individual and the group. The pattern is so prevalent across cultures that it constitutes a primary archetype identified by Swiss psychoanalyst Carl Jung and American professor of literature Joseph Campbell, who believed all mythic narratives derive from a single myth (monomyth) around a hero's journey.

Despite its ubiquitousness, hero stories and the glorification of individuals can have a dark side. First, they downplay the hero's flaws or, even worse, assume that those qualities are needed to succeed. As it turns out, Steven was not just the "brilliant little boy" we learned about in the beginning of this chapter. He was also an "arrogant chronic overachiever" who became a "surrogate for his father's frustrated career desires."[8] A perfectionist and hypercompetitive individual, Jobs was considered an angry, mercurial, and demanding customer. He often saw others as competitors, not collaborators, and was "notorious for throwing temper tantrums and showing intense anger toward those who disagreed with him."[9] He was a leader who lacked empathy and cared very little for what others had to say. These are not positive traits. True leaders are role models who demonstrate the ethical and positive behaviors they want to see in others and who recognize and give credit where it is due. The second consequence of hero worshipping is that it tends to dismiss the multiple people and factors contributing to someone's success. To attribute the accomplishments of an entire organization of more than 63,000 people—the size of Apple in 2011—to a single individual is to be reductive at best. It's an unbalanced narrative that fuels an outdated view based on centralized control and strict organizational hierarchy.

Design, as with many domains of knowledge, is filled with hero stories—from ancient creative minds that imbued grandiose buildings and timeless objects with formulas of perfection, to modern-day heroes of simplicity and sophistication, like Eileen Gray, Coco Chanel, Ludwig Mies van der Rohe, Ray and Charles Eames, Milton Glaser, Dieter Rams, and Jonathan Ive, to name a few. These are not just individuals who did their jobs well. For the most part, they saved the world from the mundane—the ugly, broken reality inherited from the past. While their achievements are worthy of recognition, the hero cult they embody propagates the wrong idea that great design, like art, is about the singular mind. Anthropologist Daniel Miller explains how despite a contemporary focus on the user, design is still tied to the notion of the luminary intellect: "Design in general tends to look upwards to the arts and crafts in emulation," writes Miller, "areas where it is the figure of the producer as artist or crafts person that commands attention, rather than the mere consumer."[10] Hero stories in design can reinforce the old notion of design as a form of art for the cultural elite.

For most part of history, if you were lucky, you couldn't be a genius, but you could have a genius by your side. In Roman and Greek mythology, a genius was a protective spirit, a guardian angel of sorts that would protect and follow an individual from birth to death. A genius was also a catalyst for the creative mind, with many poets from classical history being blessed by one. The idea of attributing creativity to spirits or divine intervention slowly went out of fashion during the Renaissance. The refocusing on the self and individual meant that now some of the most prominent creative forces—like William Shakespeare, Leonardo da Vinci, and Isaac Newton—were themselves geniuses. While this was an important milestone in human emancipation, it meant that all of a sudden, humans had an unprecedented pressure on their shoulders. As the author of *Eat Pray Love*, Elizabeth Gilbert, mentions in her TED talk seen by more than twenty million people, this was simply "too much responsibility to put on a fragile, human psyche,"[11] which ended up creating "unmanageable expectations about performance."

It also meant that if any mere mortal could be a genius, what's stopping anyone else from trying? This, in turn, led to generations of anxious and gloomy individuals, most notably writers and artists and, yes, architects and designers, who dreamed they could reach that pedestal. But the flame for self-reliance had been lit. Humans could not just be geniuses; they could be anything they wanted, if they only worked hard enough. Independent entities that were able to achieve the greatest deeds on their own. Such self-centeredness appears to have hit an apogee at the present time. If not, how can we explain the growth in popularity of selfies, celebrities, influencers, self-branding, and all self-aggrandizing mechanisms on display today? Curiously, such widespread emphasis on the personal ego appears to be correlated with the widening of the "self-help" section in most bookstores, as many of us react with some existential anxiety to the failure of self-actualization and the myth that "you can achieve anything." It is therefore not surprising that perfectionism is on the rise—with all the consequences we saw in the previous chapter—particularly among young people, according to a research study that looked at 41,641 American, Canadian, and British college students between 1981 and 2016. One of the main culprits they pointed out was "competitive individualism."[12]

An increase in individualism is noticeable even at a global level. In a study published in *Psychological Science*, researchers Henri Carlo Santos, Michael E. W. Varnum, and Igor Grossmann looked at fifty-one years of data (1960 to 2011) on individualist behaviors across seventy-eight countries.[13] They analyzed a series of practices (such as household size and rate of divorce) and values (such as the importance of friends and independent children) normally associated with individualism in opposition to collectivism. Individualism appears to be a global trend, with thirty-four (out of forty-one) countries showing a rise in individualist practices. The authors also tried to explain this growth by looking at three possible factors—increases in socioeconomic development, increases in disaster frequency, and decreases in pathogen prevalence (spread of diseases). Even though Santos and his team were careful not to infer a causal relationship, socioeconomic development was found to have the strongest effect in the growth of individualism. "More affluence leads to a greater sense of self-reliance and a detachment from others,"[14] says professor of leadership and organizational psychology Ronald E. Riggio.

Such progress wouldn't seem so bad if it weren't undermining our ability to empathize and collaborate with others. As we get more isolated in our personal bubble, collaboration becomes more of a mere zero-sum game where only the strong survive. Such self-absorption can even become tied with a nationalistic mindset. The outer limits of your own body and mind are transposed to a nation's borders. What happens inside matters much more than whatever might happen outside. It's a form of national egocentrism. This increase in division is not only a threat in the highly polarized political systems that have evolved in many countries, but it also can undermine global challenges such as hunger or environmentalism, which can be mitigated only by increased multinational cooperation. When taken to an extreme, the myth of individualism can have severe global repercussions that go well beyond design. It is not, however, the only misconception giving force to the sole genius ideal.

1. Cooperation wins

"This survival of the fittest, which I have here sought to express in mechanical terms," wrote English philosopher, biologist, and sociologist Herbert Spencer in 1864, "is that which Mr. Darwin has called 'natural selection,' or the preservation of favored races in the struggle for life."[15] Charles Darwin initially enjoyed Spencer's analogy of "survival of the fittest" with his original "natural selection," and he even introduced the expression in a later edition of his groundbreaking *On the Origin of Species*. As with many scholars of his time, Spencer was absorbed by evolutionary ideas, especially how they could leap the confines of biology and be applied to society, politics, and war. His reframing of Darwin's original "natural selection" as a matter of competition among the fittest led to a series of misinterpretations, the darkest of which was social Darwinism. Under the idea that only the strong survive, social Darwinism bolstered numerous social maladies—imperialism, scientific racism, eugenics, fascism—that caused suffering for countless human beings.

One popular belief in Europe circa 1900—that "those members of the human species most subject to painful sunburns were the most recent, highest, and, in all likelihood, final twigs on the exfoliating tree of evolution"[16]—provided the moral backdrop for the violence and brutality of European imperialism. In such a social hierarchy, the strong and powerful are deemed innately superior, and therefore their dominion over others is justified. In reference to the social inequities caused by such abhorrent ideas, American political scientist Virginia Eubanks reflects on how they still permeate many facets of our lives today: "We have always lived in the world we built for the poor. We create a society that has no use for the disabled or the elderly, and then are cast aside when they are hurt or grow old. We measure human worth based only on the ability to earn a wage, and suffer in a world that undervalues care and community. We base our economy on exploiting the labor of racial and ethnic minorities, and watch lasting inequities snuff out human potential. We see the world as inevitably riven by bloody competition and are left unable to recognize the many ways we cooperate and lift each other up."[17]

However, social Darwinism was not the longest-lasting ideology cultivated by Spencer's misreading of Darwin's evolutionary mechanism. His outlook on history as being naturally shaped by those with greatest strength inspired many economic and political views still held today, such as laissez-faire capitalism, unrestrained competition, and market aggressiveness. We can still see many remnants of this creed in today's workforce. Competition drives success, so they say. Eat or be eaten. Business is cut-throat. You must be fierce in order to win. Always stay ahead of the pack. This is the type of mindset that sees enemies and competitors around every corner and that forces people to be suspicious of every client and coworker. There's only one problem with this reading of Darwin's work: it is completely wrong. What Darwin meant by "fittest" was simply the most adaptable, not necessarily the strongest or most adept. "The best adapted may not always be the strongest or the most beautiful or even the most pro-lific,"[18] argues philosopher of biology Robert N. Brandon, but simply the one able to adjust to the local, changing environment.

We have seen how a more competitive and individualistic society is leading to a rise in perfectionism, narcissism, anxiety, and other ailments of the heart and mind. In part, we have been led to believe that evolution favors selfishness. Brian Hare, a professor in the department of evolutionary anthropology and the Center for Cognitive Neuroscience at Duke University, and Vanessa Woods, a research scientist and award-winning journalist, have tried to change this misconception with their tour-de-force *Survival of the Friendliest: Understanding Our Origins and Rediscovering Our Common Humanity*. In the book, Hare and Woods make a compelling argu-ment against the idea that the strong, ruthless, and aggressive type normally wins, claiming instead that "cooperation is the key to our survival as a species because it increases our evolutionary fitness."[19] This is indeed something that Darwin himself observed in *The Descent of Man*: "those communities, which included the greatest number of the most sympathetic members, would flourish best and rear the greatest number of offspring."[20] Here we have his original idea of natural selection tied with the notion of sympathy, which as American psychologist Paul Ekman argues, "today would be termed empathy, altruism, or compassion."[21]

The role sociability and cooperation played in our evolu-tion as a species has been further attested by a 2016 paper led by mathematical ecologist George Constable, which showed that altruism is more evolutionary advantageous than selfishness.[22] In many ways, this is not surprising. We are social creatures. Our brains, language, and tools have evolved to meet an increasingly high demand for social engagement and organization. We wouldn't be where we are today if we hadn't relied on each other for survival and for carrying through major inventions in history. If we look at some of the biggest design achievements of the past and present, we understand their inherent complexity could have been tackled only by a large group of cooperative individuals. This is the case with the International Space Station or with CERN's Large Hadron Collider, which is the largest machine in the world and employs ten thousand scientists from over a hundred countries. Even a small, modern object of desire such as Apple's iPhone is achieved through deep, interdependent cooperation. In 2015, Apple had eight hundred engineers and specialists working on the two hundred individual parts that make the iPhone's single camera module.[23]

The focus on the isolated hero aligns with the modern-day, capitalist narrative of individualism, competition, and self-affirmation. It also takes us away from the value of cooperation in human development. If you drank too much of the selfishness potion, you can be tempted to think that becoming a sole genius is the only path to success, and in the process, you will likely underestimate how dependent you are on others. You might overlook the important fact that your labor is interdependent with a multitude of individuals and their voices and skills. Evolving, maturing, and succeeding as creative professionals start with recognizing the contributions of others. We can achieve our greatest successes through collaboration, not through conflict or competition. Henry Ford recognized this early on when he said, "Coming together is a beginning. Keeping together is progress. Working together is success."[24] Ford's observation is as relevant as ever, particularly at a time where we have multiple existential threats, from climate change to ecological collapse, overpopulation, and global pandemic. Cooperation is the only way out.

2. You are not alone

By all accounts, Josie Esquivel was a successful Wall Street analyst. When she turned forty, the Harvard graduate was named number one in her industry by a prominent magazine. Compensation was rising, and she had other firms interested in hiring her. Two weeks after her first-place ranking was announced, after seven years at Lehman Brothers, a company she respected for how much it taught her, Esquivel interviewed for a position with Morgan Stanley. Esquivel had the skills that Morgan Stanley was looking for, and its hiring committee was keen on having such a star join their team of analysts. The fact she could bring many of her established corporate relationships with her was also appealing. Esquivel's decision was not easy, but eventually, she decided to accept the offer, and in 1995 she joined Morgan Stanley, a move she came to regret after a few years when she struggled to adjust to the new firm's culture and conservative standards. Her ratings declined shortly after, and by 2000, her standing declined to a runner-up.

Esquivel is one of many analysts surveyed in the 2012 book *Chasing Stars: The Myth of Talent and the Portability of Performance* by Harvard Business School professor Boris Groysberg. In a 2004 article titled "The Risky Business of Hiring Stars," Groysberg and his colleagues Ashish Nanda and Nitin Nohria also examined the careers of 1,052 analysts who worked at seventy-eight Wall Street investment banks between 1988 and 1996. These were not typical analysts. They were high achievers—star performers. They had all been named best in the industry by *Institutional Investor* magazine at least once in that period. According to Groysberg and his colleagues, analysts were an interesting target because they best represented free agents with portable skills—independent professionals who didn't care who they worked for. For such top performers, changing jobs was as easy as crossing the street. They had nothing to lose. They could simply move on and take their clients with them. For many, it was hard to resist the temptation. However, these three researchers discovered that when stars were employed by new firms, their performance "plunged." This was not just a momentary adjustment to the new culture. The decline persisted for up to five years. Furthermore, the weakening extended to the functioning of their new team, which sometimes returned to normal only after the star eventually left the company.

Why was that the case? As the study shows, it is not as if these stars "suddenly become less intelligent or lose a decade of work experience."[25] It's simply that their performance does not depend exclusively on them. For a star to succeed, numerous forces—an array of resources, capabilities, and processes that are unique to the organization—are needed. There's also the irreplaceable combination of human talent that has harbored and upheld the star. When stars transfer to another organization, they leave behind their team and entire support system. The star then struggles in an environment that frequently is hostile, particularly to incoming celebrities, and is forced to learn the "procedures, personalities, relationships, and subcultures"[26] of their new reality. Unable to quickly adopt fresh strategies—in part because of their past successes, in part due to their perfectionist tendencies—their performance starts to slip away from them. They are likely to leave their new role within just two or three years.

Context, culture, and interpersonal relationships matter tremendously in anyone's success. As a twenty-first-century knowledge worker, you might attribute your job performance largely to your own aptitude and skills and thus regard yourself as "equipped to be equally productive in any appropriate workplace."[27] This is true, at least in part. As Groysberg's research demonstrates, your team is as responsible for your success as you are and sometimes even more. Acknowledging their contributions is not just a sign of humility, maturity, and great leadership but a vital step in adapting to an ever-changing work environment. As the scale and difficulty of our problems grow, so does our reliance on others. In a society increasingly driven by individualism, it's hard to acknowledge that the design profession, once the activity of sole geniuses, is now evolving in the opposite direction. Today's design challenges are of a completely different magnitude and complexity than they were just twenty or thirty years ago. They also require a scale of cooperation that would baffle any twentieth-century designer. As never before, interdependence is far more important than independence.

No longer do we have the singular design hero figure we've become accustomed to study and revere, such as Ludwig Mies van der Rohe, Alvar Aalto, Dieter Rams, Paul Rand, Philippe Starck, and Florence Knoll. For better or worse, design today is rarely about the individual or the individual's idea. In many ways, it never should have been. Today, designers are immersed in large, multidisciplinary teams working in complex systems that require a great degree of coordination. They work closely with people performing a myriad of specialized design roles, some of which have only emerged in the past decade, and with people working in other disciplines, including product management, engineering, quality assurance, and sales. And the intricate network of people they interact with outside the internal team hasn't become any simpler either. Instead of a single client or stakeholder, designers have a multitude of dedicated points of contact, sometimes across several organizations. The customer landscape has changed, as well. Many designers today work on products that are used not by just thousands or even millions of people but billions. The magnitude and impact of such work are enormous.

What designers are building has also changed dramatically. We no longer are doing just chairs, logos, posters, dresses, and packaging. Instead, we are developing experiences, platforms, services, organizations, and communities, often on a global scale. We are building complex systems that are bigger than any distinctive part or person and that cannot be built by a single designer. And the changing landscape does not affect only design. Can anyone today claim individual responsibility for the release of a movie or the making of a car, house, building, bridge, or dam? Even in art, the common flagbearer for the sole genius myth, we can witness a considerable shift toward the collective. Andy Warhol is known for his Factory in Manhattan, which was more of a workshop than a factory. Contemporary American artist Jeff Koons, on the other hand, has moved much closer to our mental image of a large industrial complex. At one time, Koons employed a team of more than one hundred people in a 1,500 square meter (16,000 square foot) factory setting in Chelsea, New York City.[28] His assistants reproduce a vast assortment of sculptures and paintings by hand, frequently through a color-by-number system developed internally.[29] As an example, Koons's famous 2014 sculpture *Liberty Bell*, which took eight years to produce, involved a variety of specialists who were responsible for structured-light scanning, 3D computer modeling, laser cutting, and wood and metal milling and who worked in locations extending from Walla Walla, Washington, to Germany.[30]

It's not just the scale of collaboration that's different; it is also its very nature. We are no longer working elbow to elbow in a physical office, presenting our work in a boardroom, and giving handshakes throughout the day. We are increasingly working apart from others physically. We collaborate across multiple locations and time zones, communicate and share content through a variety of online digital tools and platforms, and present our work virtually to large, unfamiliar audiences. Our teams are spread across the world, embodying a vast array of languages, cultures, backgrounds, and behaviors. Many of us are working from home, not just because of a global pandemic but because we care deeply about our families and our work-life balance. We are ever more interdependent and more distant at the same time. This societal shift means we need better methods, skills, and tools to face this new professional reality. It also means we will become more eager for ties, relationships, and the types of social structure that uphold our performance, just as Josie Esquivel did. Conventional approaches and individualism don't work anymore. We need to do it together.

3. Be humble

Humility requires a delicate balance. With too much of it, you can end up with insecurity. With not enough, you end up with conceit. You fail to see new evidence and knowledge even when it is right in front of you. And arrogance is what has persisted within the design community for too long—the idea that problem-solving is the exclusive domain of design, that designers somehow are the only people able to understand the needs and desires of our fellow human beings and come up with the most effective solutions to their problems, that only designers hold the secret formula to the eternal balance between form and function. Design exclusivism is dangerous. It stems from fear and insecurity. It is a form of snobbery that stops us from collaborating with others and having a meaningful impact as a designer. We tend to disregard the insights of other disciplines and are offended whenever we must justify our own decisions. It is an attitude that disengages alternative views and seeks consensus instead of a diversity of opinions. Ultimately, it shows a lack of openness and humility.

In a desire to uncover the importance of humility in the work environment, Bradley J. Owens, Michael D. Johnson, and Terence R. Mitchell reviewed the literature on humility across many philosophy and psychology journals with the goal of identifying the effects of humility on organizational outcomes.[31] According to their findings, humility is comprised of three things. The first pertains to a willingness to see oneself accurately. Self-discovery is a long journey, and humble individuals are open to navigating that meandering path and embracing any shortcomings that might be discovered along the way. They are open to acknowledging their flaws, which means they are more grounded and less prone to illusions of grandeur. "Individuals who maintain more realistic self-views tend to be more psychologically healthy and have higher general well-being," while people who lack self-awareness become more prone to overconfidence, "which is the root of a myriad of organizational problems, poor decisions, and self-complacency."[32] Confidence is one thing. But don't let it go to your head.

The second dimension of humility concerns the ability to recognize the strengths of other people. Humble individuals don't feel threatened by others, even when others have skills they don't have. As Owens explains, humble individuals "see mentors everywhere."[33] They seek growth by learning and leveraging other people's skills. They don't see rivals but exemplars. Humility is like "social learning on steroids." This approach can help alleviate toxic forms of envy and contempt. As soon as you start perceiving successful others as mentors, as professionals with whom you can learn from and whose actions you can emulate and improve, you can start feeling less subjugated by them and, as a result, more secure in yourself. This can also apply to any competitive environment you may find yourself in the future. Perceiving competitors as disguised coaches can provide an effective framwork for dealing with their achievements. And guess what: you might learn a thing or two.

The third and final factor uncovered by Owens, Johnson, and Mitchell has to do with teachability. Humble people have a continuous desire to learn. They show a strong predisposition for being open to feedback and new ideas. They proactively seek advice from others because they recognize their own shortcomings and see others as potential sources of knowledge. I can relate closely to this idea. Curiosity and inquisitiveness are major drivers in my life and are things I care deeply about. Whenever I can frame a given event as a potential learning experience, it makes it easier to follow through. I still recall a time as a manager at Google when I was hiring and growing my team at a fast pace. My calendar was filled with back-to-back interviews throughout the day. This was not fun. However, as soon as I framed each interview as an opportunity to learn something new about a candidate, their background and viewpoint on the world, interviews became not just more bearable but something I looked forward to having.

Humility can also be contagious. Take moral elevation, a topic that continues to interest many sociologists. It is the positive emotions and desire to replicate positive behaviors that are triggered in others who witness virtuous gestures. Moral elevation can cascade through an audience of strangers, so imagine what it can do to a group of coworkers. Humility is more than just a personal pursuit. Together with other important human skills like passion, curiosity, and empathy, it can be part of an ingrained set of values for your team or organization. But in the same way that it can be cultivated, it can also be lost. Every manager knows how certain team members can boost or lower the morale of a group. Often, culture fit can be brushed aside in favor of a perceived super talent or genius. This can be a risky move. I had a manager who once told me there was space for only a couple of egotistical stars in the group, and she often gave the following caveat: "and they better be really good." But no matter how talented one person might be, an inflated ego can pierce through the social fabric of your team very fast, and sometimes that tradeoff can haunt you. This is the other consequence of hiring stars. It can shake your team's culture badly.

As designers, we are constantly surrounded by unpredictability as we tackle increasingly large problems whose context we know very little about. To inhabit such a world means we need to be humble, recognize our blind spots, and rely on others for help. One way to explore the limits of modesty is to learn how to partner with nondesigners, not just working in separate roles with each doing their own thing but inviting nondesigners to be involved in the creative process. Codesigning with others can be a truly humbling experience. It makes you vulnerable to potential flaws as well as quirks and behaviors you might not feel comfortable exposing. While it's almost imperative to work side-by-side with customers during the initial problem definition phase, you can involve them in later generative stages as well, through design workshops and ideation. You can also bring stakeholders into the mix. This change in dynamics can build trust and help stakeholders recognize each other's strengths and weaknesses. It can also make them feel included and heard. Participatory design can be a great tool for becoming more attuned with the needs and expectations of society through the input of customers and stakeholders and, in the process, for not getting lost in our own presumptuous minds.

4. Be authentic

Imagine being locked in a small cubicle with someone you don't know for several months, hundreds of miles away from our planet. This might seem like a farfetched scenario for most, but it's part of the job of being NASA astronauts. It is what they spend years preparing for. Spaceflights and International Space Station expeditions can be expensive endeavors but not just from a material point of view. They can also be risky social experiments. Just think of the high stakes for any personal conflicts and serious disagreements that occur among astronauts. In order to better train astronauts for such events, NASA sends its crews to wilderness training in hard-to-reach environments where they test their resilience and ability to bond. John Kanengieter is a leadership expert hired by NASA to prepare astronauts to survive in the wild. Over thirty years, he led multiple teams to remote locations in the Wyoming mountains, where they faced emotionally charged experiences. As a result, he often developed strong ties and friendships with the training astronauts.

For NASA astronauts, these missions are vital to learn to "accommodate each other's idiosyncrasies through the numerous challenges and "hard-bitten intimacy of a wilderness trek."[34] As Kanengieter and Aparna Rajagopal-Durbin explain in their article on expedition success, for a group of people to succeed in the wilderness, they need to develop a type of expedition behavior. This means "getting along in a diverse group, cooperating with teammates, effectively resolving conflict, and keeping yourself and others motivated."[35] In a harsh environment, it's hard to survive by yourself, so you inevitably must rely on others for survival. Being exposed opens a door to trust. You might think you need to build trust first in order to open yourself and be vulnerable, but as Daniel Coyle points out in *The Culture Code: The Secrets of Highly Successful Groups*, being vulnerable together builds closeness, bonds, and eventually trust. Thus, vulnerability is not an outcome of trust. Often, it is a conduit to trust.

Still, we have a hard time being vulnerable with others, particularly coworkers. We are afraid that vulnerability will be confused with weakness. This is a mistake. Just as in the previous chapter we discussed the importance of vulnerability to conquer your own fears and become a better designer, here we want to point out that vulnerability is also a powerful vehicle for building trust with your coworkers. Trust is critical not just for NASA astronauts but for any effective social group collaborating on a given a project. If vulnerability is the quickest mechanism, perfectionism and pretentiousness can be major obstacles. You might think that bringing a perfected, made-up persona of yourself is a safer path to success. But it can become a major hindrance, leading often to social alienation and an inability to collaborate with others. In a paper with the suggestive title "Perfectionists Do Not Play Nicely with Others: Expanding the Social Disconnection Model," researchers argue that perfectionism can often lead to disharmony with other people. It can underlie "loneliness, problems with perceived social support, intense interpersonal conflicts, daily interpersonal hassles, feeling deficient in the eyes of other people, hostility, and disagreeableness,"[36] among a few other concerning factors.

So it might seem like a cliché, but you should aim at bringing your whole self to work. Being authentic is critical. You can save many years of therapy if you follow this advice. This is true even for individuals who are often the target of discrimination. In a 2017 study, researchers looked closely at the impact of concealing or revealing elements of one's identity across a sample of four hundred individuals from the LGBT community. Their findings suggest that "concealing a stigmatized identity has negative consequences for individual wellbeing" and affects social interactions. Furthermore, it "reduces work commitment and job satisfaction, which is likely to ultimately affect team processes and organizational performance in negative ways."[37] In other words, hiding your real identity can hurt your career in more ways than one. One of the things that the 2020 COVID-19 pandemic taught us is that maintaining a simulated work persona is not just impractical but simply unmanageable. Switching off all the humanness that makes us human is not realistic. Such a realization will hopefully outlast a singular global pandemic so that gradually, we can relinquish the idea of a separate, better version of ourselves.

Actionable Advice

How you mature and progress as a designer will depend in large part on the people you choose to work with, the relationships you build, and the insights you learn along the way. And if it hasn't been clear so far, you cannot do it alone. Individualism does not pay off. You need others in order to succeed, so don't let overconfidence and arrogance get in the way. Also, don't aim at attaining a fictious, unreachable pedestal. Focus on doing your best work, surrounded by others who can contribute to the common goal and uphold your dreams and aspirations. As an independent knowledge worker, you will have many tempting opportunities around every corner. Don't be too eager to jump at your first opportunity at another company. You might realize quickly after the move how reliant you are on others. But also don't stay in a place that doesn't promote the values you wish to pursue. Before accepting a new role, ask many questions about the organization's culture, principles, and mission. This if often more important than the service, experience, or product it gets to build. Remember this in your next job hunt. Ultimately, wherever you are, advocate for an environment that fosters diversity of background and thought, where people feel safe to express their ideas and themselves.

By now you have realized that in order to work with others you need to nurture several personal traits that are not visible in most resumes. These skills can often be more important than the hard-earned ones you learned in high school, college, graduate school, or other professional programs. Commonly mislabeled as soft, skills such as humility, authenticity, and vulnerability are crucial in most types of collaborative efforts. If you are starting a new work relationship with someone, your priority should be to build trust, and in order to do that, it is important to embrace clarity and transparency from the beginning. When initiating a project with a multidisciplinary team, each team member needs to have a clear understanding of everyone's role and contributions. If you're exposed to new disciplines that you haven't worked with before, clarifying responsibilities upfront can alleviate many future misunderstandings. The burden should not only be on designers. When all team members explain what they do, how best to collaborate with them, and what their expectations are for success, you can start to recognize and empathize with the human being behind the job title.

To continue cementing trust with your partners, clients, and coworkers, you should aim at consistently meeting or exceeding expectations in every assignment or project. Driven by your competence and reliability, your consistent performance will bear many fruits. Competence means being capable of doing the job, caring about the craft, giving attention to details, and having pride in craftmanship. Reliability is all about delivering on time with the highest level of quality. It's about following through consistently, respecting deadlines, showing up at meetings, being available for questions, and communicating about issues early on. It means being able to do what you say and say what you mean. This brings us to honesty and integrity, key factors in building trust. You should aim to speak the truth, keep your word, not gossip, and not be afraid of expressing yourself. And remember, the best way to cultivate a reputation for being honest, competent, humble, and fair is to behave as such—not by showing your best self but by being yourself.

All advocacy is, at its core, an
exercise in empathy.

—Samantha Power[1]

Every great design begins
with an even better story.

—Lorinda Mamo[2]

3

Design is about ideas

Jean-Michel Basquiat is known as a graffiti prodigy who lit up the 1980s art scene in New York City with his bold, provocative, social commentary paintings. After his death at age twenty-seven, Basquiat went to become an influential pop icon. His interest in graffiti was influenced by his friend Al Diaz, whom he met in high school. Diaz had been immersed in New York's underground movement since he started writing graffiti on trains at the early age of twelve. Bonded by their artistic pursuits and a shared Puerto Rican ancestry, the boys' first joint project was a satirical school newspaper, which gave them a lot of creative freedom. In a popular article for the paper in 1977, the duo featured a fictional dialogue between two characters discussing the benefits of an imaginary "guilt free religion"[3] called SAMO. Later that year, they began spray-painting buildings in lower Manhattan under the tag of the new religion. Despite their friendship, it was a short-lived collaboration. In 1980, Basquiat inscribed "SAMO IS DEAD" in a Soho building after an argument with Diaz. A low-key type of person, Diaz has continued doing art to this day. Basquiat went on to become one of the most influential artists of the twentieth century with several of his paintings being sold for more than $100 million dollars.

According to American Hungarian Romanian physicist Albert-László Barabási, this tale is the artistic equivalent of scientific twin studies, conducted to evaluate the effects of social upbringing on individuals with the same genetic material. "Two students who are the same age, from the same environment, make art that's impossible to tell apart. Suddenly they become untwined, breaking abruptly out on their own."[4] One achieves tremendous success, the other remains fairly anonymous. What could explain this outcome? A lot has to do with nature and personality. Diaz was more solitary, and Basquiat was more outgoing. Perhaps more fundamentally, they had very different approaches to what they did with their ideas. "This was evident even during their adolescent SAMO phase," writes Barabási, "when Diaz insisted that they keep their shared identity a secret. Basquiat? He outed the partnership to the *Village Voice* for one hundred dollars."[5] Even more important, Basquiat was an "unapologetic networker." During his short career, he connected with and befriended some of the most influential names in the contemporary creative scene, such as artists Andy Warhol, Keith Haring, and Debbie Harry, as well as art critics, editors, and curators like Glenn O'Brien and Diego Cortez.

Basquiat embodies an important lesson for any designer. Ideas alone don't necessarily go far. For ideas to go somewhere, they need to contaminate others. They need to spread their wings and inspire minds beyond their creator. Therefore, you need to set them free. Instead of being protective of your solution and locking yourself in a comfort zone, whose downsides are discussed in chapter 1, you need to expose it widely. The notions of virality and contagion are appropriated from epidemiology and rightly so, since there are many parallels between the spread of information and the spread of diseases. An example of this is found in the study of memetics, which investigates how an idea or a meme can propagate in a human population through social contagion. A meme (the term was coined by British evolutionary biologist Richard Dawkins in 1976) is a unit of cultural information that, similarly to the gene, can self-replicate, in this case in the mind of a given host.[6] An idea might "start with a small set of individuals or organizations and spread, often from person to person, almost like a virus,"[7] says marketing professor Jonah Berger. Basquiat leveraged the idea of word-of-mouth to his advantage, relying on others to spread the word and slowly infect a much larger audience. With time, recognition, prestige, and eventually money came to Basquiat in abundance. At only twenty-two, he was the youngest artist to ever showcase his work at the Whitney Biennial.

The dynamics of information diffusion, like those of disease infection, obey different patterns—at times, a persistent and predictable ebb and flow and at other times, a sudden burst followed by an immediate demise. On a few occasions, like a pandemic, ideas, fads, innovations, and memes can catch on and reach an outbreak. In his highly acclaimed book *The Tipping Point: How Little Things Can Make a Big Difference*, Canadian author Malcolm Gladwell describes the various elements that can contribute to a potential outbreak or information epidemic. In what he labels "the law of the few," Gladwell introduces three types of people who can play a critical role in propagating an idea—mavens (knowledge seekers who have a message to share), connectors (highly connected individuals who can spread the message), and salesmen (natural communicators with strong persuasion skills). Designers are essentially *mavens*. They accumulate knowledge and expertise and are happy to share it. They generate innovative viewpoints and solutions to a given problem. They are originators and idea brokers at the same time. Not all ideas will be good, but a few good ones might catch on.

Why do some ideas become popular while others fade into oblivion? One reason is quality. Some ideas are simply better than others. So what makes a good idea? There is no single formula, but it probably starts with originality. A solution that solves a problem in an unexpected way tends to have more traction. Why? Novelty improves recall. It is one of the oldest mnemonic techniques, well studied since the High Middle Ages, as part of a group of principles known collectively as *ars memorativa* (the art of memory). A modern manifestation is the *Von Restorff effect*—which tells us that we recall better what is unexpected—a principle widely used today in marketing and advertising. The second ingredient is elegance. A solution is elegant when it achieves great effectiveness with grace and simplicity. You could call it beauty. However, the word *elegance* invokes fewer negative connotations and is similarly understood by both science and art. Finally, a solution must be relevant. A good idea makes people feel good because it has practical value from which they can benefit. As a result, they are likely to establish a strong emotional attachment to it. This also highlights the importance of affect, an element explored by designers throughout the ages. What is emotionally compelling to us makes it more engaging, memorable, and therefore shareable.

If you have a good idea, you also want to make sure it sticks. This can be difficult, since most people are busy with their lives, frequently multitasking and thinking of their next deadline. However, regular contact can have consequential effects. We tend to develop a preference for things we are often exposed to. This is known among psychologists as the *mere-exposure effect*. Branding and marketing have long capitalized on this familiarity bias. After all, it is better to see a bad logo many times than a good logo only once. I remember an episode that highlights this principle. I once had a talented designer on my team who set out to create a series of elaborate user-interface concepts for an existing product. It was a powerful idea. The designer went out of his way to schedule meetings with senior leadership across the organization to expose the work, sometimes more than once. Soon, everyone was talking about it, and later, many of his original ideas found their way into the product. Grit and persistence can pay off. And so does exposure.

Now that we know what a good idea is and how it can become sticky, it is time we make it contagious. If the numerous connections Basquiat established during his lifetime were mapped, that map would be a highly intricate mesh of artists, critics, and editors. This is not necessarily unique to Basquiat. Any social group you can think of is comprised of a network of individuals, where every person or node has a given ability to disseminate information. However, it is not an equal game. A few individuals have a much higher chance of circulating a given message. In network science, this is known as the *law of preferential attachment*. Whether it is an arrangement of airports, servers, websites, or people, the recurrent underlying structure is one where most nodes are of small or medium size. A few nodes known as *hubs* have a much larger degree of connectivity. This discrepancy increases over time, as new nodes tend to connect to the hubs due to preferential attachment and prospective influence. Therefore, it is not surprising this network law is also known as "The rich get richer."

Within a given community, *connectors* are the hubs of its social network. Due to their privileged situation, they can circulate an idea much more broadly and effectively than any large group of less influential individuals. They are also central to the stability of the network, functioning as the social glue of their group. As we saw before, Basquiat became considerably more popular because of his ability to connect with the right nodes in the network, many that were dominant in the art scene of the early 1980s. Some truly powerful connectors, known as *superspreaders*, can make your idea literally explode in popularity. In modern-day marketing, this measure of influence is also called *social currency*. Yet social media has only capitalized on an organizational system that has been with us for a long time. While in the past connectors would have been defined by their rank, authority, or prestige, in today's social media–driven society, the number of followers on a given platform is usually what grants a person the status of a connector and therefore the ability to broadly propagate any meme.

But even the most talented designer working with a well-established connector can go only so far. This is in part because what is being exchanged between the two is just a concept. An idea, after all, is only a projection of potential impact. It can be immensely effective just as a projection. Ideas are eternal. They live beyond space and time. They are also immensely powerful. They can move mountains, as the popular adage says, inspire people and transform societies. Yet they are still just a thought or an ideal. A mental representation, according to Plato, is separate from reality. For designers, an idea cannot just be a perfect pattern. In order to exist, it must become manifest, not necessarily visible. Designers are now involved in many invisible pursuits.[8] But ultimately, it must affect change in the real world. Designers are practical and utilitarian problem-solvers, so simply coming up with a concept in abstraction is one step too short. Design can have a voice in what ought to be, but showing is often the best way to reach a desired goal: show, don't tell. However, putting a plan into effect is hard and often needs more than a good idea.

As it should be clear by now, an idea—no matter how original, effective, or ethical it might be—is just an idea. If you don't know how to express it, how to put it in to words, it will never go anywhere. Designers can be great originators but are not always good catalysts. To use Gladwell's metaphor, they are great mavens but not necessarily great *salesmen*. Designers need to learn to sell their ideas. This can truly be the most critical skill in their career or, when lacking, the biggest impediment to their success. It is also true they don't always have to do it alone. A famous example is English biologist Thomas Huxley, known for being a relentless advocate and fierce debater in support of Darwin's theory of evolution, earning him the title of "Darwin's bulldog." As a shy and secluded family man, it is hard to speculate how far Darwin's arguments would have gone without Huxley's combative and brilliant orator skills. Would Al Diaz's fate had been any different if he had had a Huxley pushing him forward and advocating for his work where it mattered? It's hard to say, but one thing is sure: you shouldn't have to rely on someone else to do the job for you.

Designers must aspire to be more than just creative instigators. They should be effective mavens and connectors but also convincing salespeople who are able to influence and sway other individuals. Remember that the goal is to transform an idea into something more than a mere projection. For this materialization to happen requires passing through a few gateways and gatekeepers, so you need to learn the awkward, delicate dance of persuasion. This dance combines character, personality, and social skills that go beyond any tool or methodology you might have learned at school or at a previous job. Your posture, knowledge, self-confidence, expertise, assertiveness, and credibility can all play important roles, yet none of these traits alone is enough to sell your idea. If you want your design solution to see the light of day, you need to build the right strategic toolbox for persuasion. The following series of tips can help you get there.

1. Build a defensible rationale

Stepping into a design review can sometimes feel like entering a hot zone. When change is introduced, resistance is to be expected and is likely to increase as the implementation costs of the proposed solution are presented. People have a strong propensity to maintain the current state of things, and this *status quo bias* can lead audience members to question your judgment and design options, sometimes in an emotional way. They might skip some presented information and jump straight to their own assumptions, conclusions, and even prejudices. This is happening while you are surrounded by your peers, cross-functional partners, clients, or the senior leadership of your organization, which can make a design review an intimidating experience. The worst thing you can do in such a scenario is resort to subjective explanations. It's great to have a point of view, but design is not about opinions. If you ground your design solution on your individual beliefs, you are doomed to let yourself down, as well as the entire design community. You will be amplifying the misconception that design is subjective and is just a matter of interpretation. You must underpin your argument with clarity and reason. You need to arm yourself with evidence.

As you build a defensible rationale for your design solution, you should consider qualitative research, quantitative research, and cognitive science. You don't always need all three, but as much as possible, you should leverage these important tools in your design defense strategy. Let's cover a little bit what each one can do individually.

Qualitative research

When it comes to building a defensible rationale, qualitative design research—the observation and collection of nonnumerical data, such as thoughts, opinions, reasons, perceptions, attitudes, motivations, and behaviors—tends to earn a high dividend. Such insights can be fundamental in better understanding the human problem and stimulating subsequent design solutions. While relevant at all stages of design development, the early-stage exploratory research can truly light the path for designers. It does not have to be a lengthy and expensive process. Research is not a luxury. You can rely on past studies relevant to your question and pursue a variety of lean and agile research approaches, such as surveys, cafe studies, phone interviews, design sprints, and participatory design sessions. Even a few observation sessions can yield great results. Light research is always better than no research at all.

Human-centered research can still be the target of occasional sneering. Critics of the practice use the familiar argument that users don't know what they want. And that's certainly true in most cases. Users will hardly give you a prescribed list of requirements for you to build. However, this is a mischaracterization of the discipline. Design research does not ask people what they want. Most people don't know what they want. The goal is to identify specific needs, both met and unmet, through direct contact with users so that those needs can be translated into opportunities and, ultimately, design solutions. Research also aims at understanding context and asking relevant questions to customers, stakeholders, and organizations. Without this important bridge that connects the problem to the solution, designers would become merely solvers, creative wanderers. Being the voice of the user is an obligation of the designer. It can also yield tremendous dividends even in the fiercest of design reviews. After all, it is hard to argue against the explicit needs of your customer.

Quantitative research

Quantitative research can collect and analyze large volumes of user data in order to find patterns and correlations. At a time where many digital design products are being measured and instrumentalized, it's easy to collect a wide assortment of metrics on things like clicks, taps, scrolls, swipes, pinches, movement, time spent, pages per session, and purchases. Almost every interaction with a screen and user interface—either as an early prototype or a finalized product—can be tracked and measured. It can also be visualized in different ways to better understand the unique tasks, behaviors, and paths undertaken by users within a digital experience. It can show us product dead ends, bottlenecks, transition cliffs, desire lines, preferable features, as well as the continuous ebb and flow of traffic. While the ethical implications of this process are covered in the next two chapters, when done well, the resulting user journey map can lead to substantial improvements in a product. Therefore, quantitative research is an important tool in building a defensible rationale because it can objectively validate your design problem, hypothesis, or solution. You should leverage such a weapon as part of your evidence arsenal.

Cognitive science

Design can sometimes feel like an echo chamber. Over the years, as design became more specialized, we lost our ability to think broadly across multiple domains, but more important, we lost touch with the accumulated knowledge of other disciplines. This can lead to a design elitism that works against the cross-disciplinary approach needed in the modern workforce.[9] Evidence that substantiates good design practices can come from many fields, including economics, visual perception, marketing, and evolutionary psychology. When applied correctly, these cross-disciplinary strategies can be both generative (by inspiring and guiding the design process) and evaluative (by assessing its effectiveness through a set of proven heuristics). You can even align them with your product mission, vision, and key performance indicators. They go by different names—laws, rules, paradoxes, effects, biases. I tend to prefer the word *principles*.

I'm particularly fond of principles because they encapsulate a general idea or consideration instead of a prescriptive, step-by-step instruction. Some of my favorite design principles, which I've taught over the years—such as *horror vacui* (a fear of empty space), Hick's law (decision-making time increases as options increase), or the aesthetic-usability effect (the preference for beautiful products)—highlight innate human biases or shortcuts uncovered over the years by cognitive science. In talking about design principles, I've noticed two recurrent patterns in my audiences. Designers are often delighted to discover that many of their "intuitive" options are grounded in science, while nondesigners are surprised to know that design can be objectively scientific. Many of these powerful principles provide designers with a tool to better understand the human brain. But perhaps more crucially, they allow designers to verbalize design choices based on rigorous, well-established research.

2. Tell a compelling story

Now you've built a defensible rationale based on evidence and reasoning, but unfortunately, it is not enough. The art of persuasion can be hard to decode, and it is swayed by multiple unpredictable variables. One highly effective way to package your evidence and argument is through storytelling. Stories have been an effective mechanism for communicating and memorizing information for thousands of years, long before we invented symbols and written language. Designers need to master this important skill. Here's the good news. Every design solution contains the perfect recipe for a compelling narrative. If you are bringing ideas to life, you're already telling a story. Like design, great storytelling stems from a problem that we are compelled to know more about. Through stories, we are often led on empathic journeys with the characters and the struggles they face as the storyteller gives them choices and possible solutions.

Designers are well equipped for storytelling since they are the ones asking the questions, framing the problem, and understanding the context. So don't overthink it. You can contemplate it as just another design project. "The process of selecting what to include and what to exclude in your story is a design decision," says author and designer Cheryl Platz. "You're asking important questions and identifying where you might not have answers, where you might be making assumptions, and where your key insights lie."[10] So what are the key ingredients of a great design narrative? In *The Storytelling Animal: Stories Make Us Human*, American literary scholar Jonathan

Gottschall explains that the elemental function of a story is composed of three key elements, respectively:[11]

Character + Predicament + Attempted extrication

If this formula were translated to design, it would look like this:

User + Problem + Solution

The first element of your story, your main *character*, is the human or humans who will benefit from your design. Not always, as we will explore in chapter 7, but often. Providing as much context about them is paramount in creating empathy and in understanding some of the nuances and challenges they face, for which your design solution will prove effective. The English journalist Christopher Booker spent thirty-four years trying to identity the elemental essence of a story by analyzing hundreds of pieces of fiction. Booker identified seven archetypal plots, including obvious ones such as "rags to riches," but if there is a metaplot, it is one centered on the main protagonist. As Booker explains: "However many characters may appear in a story, its real concern is with just one: its hero or its heroine. It is he or she with whose fate we identify, as we see them gradually developing towards that state of self-realization which marks the end of the story."[12] Focusing on the hero or heroine of your story means you are leveraging an ancient narrative archetype that is almost innate to humans. Drawing on in-depth customer research, you can bring your characters to life through *user segments* (users who are grouped by shared characteristics) and *user personas* (fictional users who represent qualities of the target audience), while focusing on their personality, behavior, attitudes, and needs. You can also provide quantitative evidence for your solution, yet focusing on a single individual and conveying a unique story is a more compelling strategy and is also intrinsically human.

The *predicament* is the problem you're trying to solve. It's important to substantiate it with enough details so that the urgency or gravity of the challenge is communicated. This is an area where qualitative design research can help. Use your hero or heroine once again to highlight the specific hurdles they face on a regular basis. You can measure their struggle in ways that are pertinent to your design story, such as the amount of wasted time, unnecessary steps or tasks, inability to overcome obstacles, or failed actions. These struggles should be a series of hurdles that can normally result in real human consequences, such anxiety, stress, or injury. It is critical to get the predicament right, since it is the primary means for evaluating the success of the solution. But you must strike the right contextual balance. I've seen designers do this part wrong in two ways—either by jumping too soon to the solution and getting a lot of contextual questions as a result or by providing too much context when none is needed. The key is knowing the right balance, which requires getting to know—ahead of time—your audience members and their grasp of the challenge at hand. This way you can target the most appropriate frame of reference without being too terse or verbose.

Finally, the *attempted extrication* is your effort to solve the problem for your character. You can think of it as an attempt to rescue them from a previous impediment, your observed problem. Here you have a free rein to expand on the benefits of your solution— why it effectively solves the observed, well-document challenge for your hero or heroine. Provide evidence of success even if it's only preliminary. You can rely on visual aids and presentation design, yet don't feel trapped by a tool. If you are applying your storytelling skills right, you can triumph with pen or paper or even by your spoken words alone. When packed in the right sequence with the right evidence and context, your design story can be empathic, convincing, and persuasive. On the other hand, your story does not have to end here. It continues living, sometimes long after you are gone. As is shown in chapter 8, design stories often disregard a critical last stage that validates our designs as well as our ethical responsibilities—the lasting impact of our solution.

3. Persuade with empathy

Empathy can be a design superpower, not just in interpreting users' needs and desires but also in persuading stakeholders. Despite its modern-day limitations, user empathy[13] has been widely publicized, but here we explore a lesser known type of empathy in design— stakeholder empathy. In essence, it describes an affinity with the person a designer must persuade when selling an idea. This is normally a client, executive, director, product manager, or peer. Stakeholder empathy can be pivotal in making sure your original solution is accepted. As the ultimate gatekeeper between your idea and its implementation, you need to develop the right empathic strategy for persuasion. But this is not unique to design. It is hard to find a job where there isn't a human gatekeeper—a boss, a client, a customer, a reviewer, an editor—that you need to persuade in order to have your work accepted. This is true in academia and in industry at large. Such a validation process has its benefits, but it can be prone to biases of all sorts.

Even before trying to convince anyone, designers should understand that every idea has an associated cost. An idea is a bet on the future. From a stakeholder viewpoint, saying yes to a solution requires an investment in time, money, and resources. It takes a certain leap of faith since a cost can be calculated, but a benefit might not be as apparent. Stakeholders have a lot to lose, including their reputation, so to bet on an idea, they require some level of assurance in its success. Also, people tend to be less driven by reason in decision making than they might think they are, and stakeholders are no different. They are also probably busy, with competing proposals or other matters to oversee and approve. You can provide enough evidence packaged in a compelling story. You can even reduce uncertainty and risk by showing what the result will be, either through advanced prototypes or through live executions of the intended solution. However, none of that will change the fact that an interaction with a stakeholder can be a charged experience.

It can be a power struggle at times, where aversion to change is to be expected.

Stakeholders who are at the top of the decision-making chain often feel that their viewpoint is what got them there. As such, they can be confident in their judgments and not see a reason to change things. They sometimes are not looking to be convinced either. There's a tremendous amount of fear and status anxiety in organizations, and no one, particularly people at the top, likes to be judged or proven wrong. They are also driven by social proof. What are my peers doing? Will my boss endorse this decision? Will it make me look good? You must somehow circumvent this apprehension. Avoid pushing too hard since people being pushed become defensive and eventually react. Presenting more evidence or expanding on your own view of the matter will likely not go far. However, appealing to something that is closer to them and their interests, passion, and priorities will make your view more relatable, personal, and therefore worthwhile. You must sway them through empathy by aligning with their narrative, frame of reference, and sphere of knowledge and concern.

As social psychology professors Matthew Feinberg and Robb Willer uncovered in a study in 2015, empathy plays a key role in persuasion, even in the most challenging scenarios.[14] Facing an increasingly polarized political landscape in the United States, Feinberg and Willer decided to test how successfully liberals and conservatives could convince each other to adopt their respective viewpoints. As the study showed, arguments that relied on the moral principles of their political opponents (what they valued and cared about) had a much higher success rate than arguments based on the opponents' self-interest. This is easier said than done. "Most people are not very good at appealing to other people's values,"[15] says Feinberg. We're often stuck in our own minds, on what's important to us—our priorities, interests, and desires. Left unchecked, these priorities can lead us to fall into a consensus bias—the assumption that one's judgments are shared by others and hence appropriate in a given context—and to become a victim of overconfidence. Worse, they can lead us to believe that the presented facts or solutions are self-explanatory, when alone they will rarely suffice. What do you do when a stakeholder doesn't see eye to eye with you on the value of your solution? Do you just send a slide deck filled with more examples?

Changing minds is hard and can't be done by just providing more facts and evidence. A better approach for this is active listening and building trust. Jonah Berger, marketing professor at the Wharton School at the University of Pennsylvania, compares this tactic to the careful dance used in hostage negotiations. A good hostage negotiator never goes too hard on the perpetrator since it might push them over the edge. "Push them too hard and they'll snap. Tell them what to do and they're unlikely to listen,"[16] explains Berger. "Instead, they identify what's preventing change from happening and remove that barrier. Allowing change to happen with less energy, not more."[17] This should be a great goal for any designer. As shown in the previous chapter, building trust is useful for establishing ties with your team members and peers and also with your stakeholder. Trying to get to know them at a personal level goes a long way. It brings down barriers while providing valuable insights into what they care about, what's worrying them at that moment, and how they prioritize those concerns. It makes it easier to put yourself in their shoes and ask, "What's in it for me? Why should I listen to this?"

Finally, a commonly forgotten facet of stakeholder interaction involves organizational context. By doing research on your stakeholder, you can identify common points, interests, and past events that can be relevant in the current discussion and subsequent approval. But your research shouldn't stop there. If you are pitching your idea to a new client, you need to do some background investigation on the organization. You need to understand their culture and operating methods. This will inform what drives stakeholders in that group and provide valuable insights into their appetite for innovation, their degree of customer centrality, and their overall business strategy. You cannot just jump straight into a design problem, talk with potential customers, and apply a given design methodology without understanding the underlying culture of the organization. Context is critical and can save you a lot of pain points and disappointments down the line.

Actionable Advice

Don't fall into the trap of believing your idea is powerful enough to convince others on its own. When it comes to advocating for a given design solution, don't rely on your opinion or anyone else's. Advocate for evidence and aim at building your own defensible rationale. Arm yourself in a way that every angle and possible drawback has been considered and evaluated. You will become a much stronger designer as a result. Package your solution in an engaging way by means of a memorable story, which provides details on your target user, the problem at hand, and the potential benefits of the solution's implementation. If you want to disseminate your idea more broadly, this is easier than ever before. From podcasts to blogs, social networks to webinars, there are numerous tools that can help make your voice be heard. So take advantage of them. Tap into your existing network or strive to expand it considerably. Be pragmatic, and focus on the few connectors who can help propagate your innovation. Be persistent, and don't give up at your first hurdle.

Before going into a meeting room or conference hall, you must understand the context that you are entering. Every time I'm invited to a conference, my first question is about the size and composition of the audience. The answers to these questions affect how much emphasis should be given to a given topic. You don't want to be too superficial or spend too much time on unnecessary details so that it seems you are preaching to the choir. Context also affects the type of language used, such as acronyms and technical jargon. When meeting a stakeholder, do your homework ahead of time. Learn all you can about their values, motivations, goals, constraints, and strategy. Try to also understand the organizational culture they foster. One way to build trust is to get to know stakeholders at a personal level. Sometimes scheduling an informal meeting ahead of time can help. Start with a genuine compliment, which can lower defensive mechanisms, put people more at ease, and create a more productive atmosphere. Provide a clear structure that's easy to follow. Focus on high-priority issues. Be explicit about what you need. Sincerity and honesty always go a long way.

Learning how to persuade and influence others can be a lifelong pursuit. It starts by paying attention to your "soft skills." These are human skills that can be vital in making your idea come to fruition and in allowing you to succeed as a designer. You should constantly calibrate yourself along the way since self-perception is always distorted. Ask for regular peer feedback in addition to regular performance evaluation cycles. If you work in an environment that doesn't have such measures in place, there are other informal tactics you could consider. Send your peers, coworkers, stakeholders, or clients a simple questionnaire on your performance. This can give you valuable data on areas you might be able to improve. You can also ask them directly, during a private conversation, "How am I doing? What can I do better?" Finally, you can take workshops and training courses that can be revealing of your own personality traits, triggers, and areas of focus. Through these, you can become a more confident and convincing presenter and, perhaps more important, understand how others might perceive you.

Societal Impact

We reduce people to statistics in ways that dehumanizes them, keeping ourselves at a distance from the ugly realities of our decisions.

—Jacqueline Novogratz[1]

Treat different people differently. Anything else is a compromise.

—Seth Godin[2]

4

Design is about tasks

At twenty-eight, James Wisniewski struggled to have any meaningful personal relationships. Gaming up to fourteen hours a day can make dating hard. It can also have a negative effect on your health and well-being. A driver in Wales, UK, Wisniewski spent most of his time sitting down, either in a vehicle on the road or on a chair in front of a computer monitor. As soon as he returned to his home at around 6:30 p.m., he started playing video games, sometimes well into the night. The many hours that he spent sitting took an undeniable physical toll on his body. He suffered from constant back pain, slept poorly, and often felt exhausted. Unfortunately, James was not the only or the most severe case of gaming addiction. In 2005, a thirteen-year-old

Chinese boy called Zhang Xiaoyi committed suicide after spending two days straight playing an online role-playing game. Gaming-related suicides have also occurred in South Korea, India, and the United States. The addiction is so pervasive that in 2018 the World Health Organization (WHO) adopted gaming disorder as a mental health condition in the eleventh revision of its International Classification of Diseases (ICD).

"It's the priority of my life—I wake up and think about it, I go to bed and think about it," said Wisniewski regarding his gaming addiction.[3] These words seem to echo the criteria of gaming disorder as defined by the WHO—the "lack of control over playing video games (when and how often), priority given to gaming over other life interests and being unable to stop playing games even when negative consequences have occurred as a result."[4] Besides the anxiety, depression, and social phobia it can cause, gaming addiction can put youngsters on a dangerous path for gambling. This happened with a young man in Great Britain who started playing video games at age twelve and by his early twenties was recovering from compulsive gambling disorder.[5] Jack Ritchie started using his dinner money for gambling at age seventeen and seven years later took his own life. To help with similar cases, UK's National Health Service (NHS) finally opened a gambling addiction clinic in September 2019 to help children as young as thirteen.

If you think gaming is the rare industry that triggers addictive behavior and mental disorders, think again. Gaming has just been around for longer than some newer technologies. Research on the negative effects of gaming date back to the 1980s, and the press started covering the topic more attentively after a 1993 *Wired* article was published about a college student who failed to attend classes so that he could spend twelve hours a day playing in a multiplayer real-time virtual world.[6] Today, often inspired by gaming tactics, we are developing highly addictive technologies that serve no apparent purpose apart from making us more anxious and depressed. In his book *Irresistible: The Rise of Addictive Technology and the Business of*

Keeping Us Hooked, Adam Alter, of the marketing and psychology departments at New York University's Stern School of Business, mentions a study that found that 40 percent of people nowadays have some type of internet-related addiction, such as games, social media, email, or pornography.[7] People check their mobile phones 150 times a day on average and their emails thirty-six times an hour. We do this because we derive some apparent gratification from social validation but also because these tools behave as highly addictive games that explore numerous cognitive biases and shortcuts. Many of us are simply hooked. Alter refers to this as the "tech zombie epidemic."[8]

Although social media addiction is a fairly new area for research, it seems to have spread across all age groups around the world. Experts estimate that up to 10 percent of Americans have problematic social media use, and the number of rehabilitation centers and youth clinics targeting this problem has grown substantially in recent years. As with gaming, people with impulsive behavior might be more susceptive to developing an "impaired response inhibition."[9] At the time of this writing, social media addiction has not yet been included in the WHO's list of mental disorders, but this could certainly change in the future. With all these deeply worrying signs, you would think that the people building online games and social media platforms would be concerned about their negative impact on society. You would expect designers to be troubled by treating their users as passive zombies. But you would have to think again.

If we look behind the scenes of these troubling use patterns, we see a whole different picture. For the designers, product managers, and engineers who work on a given product feature, twenty-eight-year-old James Wisniewski is just another number on a spreadsheet, another pixel on a chart. The fact that he spent fourteen hours a day logged into the system was not a cause for concern but an intended goal. It was happening by design. Likely driven by a need to document demonstrable growth, the product team aimed at showing progress on various engagement metrics, such as *average session duration* or *bounce rate*. Perhaps more critically, the team aimed at minimizing friction on tasks like buying another weapon or upgrading a team pack. When tasks in a game rely on paying for extra products, decreasing the amount of time for completion will improve its conversion rate and, as a result, increase revenue. It will also instill in young users the addictive thrill of gambling. As Israeli historian Yuval Noah Harari eerily points out in *21 Lessons for the 21st Century*, "online giants tend to view humans as audiovisual animals—a pair of eyes and a pair of ears connected to ten fingers, a screen and a credit card."[10]

A lot of digital designers spend their days fine-tuning every step along the user journey to reduce friction and increase adoption. If all of the products they built were benign and meant to improve people's lives, perhaps this wouldn't be a concern. Yet despite the nature of the product, reducing humans to simple task operators on a funnel is the first step in distancing ourselves from our responsibility as designers. When task completion becomes the primary measure of success, we're failing to understand the true repercussions of our work, we're overlooking the cumulative effect of multiple tasks over time on human behavior and well-being, and we're failing to perceive humans as the unique entities they are. Seeing people as data points is the first level of abstraction, the first dehumanizing step. When every click, swipe, pause, eye movement, and purchase can be tracked, it's also the first step in accepting design as a measurable instrument for profit, a topic explored more closely in chapter 5.

Seeing humans as data points is not just narrow or unhuman; it's also the wrong approach. Reducing design to a series of tasks is a simplistic way of looking at a problem. Humans are idiosyncratic creatures, unpredictable in many ways. According to the cofounders of the consulting firm Red, Christian Madsbjerg and Mikkel B. Rasmussen, "companies that rely too much on the numbers, graphs and factoids of Big Data risk insulating themselves from the rich, qualitative reality of their customers' everyday lives. They can lose the ability to imagine and intuit how the world—and their own businesses—might be evolving."[11] Yet designers continue to fall into this self-preserving, distancing trap, withdrawing ourselves from the humans we are meant to help, from the impact we can have in their lives, and from our own burden of responsibility. While design used to be seen as an art form, design now is a means for measurement and revenue. If we want the righteous nature of design to prevail, we must change our direction. If not, human-centered design could become stuck between the extravagant design-as-art of the past and the worrying, design-as-a-tool-for-control of the present.

One way to avoid such dehumanizing behavior is to rely on a design superpower—the ability to read the minds of users and understand their needs, or empathy. This prescient skill can pay off tremendously in the success of a product. However, user empathy is challenging, since designers are often dealing with strangers. And don't get fooled by your perceived telepathic capabilities. As Malcolm Gladwell explains in *Talking to Strangers: What We Should Know about the People We Don't Know*, we have a recurring tendency to overestimate our ability to judge and understand strangers.[12] It is easier to connect with an end user when the designer is also a customer. Let's say you are designing the interface for an online music service or a logo for a coffeehouse chain that you use frequently. Putting yourself in the shoes of the customer might not seem difficult because you and some of your friends and acquaintances are consumers as well. In these cases, empathy is linked closely with familiarity.

Empathy however, becomes more challenging when you are commissioned to work in a domain or an industry you are less familiar with. It's even harder when you're designing for thousands or even millions of users on a global scale and have to consider a wide array of languages, customs, and behaviors. While well-intended, the importance of empathy in design describes an outdated, one-to-one relationship between a designer and a customer, which changed a long time ago. Today, that relationship is not even one-to-many or few-to-many. In most large-scale contemporary digital platforms, it's a many-to-millions relationship. How is it possible for an individual designer or even a collective of multidisciplinary designers to empathize and understand the unique needs and viewpoints of such an overwhelmingly large audience?

Empathy helps, but it can go only so far. No matter how much you try, it won't bring the human back to the equation. In order to do so, we need to aspire to a more humane design practice. Harari adds to his eerily depiction of humans as audiovisual animals by saying that a critical step in fixing this view is to "appreciate that humans have bodies."[13] I would go a step further and include mind. We can fix this by acknowledging that humans have a unique body and mind. What exactly does that mean? It means understanding our diverse idiosyncrasies and abilities, as well as our shared irrationality; respecting our time, privacy, and personal data; respecting our human dignity and free agency; seeing users as a whole person, not as dots plotted on a chart. Above all, it means including everyone. Such an approach is far from restraining. In fact, it can be an important catalyst for new, compassionate ideas that respect humans in their full magnitude.

1. Diverse range of idiosyncrasies

Johann Sebastian Bach had very large hands. The eighteenth-century composer and organist could reach a span of twelve white keys (a twelfth) on a piano) with a single hand, while most people can reach only eight (an octave). This physical characteristic, uncovered by a German anatomist who analyzed Bach's skeleton in detail,[14] certainly must have been advantageous. Reaching a twelfth is not easy for most people. Many musicians have struggled with their own physical limitations, including Elton John, who gave up on a career in classical music because he could not reach certain chords. But small hand size afflicts primarily women, who are constantly reminded of the challenges of inhabiting a world designed for men. "Several studies have found that female pianists run an approximately 50% higher risk of pain and injury than male pianists"[15] while attempting an unnatural stretch, says British journalist Caroline Criado Perez. The average hand span for a woman is between seven and eight inches, 0.88 inches (2.2 cm) smaller than the average male. Bach's hand span was 10¼ inches (26 cm). And Russian composer Sergey Rachmaninoff's was an impressive 12 inches (30.4 cm) from thumb to last finger. Designed for the average male hand, the standard piano keyboard has put some men and most women at a serious disadvantage—87 percent of adult female pianists to be precise.[16] It is the type of design tunnel vision that discounts a large segment of the population by not considering our differences.

We live in an inequitable world—with voice recognition systems that fail to recognize female voices, cars that are built around male measurements (which make women 74 percent more likely to die or be severely injured in a car crash), and public toilet designs that are inhospitable for women and children—where design is often a vehicle for exclusion. And women are not the only ones who are ignored. Many underrepresented social groups, races, cultures, and ethnicities experience this type of situation every day. The tech industry is filled with examples of racial bias—in soap dispensers, fitness trackers, heart-rate monitors, face identification or image recognition software, and many other applications and devices. Either because the training data for the underlying algorithms is skewed or because the product wasn't tested with a broad segment of the population, these designs fail to grasp an ultimate truth about human nature: we're not all the same.

Humans are not one-dimensional, formulaic task operators. We are idiosyncratic creatures with a variety of body shapes, interests, and backgrounds. We are complex individuals who are filled with riddles and contradictions, lies and pretenses, and above all, unpredictable behavior. Our circumstances are multifold and determine how we look, think, and behave. We are made up of our singular traits. Our human makeup includes race, gender, age, culture, ethnicity, nationality, language, lifestyle, personality, education, religion, profession, and income. Consider the myriad ways we can be different in one single trait to understand how varied we can be. We are also ever adapting. Even well-intentioned approaches like customer segmentation and user personas, which are bedrock tools for building user empathy, can show only an immutable facet of an individual person and too often focus on demographics and stereotypes instead of needs. However, our goals, desires, moods, and behaviors can change frequently, sometimes in a single day. Furthermore, we are multitasking on various devices over several hours and often at the same time. We are always distracted and interrupted by technology as well as by other people. We are multitaskers in a multimodal world.

To design for a single task, by a loosely defined human archetype, in a single snapshot of time, is an unrealistic shot in the dark. You're choosing to ignore a large slice of humanness and all the variations that come with it. It is not the type of humane design we should seek. We must work side-by-side with communities that have been marginalized in order to find more inclusive solutions. "Recognize who's most excluded from using a solution and then bring them into the heart of the design process," says author and design director Kat Holmes. Furthermore, diversity can be a force for innovation. "People who navigate mismatched interactions every day of their lives will bring ingenuity and deep expertise in how to solve those design challenges."[17] A lot of the design work should be about observing, hearing, and working with people different than yourself—just as producer David Steinbuhler and pianist Christopher Donison did when they created a set of reduced-width keyboards, known as the DS Standard, and hence leveled the playing field for thousands of aspiring musicians. Human-centric means all humans are equitably represented. Anything else is a compromise.

The most obvious way to design with diversity in mind is to embrace a diverse team. According to the British Design Council, 78 percent of those working in the design industry in the UK are male,[18] and approximately 86 percent working in the UK and US are Caucasian.[19] This means that in a team of twenty designers in either of these countries, roughly sixteen will be white males. The problem with such a skewed situation is that it creates a type of monoculture that is oblivious to the wide range of problems and experiences of a diverse population. This would be worrying if the team was responsible for any product, but when it oversees products used by millions around the world, as is often the case in big tech, the harm is much greater. A lack of visibility and understanding is a limiting factor to human imagination. A monoculture becomes a stale environment for ideas to flourish in. There are many known unknowns out there that designers are either unconsciously unaware of or consciously ignoring. You should aspire to neither outcome.

At one point at Google, I was managing a team of more than thirty people from twelve different countries, across six locations, with multiple ethnicities and an equal gender split. This diversity of experience, background, and mindset made for the best type of interpersonal interaction and discussion. Each unique perspective enriched the group in a critical way, and there was rarely a time when I was not surprised by the team members' different ways of looking at life. The world felt somewhat smaller and each corner of humanity easily reachable, even by a small collective like ours. Embracing a diverse workplace starts by hiring diverse talent and evading the prevalent tendency to hire people who look and think like you. With more perspectives, you can have a wider range of thought and problem-solving skills, as well as more representation from the population at large. The team becomes more sensitive to the differences in experience and context of their product audience. As a diverse group of problem solvers, you can detect a much larger quantity of known unknowns.

2. Full spectrum of normalcy

Despite occasional pain from arthritis in her hands, Betsey Farber loved to cook. In the late 1980s, she struggled with the existing vegetable peelers that were available in stores. These objects hadn't changed in decades. Predominantly made of metal, they were hard to grab and maneuver properly. The discomfort was aggravated by Betsey's arthritis, a condition that afflicts roughly 23 percent of adults in the United States, or about 54 million people. Despite her background in architecture, which made her sensitive to issues of ergonomics, her frustration had a more profound effect on her husband, designer Sam Farber. While cooking a meal with Betsey and hearing her complain about the issue, Sam decided to take matters into his own hands. In 1990, Sam Farber came up with a better solution—in fact, a whole series of solutions. The result was the now iconic OXO line of kitchen utensils, with their soft rubber hand grips that allow for a firm grasp with less pain. Its flagship product, the swivel peeler, was a tremendous success. It was added to the Museum of Modern Art's collection four years after its launch and won multiple design prizes. Thirty years later, it's still a highly popular, timeless piece of design.

Apart from its commercial success, the OXO peeler has also become a revered example of inclusive design. It showed that when designers focus on the needs of people outside the norm, with impairments or disabilities, everyone can benefit from the outcome. The thirty-year-old peeler is not the only case of what we now call *inclusive design*. Many inventions now available for the general public started when someone focused on a problem seemingly experienced by only a few. In the dental hygiene aisle, there are the flip-top toothpaste cap, which allows people to open the cap with a single gesture and only one hand versus the previously ubiquitous screw top, and the electric toothbrush, which alleviates an arm movement painful for people with arthritis or aging joints. Subtitles, which allow people to follow a TV show in a noisy or busy environment, and text messaging, a widespread technology that has changed the world, were originally invented for hearing-impaired individuals.

However, this inclusive mindset is quite recent. For most of Western history, we have aspired to an ideal human body. The earliest documented desire for perfect anthropomorphic proportions can be traced back to the Roman architect Marcus Vitruvius (c. 90–c. 20 BCE), later to Leonardo da Vinci (1452–1519), and more recently, to Swiss painter and architect Le Corbusier and German architect Ernst Neufert.[20] Over time, out of a desire for an idealized form, we created a standard that was unrealistic and completely arbitrary. According to Corbusier himself, his *Modulor* drawing from 1945 was based on the body of a French man who was 1.75 meters (5 feet 9 inches) tall, but it was changed to 1.83 meters (6 feet) in 1946 for no apparent reason other than "in English detective novels, the good-looking men, such as policemen, are always six feet tall."[21] The idea of a standard was also pursued through numerical inference. Design researcher Sara Hendren points to 1840 as the beginning of such attempt, when French statistician Adolphe Quetelet attempted to measure and rank "the average man" by statistical means.[22]

The effort to have an entire population represented by a normal type was the beginning of a cult of normalcy that understandably caused great harm and inequality and persists today. Such statistical averaging has had a dehumanizing consequence, since as Hendren explains, "the habit of statistical thinking, broadly applied, creates a distancing effect, obscuring the specificities that also matter."[23] This is what is known as the *aggregation bias*—an incorrect assumption that trends in a group apply to individuals or, in other words, confusing the forest for the trees. Ernst Neufert's widespread influence in today's design and architecture practice means we are still, for the most part, designing for the peak of a bell curve— designing for an abstract standard to which no one conforms. People outside of the peak are simply peripheral and seen as anomalous or impaired in some way. As American designer Ellen Lupton and her colleagues mention in this context, "Eurocentric principles of modern design were conceived as egalitarian tools of social progress, yet they served to suppress differences among people across the globe."[24] This is a critical misconception that every designer should fight to change.

Central to inclusive design is the notion of *accessibility*— historically, the design of products, services, and experiences that aimed at being used by people with disabilities. However, accessibility is not only for people with a physical impairment. In 2017, Microsoft launched the Inclusive Design toolkit, one of the most comprehensive resources for accounting for diversity and inclusion as part of the design process. The toolkit introduces the important distinction between *permanent* disability (say, a person with one arm), *temporary* disability (a person with an arm injury), and *situational* limitations (a person holding a baby with one arm). When the notion of accessibility is expanded to include more than permanent disability, you can include almost every human. In fact, almost all of us at some point in our lives will suffer from one type of disability. As Microsoft researchers point out, "in the United States, 26,000 people a year suffer from loss of upper extremities. But when we include people with temporary and situational impairments, the number is greater than 20M."[25] This speaks to the importance of seeing users not just as a single snapshot in time but as an entity in constant flux who is subject to change, transformation, and injury.

Accessibility is therefore about inclusion. It's about broadening the spectrum of abilities and embracing all humans on the curve. It's about respecting their unique skills and capabilities. As we learned from Betsey Farber and Sam Farber, aiming at solving a problem for a seemingly few "actually results in designs that benefit people universally."[26] When you design with a specific visual, hearing, motor, or cognitive impediment in mind, you are led to think of edge cases—elements you would have missed by looking only at the norm. And this is what well-rounded design practice should aspire to. The best design will emerge from the toughest constraints and must consider not only budget, materials, and team size but also the unique constraints imposed by humans. Such an inclusive mindset is a powerful tool for innovation and creativity. You should think of constraints as an invitation to think outside the box and break the mold. Ultimately, practicing universal and inclusive design can also be a humbling process. It makes you realize we are all flawed.

3. Shared irrationality

Humans are not rational beings, at least not as rational as we might think we are. As behavioral economist Dan Ariely says in his book with the same title, humans are "predictably irrational."[27] We assume that most of the decisions we make are driven by reason and facts and, for the most part, are in our own self-interest. However, psychology and behavioral economics have shown us over the years that our brains make systematic errors in judgment and decision making. We have a myriad of cognitive biases that keep deviating us from rationality. Some of these internal triggers are also universal, things we share as a species across gender, race, culture, language, and geography. While we are diverse and unique in many ways, we are also united by our perceptive patterns, shared tendencies, and irrationality. As designers, we must pay attention to what makes us different and, at the same time, what unites us as a group, society, and species.

Cognitive biases are mental shortcuts, evolutionary triggers that we have adapted and evolved over thousands of years, even before we were surrounded by the beeps and bells of modern-day technology. They often determine how and how fast we react to different types of stimuli. The most obvious evolutionary bias is the *savanna preference*, an innate inclination for open environments with a stream (source of water), greenery (food), scattered trees or high grass (refuge), and blue sky. Such scenery has been employed over the years in countless paintings, posters, wallpapers, and monitor screensavers. Who doesn't remember *Bliss*, the default Microsoft Windows XP wallpaper, with its iconic blue sky and field of green grass? Other tendencies, such as the *attractiveness bias* or the *Von Restorff effect* (which tells us that unusual things are easier to remember than usual things), have been central to domains such as marketing and advertising.

Several perceptive tendencies can be applied intuitively as design best practices, constituting a well-informed ethos of good design. Most of design is experienced by the human brain as sensory information. Hence, a better understanding of how sensory processing occurs—through the lens of various fields of psychology, such as perception, memory, attention, and emotion—can be valuable. Take the *serial position effect*, which tells us that humans tend to better recall the first items on a list (the *primacy bias*) and the last items on a list (the *recency bias*). Or consider Gestalt's *law of proximity*, which explains that we perceive elements closer together as more related than elements farther apart, or one of my favorites, *horror vacui* (horror of the void)—the tendency to fill empty spaces, physical or digital, with things. Such principles are fundamental to design practice and guide the way we structure, prioritize, and display information. As is mentioned in chapter 3, they can also be an important source of evidence for building a more informed and defensible design solution.

When coupled with design and research, cognitive science can furthermore provide us with meaningful answers to the question of "Why?" Despite all of the technological artifices of today and the use of big data and artificial intelligence, companies cannot answer why we act in a certain way—why we do what we do. At best, they can gather data on a given behavior, preference, or attitude; collect an absurd quantity of figures on views, clicks, and sales; and plot the data in a complex dashboard. Yet no singular chart will explain why. This is where the cognitive and behavioral sciences can come in. They can provide us with an "emotional, even visceral context in which people encounter their product or service"[28] and help us identify the often opaque triggers that affect the human psyche. This knowledge can be powerful, as well as dangerous, particularly in the wrong hands.

Over the years, in seminars and workshops across the world, I have advocated for translating cognitive behaviors into design principles. I still believe that cognitive and behavioral insights can be an invaluable toolbox for designers—so that they can become more knowledgeable about what they do and, perhaps more important, about what they shouldn't do. Delving deep into human psychology allows designers to understand the inner workings of the brain and how easy it is to fool, influence, and sway human memory and perception. There is a delicate duality and often a conflict between nudging users in the right direction and manipulating them in the worst possible way. As we know today, many digital platforms and highly addictive applications on our smartphones are leveraging this knowledge for their own profit. They are manipulating our behavior and exploiting our ancient cognitive biases and fallacies, and they are doing so by design.

In 2003, American social scientist Brian Jeffrey Fogg published *Persuasive Technology: Using Computers to Change What We Think and Do*. The book focuses "primarily on the positive, ethical applications of persuasive technology."[29] This benign view of "persuasion in the digital age" opened the door to a research area known as *captology* (the study of computers as persuasive technologies) and a dedicated research lab at Stanford University,[30] which inspired numerous digital platforms to make users captive to their addictive, habit-forming products. Despite a recent change of tone, now highlighting the ethics of persuasive technology, captology had done a lot of harm over the years. Today's pervasive design elements—such as infinite scrolling, pull-to-refresh, streaks, likes, and notifications— are highly addictive mechanisms that draw users into "ludic loops or repeated cycles of uncertainty, anticipation and feedback."[31] Platforms such as Facebook, Tiktok, Twitter, and YouTube have taken captology's handbook to heart by using "methods similar to the gambling industry to keep users on their sites,"[32] explains cultural anthropologist Natasha Schüll. In a 2018 article in *The Guardian*, which describes in detail the devastating consequences such tricks can have on the human psyche, journalist Mattha Busby writes: "these methods are so effective they can activate similar mechanisms as cocaine in the brain, create psychological cravings and even invoke 'phantom calls and notifications' where users sense the buzz of a smartphone, even when it isn't really there."[33]

Human attention is a commodity. The new digital swipe and clickbait ecosystems are called the *attention economy* because they play with our perception and explore our biases, with the goal of mining our most precious resource—time. Anyone interested in the ethics of design should start by understanding cognitive science, since it paints a map of possible flaws to explore. It's truly impressive how effortlessly the human mind can be tricked. We're all impaired in some way, so exploring these shortcomings for profit is unethical at its core. If someone was exploiting another person's physical disability and living off someone else's limitation, an innate sense of injustice and immorality would be triggered in observers. Yet many modern-day digital platforms are doing exactly that. They are abusing perceptual weaknesses and are doing so in a camouflaged way to make their actions harder to detect. Invisibility can be an effective subterfuge for exploitation. Respecting users means we won't be distracting, manipulating, and enslaving the human mind for profit. We won't be interrupting users' time and attention for our own self-interest. Design cannot be used as a weapon for abuse. Instead, it should be a tool against it. It should protect users and provide transparency and quietness amid the digital chaos.

4. Personal data trail

Imagine walking into a store and browsing through a few items. The store manager approaches you with a smirk and says, "I know we already provide a great service, but we are trying to make it even better." And he continues with a curious proposition: "In order to do so, we would like to have your email address, phone number, and street address; take a careful look at all the names and their contact information in your address book; review your financial statements and all of the purchases and payments you've made in the past year; inspect everything you have searched for and browsed through while on the internet; follow you around the supermarket, in your neighborhood, out of town, and across the globe; analyze your health and fitness data to see how well you are; take note of all the apps you have installed on your phone and how often you use them; and meticulously track every action you take in this store and every article and advertisement you look at and for how long." If someone came up with such a proposal in the physical world, you would think they were out of their mind. You would push them away without hesitation and likely call the police. Yet it has become somehow acceptable for this level of exploitative spying to occur online.

This has not always been the case for digital products. In the past, most software applications on computers did not gather a substantial amount of data on users. When smartphones emerged, most applications collected a couple of personal data points, essentially to form a unique identifier, such as your name, phone number, or email address. Even by January 2021, Apple's mobile phone application iMessage gathered "only" your contact info, the device ID, and your search history. Other present-day messaging tools, particularly Facebook's WhatsApp or Messenger applications, are tracking an unnervingly long list of actions—purchases, financial information, contacts, location, and usage data. Every conceivable data point on you is being tracked. It gets more worrying when you realize the personal data is collected not just to use for "improving" product functionality and personalization, as companies like to proclaim, but to sell it to third parties so they can sell more targeted stuff to you.

This shift underpins what has been labeled *surveillance capitalism*, a new economic system fueled by the commoditization of personal data—yours and mine. Under the pretense of optimization, personal data collection and processing have become normal procedures at many large-scale digital empires such as Google and Meta, as well as many aspiring startups over the years. While it's easy to perceive the services provided by these digital platforms as "free," we are paying for them with our own individual data, amassed with varying degrees of intrusiveness. Your data has become a commodity, the digital currency of multiple applications on your smartphone, laptop, TV, and car. "In this framework, our habits, our choices, our likes, and our dislikes are not unlike soybeans or petroleum or iron ore—natural resources that are extracted and processed by huge firms, for massive profit."[34]

They are mining our own data to sell increasingly better and smarter tools to further spy on us. This is a truly frightening scenario. At a 2019 National Book Festival lecture, American media theorist Douglas Rushkoff sounded the alarm in a powerful way by saying we are being "consumed" by our digital technologies. "Human beings are no longer the users of our technology," said Rushkoff, "we are the used." As our smartphones are getting smarter about us, we are getting "dumber about it." And if you want to look under the hood, "you go in there and find out oh, these are all proprietary algorithms in black boxes that I'm legally prevented from even finding out what my phone is doing to me."[35] The true purpose of many media platforms today is the monetization of the human experience. In that sense, Rushkoff's observation that we are being used is almost inescapable. And his warning not entirely new. Back in 1950, the American philosopher Norbert Wiener wrote *The Human Use of Human Beings: Cybernetics and Society*, where he points out the "social dangers of our new technology," which was a way of predicting our present-day profiteering of personal data. Yet his foresight came with an ethical call so far unheard by the tech giants. "The social obligations of those responsible," writes Wiener, are to see "that the new modalities are used for the benefit of man [. . .] rather than merely for profits and the worship of the machine as the new brazen calf."[36]

Data mining has another nasty side effect. When you extract and process massive amounts of personal data for profit, you don't see users as humans attempting to complete a given task, no matter how human-centered your design team claims to be. Everyone in the organization starts perceiving other people as commoditized data points, even if unconsciously. Twenty-eight-year-old James Wisniewski, with whom we started this chapter, is not a

Welsh driver struggling to find a relationship. Christopher Donison is not a pianist finding it hard to play on a regular piano. They are just points on a chart—"a pair of eyes and a pair of ears connected to ten fingers, a screen and a credit card."[37] It is a dangerously dehumanizing process that allows for enough social distancing that all types of misguided behaviors can creep in. As we will learn in the next two chapters, it is one of many self-preserving strategies that help us disengage ourselves from morality and ethics.

It's too easy for designers to fall into the trap of gathering more data on users with the pretext of improving their experience and facilitating task completion, when in reality it is just so that we can sell them more stuff or use their data for other purposes, hidden in interminable terms of service. This is exploitation of the worst kind. Respecting the user is not exclusively about recognizing their unique circumstances and shared cognitive flaws. It's also about honoring their privacy and personal data. Designers must think deeply about the impact and repercussions of their work. They must investigate the context and historical background of the data being analyzed. Where is it coming from? How was it collected and treated? How did it evolve? What is the underlying goal? How is it being used? Who is benefiting from it, and who is getting hurt? We cannot continue being part of and actively contributing to the problem. This cycle of exploitation must stop.

Actionable Advice

Respect is grounded in admiration. For you to develop a high regard for the valuable qualities found in people, you must delve further into human nature by studying the mind and its internal triggers, or the variety of human customs and behaviors. You must dig into the plethora of knowledge coming from psychology, sociology, anthropology, and other related fields, and, at other times, you must empirically go out and experience it yourself by talking to your human customers and better understanding their challenges through design research and co-design, as mentioned in chapter 2 and 3. Even if your manager, team, or organization is not supportive of human-centered research, you should be its main advocate. Don't give up easily. Be smart in finding quick techniques with a high return. Research doesn't have to take long cycles and extensive reports. It can be as nimble and agile as you require. All you need is one chance to paint a fuller, more humane picture.

Respect ultimately starts with you. Even if empathy on its own won't make for a more humane design practice, it can certainly be a strong catalyst. You can train yourself to be a more empathetic designer and, in the process, become a better partner, parent, friend, and coworker. First, embrace active listening as a means of being present and truly listening to others. You should refrain from judgment, avoid the noise and distractions in your own mind, and be aware of the speaker's nonverbal cues. This is important because it allows you to "understand and empathize with a different point of view and, on this basis, search for solutions."[38] Practice in your next conversation with a stranger. Second, get to know yourself better, particularly by understanding the effect of your biases on how you perceive the world around you. Humility is a step forward in your road to empathy. Third, challenge yourself frequently. You can train your empathic muscles by stepping out of your comfort zone, learning something new, or living someone else's experience even if momentarily. I find traveling to be one of the most empathy-inducing experiences. Aim at getting to know people who are different than you, in every conceivable way, including race, culture, language, and nationality. Finally, cultivate curiosity. Ask questions constantly. Develop an attentive eye and sense of wonder for the world around you.

By becoming a more empathetic person, you develop self-awareness and become attuned to the way people prefer and deserve to be treated, irrespective of their condition. They want to be seen not as mere dots on a task completion funnel but as the wide-ranging human beings that they are. Hopefully, you can allow that openness to guide you when building products. The design world is filled with examples that seem to ignore the importance of inclusion, from creating experiences with poor contrast that are indecipherable by the elderly to designing piano keys that exclude underrepresented groups. Designing with inclusivity in mind does not mean you have to create a different product for every customer. It means designing with everyone in mind. One solution is to consider multimodal experiences. When designing a product, consider multiple ways to interact with it. Allow for different types of input and output mechanisms across different devices and an experience that adapts and scales gracefully, depending on context and need. And yes, at times, as we saw with the OXO peeler, one product is all you need to fulfill a broad range of needs.

Not everything that
can be counted counts, and
not everything that counts
can be counted.
—William Bruce Cameron[1]

When a measure becomes a target,
it ceases to be a good measure.
—Marilyn Strathern[2]

5

Design is a measurable instrument

We can witness a yearning for measurement in the rise of the first Sumerian cities in ancient Mesopotamia, which led to the oldest known alphabet approximately 5,200 years ago. Documented in numerous clay tokens that survive to this day, the proto–writing system that led to the Sumerian cuneiform was meant to represent simple quantities of goods for commercial transactions. Measurement and quantification have been deeply intertwined with business for as long as we can recall. However, during the European High Middle Ages, this craving reached a new high. In *The Measure of*

Reality: Quantification in Western Europe, 1250–1600, American historian Alfred W. Crosby describes how European scholarship at the time was concerned with the quantification of nature, which later became an important driver for the scientific revolution. This was no easy feat. Fourteenth-century European citizens lived in a hyperqualitative world and used only simple nominal scales to express measurements. The weather was either dry or wet, and the water was either hot or cold. Time, proclaimed by church bells, was based on the canonical hours—which designated when a prayer was to be said. And numbers also carried plenty of trivial and mystical meanings.

To move from symbolical properties to a full spectrum of values, medieval Europeans had to put away superstitions and develop an obsession with reliable measurement. Numbers had to become tools that were dissociated from any moral or emotional value. The transition from qualitative expressions to quantitative measurements led to a huge leap in data gathering and a significant step toward the development of science, in part propelled by the adoption of Arabic numerals, which were able to deal with very long aggregates. If measurement was about numbers, then mathematics was its language. The fascination for this new vocabulary comes across in the words of Johannes Kepler, whose faith in the discipline in 1599 was deep-seated: "What else can the human mind hold besides numbers and magnitudes? These alone we apprehend correctly, and if piety permits to say so, our comprehension is in this case of the same kind as God's, at least insofar as we are able to understand it in this mortal life."[3]

Kepler, together with Francis Bacon, Galileo Galilei, René Descartes, and Isaac Newton, launched a new approach to the understanding of nature in what became known as the scientific revolution. Because mathematics allowed people to decode numerous physical phenomena by means of formulas and equations, it was seen as the only perceptible and rightful way to measure reality. The field rose to such a high status that Galileo, like Kepler, compared it to God. "With regard to those few [mathematical propositions] which the human intellect does understand," wrote Galileo in 1632, "I believe its knowledge equals the Divine in objective certainty."[4] *Objective certainty* was a key aspiration for many scientific breakthroughs in this period and subsequently in the rise of the Enlightenment and all modern science. It's also a hidden force behind a modern-day obsession with measurement.

Medieval scholars were so infatuated by the ability to create new scales for everything, from size to weight, that they begin to think about less obvious qualities, such as motion, light, and color. As Alfred W. Crosby mentions, this is when they "forged right on, jumped the fence, and talked about quantifying certitude, virtue, and grace." If anything could be arbitrarily measured, asks Crosby, "why should you presumptively exclude certitude, virtue, and grace?"[5] This urge for factual data was unprecedented. Yet scholars in the Middle Ages eventually realized they had to draw a line somewhere. They recognized that some areas of human behavior were simply too hard or inconvenient to quantify. Our modern-day eagerness for data and quantification portrays a similar belief that anything can and everything should be measured. If anything can be converted to data and therefore measured, can we reduce design to a set of trackable parameters?

One important consequence of an overabundance of and overreliance on data is the anxiety-inducing feeling when faced with too many options, also known as the *paradox of choice*. A true conundrum of contemporary society, which goes well beyond data, is the belief that more is always better. According to this view, the diversity of choices in a supermarket aisle is a testament of our prosperity, freedom of choice, and therefore happiness. However, an abundance of options and information usually comes with a hefty price tag that often translates into stress, anxiety, and wasted time. Today, simple things such as buying a pillow can take days of research and subsequent uncertainty about whether the right decision has been made. Danish philosopher Søren Kierkegaard put it best, in reference to this modern-day dazing effect, when he wrote that anxiety is "the dizziness of freedom."[6]

Like quantification, the angst stemming from having too much information is not a new phenomenon. Back in 1255, the Dominican friar Vincent of Beauvais wrote in the preface to his encyclopedia that "the multitude of books, the shortness of time, and the slipperiness of memory do not allow all things which are written to be equally retained in the mind,"[7] and in 1685 French critic Adrien Baillet, in an apocalyptic view, wrote, "We have reason to fear that the multitude of books which grows every day in a prodigious fashion will make the following centuries fall into a state as barbarous as that of the centuries that followed the fall of the Roman Empire."[8] In *Too Much to Know: Managing Scholarly Information before the Modern Age*, American historian Ann M. Blair brings to light numerous instances where medieval scholars felt inundated by new information coming from the ancient world. They sensed that they were incapable of processing and making sense of such a large volume of data, experiencing something very much like our own modern-day trepidation in the face of a data deluge.

However, one of the most prevalent pitfalls of data overload, particularly in today's tech-driven world, is called *analysis paralysis*, which occurs when decision making is debilitated due to overthinking or overanalyzing. Even though it can happen in many domains—such as sports, games, software development, or even personal life—in the context of design validation, analysis paralysis can have a few causes. At times, the problem at hand can seem overly complex, the number of choices too daunting, or the road to consensus too steep. Victims of analysis paralysis are likely to display an aversion for things like ambiguity, error, intuition, and gut feeling and, as such, operate in a risk-averse culture. This normally results in excessive testing, leading researchers and designers into a never-ending vicious cycle of indecisiveness. The paralyzing effect is aggravated by a desire for perfectionism and a belief in data as the most accurate and objective measure of success. New media Dutch professor Johanna van Dijck calls this ideology *dataism* and describes it as "a widespread belief in the objective quantification and potential tracking of all kinds of human behavior and sociality through online media technologies."[9] This search for *objective certainty* is rooted in some key misconceptions, so let's clarify four important ones.

1. Fallacy of misplaced concreteness

In order to evaluate the effectiveness of a design solution, you have to define a set of measurable indicators. One metric is rarely enough. User research normally uses more than one method to validate a given outcome. This is called *triangulation*. Such an approach is important in order to avoid making errors and confusing correlation with causation. Take the Tech3Lab at HEC Montréal (formerly École des Hautes Études Commerciales de Montréal), the business school in Montreal, Canada. This user-experience (UX) research lab has developed groundbreaking technology that goes far beyond a typical eye-tracking study. In a single user session, its researchers can track multiple signals like facial expressions, gestures, pupil dilation, heartbeat, breathing patterns, skin conductance, and brain waves. All these data sources can be triangulated to create a rich map of a user's reaction to a given experience. Important questions for the purpose of avoiding paralysis are "When do you stop?" and "When is enough data enough?"

    In scientific research and clinical trials, there's a concept called the *hierarchy of evidence*, which defines the levels of evidence required to measure the effectiveness of a medical intervention. Yet even in a field where the quality of evidence can determine life or death for thousands of individuals, consensus on a universal framework hasn't been achieved. There are currently more than eighty grading systems for evidence, which vary across various countries and institutions. A unified hierarchy of evidence also doesn't exist in design research. Designers find it tempting to keep adding metrics to further prove an argument and support a decision, particularly at a time when data has become such a cheap and ubiquitous commodity. But data availability is not the same as data usefulness. Just because you can track and measure something doesn't mean you should. It might be a completely irrelevant indicator to the problem you're trying to solve. If so, the data creates noise, extra burden, and eventual paralysis. Such a desire for information even when it doesn't lead to action is what psychologists call *information bias*.

I've witnessed many great ideas, particularly in the tech sector, that never saw the light of day because they lacked evidence of future success. Some could have been transformational. Risk aversion is so strong that sometimes even the most mundane design decision must be validated by tangible data. One example of this symptom occurred at Google in 2009. When the product team was deciding on the right shade of blue to indicate hyperlinks throughout its online products, team members resorted to an elaborate test. Over a period of two weeks, 2.5 percent of visitors who landed on Google's homepage were shown forty-one random shades of blue to see which one received more clicks. This was not design by committee. It was design by crowd-sourcing unconscious clicks. The shade that scored highest on the test eventually made it into most Google online products, from Gmail to Search.

In 2009, when Douglas Bowman left Google as the company's first visual design lead, he referred to the widespread data-centric culture in the tech sector: "When a company is filled with engineers, it turns to engineering to solve problems. Reduce each decision to a simple logic problem. Remove all subjectivity and just look at the data. Data in your favor? OK, launch it. Data shows negative effects? Back to the drawing board. And that data eventually becomes a crutch for every decision, paralyzing the company and preventing it from making any daring design decisions."[10] Despite his stereotyping of the design evaluation phase and of engineering in general, Bowman is right in implying that testing is not always required, particularly in fairly straightforward design enhancements. This is where testing can become a form of analysis paralysis. When every move needs to be measured, the process can quickly lead to sluggishness. He's also right in saying that such a crutch eventually becomes a barrier to creativity—a concept so elusive that to this day there's still no agreement on an effective measurement formula.

When we look at Crosby's tale of medieval scholars attempting to measure abstract ideas such as virtue, grace, or love, we recognize that they fell victim to the *fallacy of misplaced concreteness*, also known as *reification*. A similar fallacy pervades many organizations today. Fueled by buzzwords like *big data, artificial intelligence, machine learning,* and *predictive analysis*, the notion that everything—including human performance, employee satisfaction, customer happiness, and product value—is quantifiable is now firmly entrenched. Designers are caught in a dreamy data storm that attempts to reduce any abstract idea into a concrete set of metrics. However, the primary touchpoints for design interaction—products, experiences, services, and brands—cannot be reduced to a series of boxes, colors, and clicks. We perceive them in a holistic way. As designer and architect Phil Best mentions in this context, "True innovation requires the adoption of a belief system that sometimes must prevail in the face of other data metrics."[11] Design as a practice is now seen as a measurable instrument whose formula has yet been decoded. Yet that hasn't stopped people from trying.

2. Ethical fading

Even if the effectiveness of a design solution could be objectively measured only by data, impartiality must be taken with a grain of salt. Quite a few cognitive biases can easily trickle in and sway the results. The most obvious one is *confirmation bias*—a tendency to look for and interpret data that corroborates your initial belief or hypothesis. Related is also *cherry picking* (or the *fallacy of incomplete evidence*), a tendency to choose facts that support your claim or suppress evidence to the contrary. The notion of *belief perseverance* explains how many people stick firmly to their beliefs despite all contradictory evidence. In fact, beliefs can even become strengthened when others attempt to discredit them, in what is known as the *backfire effect.* Even if you were to bypass all these tendencies, the process of collecting, recalling, recording, and handling data in a study is tricky and prone to errors. Many statistical biases can condition results, such as *selection bias* (choice of particular individuals and groups), *funding bias* (alignment with the interests of a stakeholder), *observer bias* (subconscious influences on the researcher), or *recall bias* (omitting of details or lack of memory). You get the idea.

The biggest danger occurs when a metric becomes the primary target for performance, control, or policy. It's dangerous because, as Jerry Z. Muller explains in *The Tyranny of Metrics*, measurement systems can be gamed.[12] Economist Charles Goodhart, in what later became known as Goodhart's law, also warned that "Any observed statistical regularity will tend to collapse once pressure is placed upon it for control purposes."[13] American social scientist Donald T. Campbell expressed a similar maxim in the context of social sciences: "the more any quantitative social indicator is used for social decision-making, the more subject it will be to corruption pressures and the more apt it will be to distort and corrupt the social processes it is intended to monitor."[14]

This behavior can be further instigated, as I have witnessed in my career, when a quantitative metric in a company is tied with an employee's performance evaluation. In such a situation, too often an employee will optimize for the measure, irrespective of whether it is ethical or good for the end user, the company, or the general public. When you are tightly focused on a given target—say, adoption, conversion, feature parity, or profitability—you can easily engage in self-deception. You simply stop seeing the ethical implications of your decisions. This is known as *ethical fading.*

A classic example of ethical fading happened recently in the German automobile industry. Between 2009 and 2015, technical personnel at Volkswagen were so focused on having their vehicles pass short-term emissions tests while also meeting sales targets that they caused one of the century's biggest auto industry scandals. The fact that a "defeat device" controlled emissions only during lab testing and not when the cars were operated by consumers was likely well-known within the company, yet only nine managers were initially suspended when the United States Environmental Protection Agency alleged violations of the Clean Air Act. Eventually, many executives were prosecuted and charged as investigators realized that the defeat devices were linked to a systemic issue influenced by the company's corporate culture. According to a case study on the scandal, when you foster a culture where "the demand and expectations of the company should be fulfilled regardless of how employees are able to perform the tasks,"[15] ethical fading seems almost inevitable.

The overall scheme was a tremendous embarrassment. By June 2020, the outrageous behavior had cost Volkswagen $33.3 billion in fines and lawsuits to compensate for the environmental harm as well as the recall of 11 million vehicles worldwide. The magnitude of this deception was dramatic. For several years, the defeat device was installed in millions of Audi and VW vehicles, which emitted forty times more nitrogen oxide than they should have. These gases are responsible for smog and acid rain and are linked to various respiratory and nonrespiratory diseases, such as asthma, heart disease, and diabetes. In a study published in October 2015, researchers estimated that the excess emissions were responsible for fifty-nine early deaths in the United States alone and many millions of dollars in associated social costs.[16]

As Volkswagen's discreditable behavior shows, ethical fading can lead to severe consequences for any company and, most worryingly, for the environment and society at large. It can be argued that a focus on metrics and a dismissal of ethics have been determinant factors in many unscrupulous practices by large corporations, some of which are explored in the next chapter. As a designer, you always need to consider the big picture and understand the repercussions of your work well beyond a single metric or performance indicator. You owe it to yourself and those around you.

3. The role of intuition

Advocates of *objective certainty* strive for the most reliable decision-making process, independent of feelings, emotions, and instincts. Humans, however, are a bit more complex. Consider the ability to respond to an ethical question, also known as *moral decision making*. As we know today, this process is highly influenced by intuition, instead of rationality. Before six-month-old babies utter a single word or are swayed by their surrounding environment, they show an innate sense of morality. For psychopaths, rationality is separate from moral behavior. These people tend to be as rational and intelligent as any of us, yet they suffer from a personality disorder that hinders their ability to develop empathy and remorse and leads to disturbing antisocial behavior.

Sure, you might say, intuition is more critical than rationality but only when it comes to morality. Well, not quite. Even plain rational choice is unachievable without emotions. People with no emotions make either very poor decisions or no decisions at all. Cultural commentator David Brooks, in *The Social Animal: The Hidden Sources of Love, Character, and Achievement*, and social psychologist Jonathan Haidt, in *The Happiness Hypothesis: Finding Modern Truth in Ancient Wisdom*, both mention the work of Portuguese neurologist Antonio Damasio, who researched patients with medical conditions that deprived them of emotions while leaving their reasoning capability somehow intact. As it turns out, many of these patients were unable to make good decisions, even about the most routine choices, such as picking a restaurant. "Emotion assigns value to things, and reason can only make choices on the basis of those evaluations," explains Brooks.[17]

Intuition is not based on baseless hunches but on insights gained from accumulated knowledge. I carry my intuition with me every minute and everywhere I go. I carry the experiences of having worked in multiple companies of varying size and in multiple industries and of accumulating learnings from my peers and stakeholders, all the books I have read and written, every research insight I discovered, every place I visited and person I encountered, every conference I attended, and every podium I stood on. My intuition is heavy and gets sharper with every new experience. I bring all of this to each design decision. And while it's true that every project is a new journey and history doesn't repeat itself, some patterns certainly persist. In part, this is because most design decisions involve humans and, across the world, most humans react in similar ways to frequently occurring situations.

In 1877 American painter James Abbott McNeill Whistler took art critic John Ruskin to court for considering the harsh criticism of his work to be libelous. During the trial the following year, and when asked by a lawyer why he charged an exorbitant price for a painting that was clearly made in a couple of days, Whistler replied: "I painted the picture in one day, and finished it off the next day. I do not ask 200 guineas for a couple of days' work; the picture is the result of the studies of a lifetime."[18]Intuition takes time to build, and the more you add to it, the faster and sharper your responses can become. A seemingly quick painting is the result of a lifetime of accumulated knowledge. Designer and Pentagram partner Paula Scher apparently came up with the Citibank logo in just a few seconds. In a Hillman Curtis documentary called *Artist Series*, Scher demystifies the common miscomprehension of the creative mind by saying that she always trusts her instinct and intuition and never sees herself as a refiner. "If I don't get it in a second, I almost never get it," she says. "How can it be that you talk to someone and it's done in a second? But it is done in a second. It's done in a second and in 34 years, and every experience and every movie and everything of my life that's in my head."[19]

So what are the implications of intuition for designers and particularly for design validation? Objective metrics are important in design validation, yet you should never relinquish your intuition.

First, learn to trust yourself. Your instinct is based on years of practice and decision making. Second, emotion is critical. You should question every time you see intuitiveness being dismissed for the sake of objectivity and optimization. They are not mutually exclusive but highly complementary. Don't let others tell you otherwise. As Haidt says, "Reason and emotion must both work together to create intelligent behavior, but emotion does most of the work."[20] Finally, designers are mirrors for society. As such, our human intuition tends to reflect what society values and cares about. This is a powerful skill that requires a great sense of responsibility to others and the world around us.

4. Automating decisions

In *Automating Inequality: How High-Tech Tools Profile, Police, and Punish the Poor*, Virginia Eubanks relates a chilling account of how her partner of thirteen years was brutally assaulted by four individuals and robbed of $35 while leaving a store in Troy, New York, in October 2015. He stayed in the hospital for several weeks, the result of multiple complications, including facial reconstruction surgery with titanium plates and bone screws. With bills accumulating and prescriptions being canceled, Eubanks spent hours on the phone with her insurance provider trying to understand what had happened to her medical coverage. As she soon realized, she probably had been flagged for a fraud investigation by an automated algorithm. After all, she had recently changed jobs, she wasn't married to her partner, and her new insurance started just a week before claims of many thousands of dollars were submitted. When trying to explain this to the customer service representative at the other end of the line, she was told that this is what "the system said," as if an oracle had laid down its final, indisputable verdict.

Just a few decades ago, most big decisions that affected our lives, such as getting a job or securing a loan, were made by fellow human beings. Nowadays however, scoring algorithms and predictive models decide who gets into a school, is qualified for a job, gets a credit card, goes on parole, receives government support, or can subscribe to same-day delivery service from Amazon. Do you want to speak with a bank officer who might have rejected your loan application? Good luck. There's no human behind the decision. And if you reach a human on the phone, they can only convey what the "system" tells them. Unfortunately, the system has determined your exclusion. That's it. If you feel somehow powerless to control your eligibility for a loan, the future holds many more opaque scenarios where computer systems and algorithms will make vital decisions on your and your family's life. We only have to look at China's infamous social credit system—which determines citizens' eligibility to travel, get financial credit, be admitted to certain schools, or even date[21]—to see how far this can go.

Underlying the recent growth of automated algorithms is a very human susceptibility to computerization. Automation bias describes a human tendency to prefer suggestions from automated machines, algorithms, and decision-making systems and to disregard contradictory information made without automation. This human bias underlies the development of a variety of computer systems we take for granted nowadays, not just in creating large, industrial complexes (such as nuclear power plants) or in moving large pieces of machinery (such as flying a plane or piloting a war drone). We trust these automated systems every single day when we ask Alexa for the weather, check the thermostat at our home, or use a spell-checking program. We trust them so much we are ready to blindly risk our lives based on their suggestions. Unfortunately, there have been cases of people who drive their cars into lakes or over cliffs because they blindly followed the directions provided by their GPS devices.[22]

It's tempting to use algorithms to make decisions and judgments. After all, humans are imperfect creatures. "We are increasingly depending on technologies built with the presumption of human inferiority and expendability,"[23] writes Douglas Rushkoff. At the root of our shared automation bias is the belief that we are inferior. We are flawed. Yes, we're human. We make mistakes. We're filled with biases, tendencies, and irrationality. We are the product of our evolution. Humans and chimpanzees share more than 98 percent of our DNA: we are "partly rational animals with adrenal glands that are too big and prefrontal lobes that are too small,"[24] which means we often act on our impulses and urges. Even assuming an imperfect nature, our overreliance on algorithms is still a curious phenomenon. "Is this humility or hubris?" asked journalists Kashmir Hill and Jeremy White in a 2020 *New York Times* article on the power of AI: "Do we place too little value in human intelligence—or do we overrate it, assuming we are so smart that we can create things smarter still?"[25]

But are algorithms better than we are at making decisions? Are they more trustworthy? This is an important question to ask, given our predisposition for automation, its undeterred growth, and the elusive myth of *objective certainty* that it carries. "There's no such thing as an objective algorithm," says American data scientist Cathy O'Neil, the author *Weapons of Math Destruction: How Big Data Increases Inequality and Threatens Democracy*. "We optimize algorithms for success," and success is normally defined by the person building the algorithm. Success means different things to everyone, so algorithms can be highly subjective and prone to agendas and interests. They are "nothing more than opinions embedded in code."[26] Did I mention they also can be temperamental and erratic?

Automated systems are susceptible to all sorts of crashes, data losses, glitches, and failures. As software developers will tell you, a good amount of their time—up to 50 percent—is spent cleaning code and resolving bugs (debugging). Some flops can be particularly worrying and embarrassing. Take the case of researchers from the Chinese tech giant Tencent, who in March 2019 found numerous ways to fool the AI algorithms running Tesla vehicles. One glitch allowed the security researchers to fool the autonomous driving system into driving over the road markings into the lane with oncoming traffic. If you think that was scary, try thinking about the increasing use of AI algorithms in the military. Another fiasco happened during the Covid-19 global pandemic when the US Centers for Disease Control and Prevention asked the consulting firm Deloitte to create brand-new, $44 million software that would be responsible for managing the US vaccine rollout. The system soon became notorious for "randomly canceled appointments, unreliable registration, and problems that lock staff out of the dashboard they're supposed to use to log records."[27] The flaws were so persistent that many states decided to hack their own solutions to managing the vaccine rollout.

Another danger of depositing too much trust in algorithms is that they are as prejudiced as we are. In order to understand this, let's go back to the early days of redlining in the United States and its discriminatory denial of services. Created in 1934 as part of an economic stimulus program during the Depression, the Federal Housing Administration was commissioned to provide mortgage loans to American families in order to stabilize the housing market after many bank failures. As part of this effort, maps were created of multiple US cities that showed the city's more and less desirable neighborhoods. Neighborhoods that were deemed hazardous or declining were drawn in red and marked with an occasional "D" grade. The red lines indicated the presence of African Americans and other minority groups. Maps like these were "codified patterns of racial segregation and disparities in access to credit," over time becoming self-fulfilling prophesies, as redlined areas were "starved of investment and deteriorated further."[28]

If we fast-forward to April 2016, Amazon was accused of racial segregation during the launch of its Prime free same-day delivery service in sixteen US cities. The service was made available in predominantly white neighborhoods and excluded minority communities in Atlanta, Boston, Chicago, Dallas, New York City, and Washington, DC. Amazon immediately said racism had nothing to do with the decision. After all, why would they exclude the Bronx neighborhood of New York City if that meant less profit for the company? The decision had been made by an algorithm. As it turns out, the geographical algorithm used to map the zip codes for Amazon

Prime same-day delivery service was built on the inherited redlining database from the US Census Bureau. Here we see, eighty years after the redlining maps were first created, how prejudice and discrimination continued to propagate into the twenty-first century and were coded in one of big tech's most revered organizations.

As designer and researcher Hana Nagel mentioned in a lecture at UXC'19 (Conférence annuelle de la Chaire UX) at HEC Montreal, Canada, racial segregation "becomes coded in the ways we design our systems, social and technical, and feeding into AI as well." This happens, according to Nagel, because we are not asking the questions about how that context came to be: "We're saying that the limited set of data is an accurate reflection of the world, and we should base all our decisions around it."[29] This is the biggest threat of automation bias and our overreliance on algorithms—accepting without questioning. This is even more damaging when such systems tend to aggravate the lives of historically oppressed groups who once again see themselves with the short end of the stick. And inaction will only make things worse. "Rational discrimination does not require class or racial hatred, or even unconscious bias, to operate. It only requires ignoring bias that already exists," writes Virginia Eubanks, warning us of the danger of passivity: "When automated decision-making tools are not built to explicitly dismantle structural inequalities, their speed and scale intensify."[30]

As is noted at the beginning of this chapter, our desire for quantification has been with us for a long time. Algorithms and artificial intelligence appear to be the pinnacle of a centuries-old pursuit—the omniscient, factual oracle we have long waited for. But knowing what we know today about its flimsiness, why do we continue to rely so heavily on algorithms to make decisions? Is it the desire for efficiency and productiveness at all costs, even at the cost of ethics and integrity? Why are we so eager to remove humans from all major decisions? Is it arrogance, ignorance, or simply shame about our own nature? Answering many of these questions requires a deep, self-evaluation as a species. And design can and should help drive the search for answers.

Stopping our eagerness for measurement might be hard and even impossible, but we can try to steer it in the right direction and validate its use through inquiry. We can also try to filter the avalanche of data and translate it into clear information and meaningful knowledge. The most important battle of our times is not to find creative ways to generate more data. We already have all of mankind's knowledge available at our fingertips. Our ability to gather data has far outpaced our ability to make sense of it. Data collection has won this battle. The challenge is to avoid becoming desensitized by it and becoming the involuntary subjects of Adam Alter's "tech zombie epidemic."[31] In this pervasive data deluge, design can shed light, filter the noise, and bring some much-needed clarity.

It can also provide an alternative type of data—what the cofounders of the consulting firm Red, Christian Madsbjerg and Mikkel B. Rasmussencall, call "thick" data. As they mentioned in a *Wall Street Journal* article, "By outsourcing our thinking to Big Data, our ability to make sense of the world by careful observation begins to wither, just as you miss the feel and texture of a new city by navigating it only with the help of a GPS."[32] Sometimes, what we need is not more data but simply better data—data that is collected by a deep analysis of a problem at hand and by "careful, patient human observation" and that is grounded in the emotional complexities of our fellow human beings, an eternal source of wonder and the key recipients of our innovation. This is the type of data that design can provide—not a measurable instrument for driving technological growth and profit at all costs, but a tool of inquiry, clarity, and observation.

Actionable Advice

I want to start with a word of caution. Data, reason, and evidence are fundamental values of human progress. The Enlightenment and the rise of the scientific method had an earth-shattering effect on human civilization, moving us away from superstition and into new realms of understanding. We owe a great debt to these transformational movements. Modern-day advances in science, technology, and medicine would be unimaginable without a strong reliance on metrics. I don't want to do away with measurement and reason or simply advocate for inward-looking confirmation bias. However, the idea that giving people more data will lead them to act differently is misguided. More charts and more analysis can be detrimental. Not only is data on its own not enough, but too much data can lead to anxiety and paralysis. As Australian designer Julia Watson stated in *Lo-TEK: Design by Radical Indigenism*, "we are drowning in information, while starving for wisdom."[33] As a designer, you must embrace this fact both as an opportunity for impact and a duty to make things different.

In chapter 3, the importance of gathering evidence and building a defensible rationale for a design solution was discussed. Acknowledging the importance of evidence is key, but it should not replace instinct. You should strive for a balance between data and intuition. As Jonathan Haidt explains, "human rationality depends critically on sophisticated emotionality. It is only because our emotional brains work so well that our reasoning can work at all."[34] Your valuable design insights are based on years of accumulated experience and emotional finetuning. They can also be an alternative to the present preoccupation with measurements and automated decisions. This alternative relies on human deduction, lateral thinking, and creativity. It expresses the needs of society and the individual as much as the needs of the business. We cannot continue reducing human problems and social decisions to mere calculations and predictive models. That route will simply not end well.

Having said that, you might find yourself amid an analysis paralysis scenario in the future. It might be self-inflicted or caused by others in your group. How can you avoid these kinds of situations? There are a few things to consider. You can impose a limit on the evaluation, either by limiting the number of tests or by setting a specific end date for data collection. This forces you or your team to stop and move on. You should abandon the unattainable desire for perfectionism and for solving problems that don't yet exist. Designers are known to be susceptible to this. You can compartmentalize decisions into categories, like large and small, high versus low priority, high versus low impact. Finally, in case you lost touch with it, return to the main goal of this evaluation—the initial problem you're trying to solve.

It is worth attempting to build a defensible rationale for your design that's not exclusively dependent on quantifiable metrics. You can try to establish human-centered targets to build consensus in the team and connect to the fellow human beings on the other side of the product—your customer. Instead of user task completion rates or clickthrough rates, aim at metrics such as time spent with family or time spent playing a hobby. Customers have a life beyond your product. If you need to add common engagement metrics as part of your research or validation process, be explicit about its added benefit. And above all, be suspicious if your design or individual performance is being evaluated by a single measure. Always question its validity. Designers must continue to be a counterbalance to the myth of *objective certainty* and expose it for the artifice that it is.

Too often, technological ease and speed
are inversely related to social progress.
—Ruha Benjamin[1]

Action indeed is the sole medium
of expression for ethics.
—Jane Addams[2]

6

Design is an instrument for good

Founded in 1926, the Book-of-the-Month Club (BOMC) was one of the largest US companies in the sector and an important distribution channel for book publishers. Its cultural significance was large enough to deserve several humorous *New Yorker* cartoons at the time.[3] The company sold books through a subscription plan, and they were delivered by postal carriers to private homes, instead of through brick and mortar stores. The precedent for this business approach was the mail catalog business. But BOMC's tactics became even more creative. Struggling to stay in business after a few months, due to a logistical process that is still challenging today, the company's partners knew they had to scale fast. Mail-order copy expert Maxwell Sackheim came up with a way to grow their subscriber list. Unless customers returned the form they received with their monthly book and revoked the subscription contract, they would continue receiving new books and being charged for the items. As it happened, life would get in the way of customers, and they tended to forget to cancel. So this business practice, nowadays known as *negative-option billing*, became a very effective profit machine. In the BOMC's first year, the firm shipped more than 232,000 books.[4]

Over time, many organizations perfected and expanded Sackheim's original tactic. It became a core marketing approach in several industries, from music to education. Today, with the advent of the World Wide Web software platform and mobile applications, negative-option billing is one of many sophisticated tricks for hasty growth, generally known as *dark patterns*. First coined by British user-experience specialist Harry Brignull in 2010, dark patterns are unethical digital design strategies meant to deceive and trick users and, in the process, increase conversion, adoption, or sales. They can take different forms, such as confusing close buttons, advertisements that are indistinguishable from content, complicated sign-up processes that lead users to subscribe to other things, hard-to-find opt-out mechanisms, items silently added to a shopping basket, or additional costs that appear only at the final checkout. The problem is pervasive. In a study published in November 2019, researchers uncovered 1,818 dark pattern instances in 53,000 product pages from 11,000 shopping websites.[5] Roughly 15 percent of the analyzed websites in this analysis included deceptive practices.

One example of a dark pattern was a seemingly inoffensive software update by Skype in 2016. While installing Skype on their computers, most users didn't notice a tiny string of text at the bottom left of the confirmation panel where two preselected checkboxes made Bing their default search engine and MSN their homepage. You don't have to be a usability expert to realize that in a multistep

installation wizard, most users barely scan the content while looking for the Continue or Next button. Options checked by default and
text in a miniscule font size are not accidents but intentional deceit.
Inattentive users might find it odd that Skype was vehemently recom-
mending an unrelated product like Bing, except for the fact they
belong to the same company. If one has any doubts about the validity
of antitrust charges against large tech conglomerates like Amazon,
Facebook, Google, Microsoft, or Uber, one needs only to look attentively at the creative ways they mislead users through dark patterns.

     Another example that received a lot of media attention hap-
pened at one of the world's most prized digital sites—Google's search
engine results page (SERP). Since ads first appeared on Google's
SERP in 2000, there has been a gradual visual convergence as ads
have grown to look increasingly similar to organic search results.
In the early days, ads had a different background, a different font
treatment, or prominent labels. You could easily spot and avoid them
if you wanted. But by 2019, almost every single differentiating visual
element had been removed, causing a public outcry. Revenue was the
driving force from the beginning. In a pay-per-click scheme, Google
and its partners earned money by deceiving users who unintentionally click on ads while thinking they were an organic result. For the
companies involved, it might seem like a win-win situation. But over
time, users who unintentionally click on an ad might feel defrauded
and eventually mistrust the brand. It is not all about money.

     As it turns out, revenue is not the only driver behind the
abundance of dark patterns we see today. Keeping users engaged—
staying on a platform, reading the next post, or watching the next
video—is also a strong motivator. In a clickbait economy such as
Facebook, dark patterns are an important tool for keeping users
sharing content, even if it is untrue, is hurtful, or incites violence.
According to a 2021 *Bloomberg* article, American journalist Judd
Legum's online newsletter Popular Information has covered the
toxic practices of Facebook extensively with tech-related, investigative journalism that cuts through a hyperpartisan, often distracted

media landscape. Legum has exposed a myriad of instances where misleading information is allowed to spread within Facebook in order to boost engagement. Often, the offending pieces are removed only when disclosed by the newsletter, ultimately showing the failure by the platform to self-regulate and enforce its own guidelines.[6]

When it comes to engagement, the biggest engine for online platforms is *personalization*—allowing consumers to read, consume, or watch content related to their previous choice. This also happens when someone visits a shopping site and sees suggestions related to items bought in the past. Yet information is another type of game. It can affect a person's mind and actions and, in the process, mold society in unpredictable ways. When lies, hoaxes, and conspiracy theories are added to this automated mechanism, it's a recipe for personal alienation. Some people end up falling into a confirmation bias cycle and inhabiting an alternate, parallel reality. An economy of clickbait becomes an economy of distortion. To see the effect of this at play, we need only to look at the presidency of Donald J. Trump. In the months leading to his election and during his four years in office, falsehoods and conspiracy theories were continually spewed and propagated across Facebook, 4chan, reddit, Twitter, and other social media outlets. When a conspiracy theorist who was investigating false rumors of a child trafficking ring housed in a pizzeria in Washington, DC, fired three shots inside Comet Ping Pong on December 4, 2016, people thought this was as tragic as a conspiracy theory would get in twenty-first-century America. But on January 6, 2021, persuaded by months' worth of lies about a stolen presidential election and incited by the president himself, a violent mob of his supporters assaulted the United States Capitol, resulting in five deaths, 140 injured men and women, and Donald Trump's second impeachment trial.

The truly dark side of dark patterns is how they take advantage of many of our innate cognitive tendencies and shortcomings. Dark patterns come disguised in slick interface components, well-written strings of text, and compelling imagery. This is the ultimate subterfuge. Good design can trigger a deep human bias, known as *cognitive easing*, where we feel more receptive to familiar, easily understandable situations. This predisposition can also apply to information. When content is clear and well laid out, it requires less mental effort to absorb and understand it. Not only do well-designed interfaces make information easier to digest, but they also evoke more favorable and positive emotions. As much as it hurts, aesthetics can be a dominant instrument for deceit. Humans perceive beautiful objects as being easier to use and, as a result, tend to be more forgiving of them when things go wrong. This cognitive tendency underlies a well-known design principle called the *aesthetic-usability effect*. This explains why a consumer, in the presence of something attractive or well laid out, might have a strong propensity to believe it is legitimate. After all, there's no way something so well-crafted could be lying to you. The control that designers have over hacking our minds and molding human behavior is truly impressive. But with great power should come great responsibility.

In a *Fast Company* article titled "The Year Dark Patterns Won," Kelsey Campbell-Dollaghan points to 2016 as the turning point for dark patterns.[7] While dark patterns previously were associated with design and user experience, during the US 2016 presidential election they went mainstream in the worst possible way: they were used as weapons against democracy. Going mainstream also meant lawmakers would eventually have to pay attention. In April 2019, US senators Mark Warner (D-VA) and Deb Fischer (R-NE) proposed the Deceptive Experiences to Online Users Reduction (DETOUR) Act. Targeting large online platforms with more than 100 million users, the proposed bill prohibits "user interfaces that intentionally impair user autonomy, decision-making, or choice."[8] While well intended, the proposed act was just catching up with what was happening in other areas of the world. Three years earlier, the European Union's General Data Protection Regulation (GDPR) was adopted as one of the most comprehensive pieces of legislation protecting the privacy of millions of Europeans. On the first day of its enforcement, on May

25, 2018, NOYB [European Center for Digital Rights] sued Google and Facebook (and its subsidiaries Instagram and WhatsApp) seeking to fine Google $3.7 billion and Facebook $3.9 billion.[9] In December 2020 alone, Amazon, Facebook, and Google were the target of several antitrust lawsuits by the US and EU[10] in a trend that is likely to continue. Although it is difficult to say where the current legislative awakening will take us, it shows a desire for much-needed regulation of big tech around the world.

It can be tough to admit that conscious designers are behind many of these deceptive practices. Sometimes they are not. Attribution, ownership, and responsibility can be hard to determine in large, cross-functional product teams. Yet the purpose behind identifying dark patterns is not to pursue blame or seek denial. We must ask ourselves, How can we justify this moral failure by design? Why do designers fall into such recurrent fallacies that are antagonistic to their aim of solving problems and helping humans?

1. Desire to fit in

As was shown in chapter 1, designers can be particularly prone to status anxiety and to a desire for perfection. This can be felt daily, particularly with junior professionals. They might land in an environment that is often not familiar with, and sometimes even hostile to, design. However, most of the friction they encounter is due to unawareness. While some designers take offense at having to explain what they do, I learned this aspect of the job from a great teacher, who told me that part of our role as designers is to explain what design is. If other disciplines would do the same, many misunderstandings could be avoided. Another common complaint within design circles is that "we" don't have a "seat at the table." This is seen as the primary reason that design is not valued enough and that designers lack influence and the ability to make decisions. This is a pretext for what many designers really seek—respect from and validation by their peers. When they do get a seat at the table, most designers come to the realization that making financial, resourcing, and operational decisions every day is not quite what they aspired to do in their careers. And those who are indeed comfortable in their new role can simply get too comfortable. They eventually conform to existing conditions and develop an aversion for change that can trickle down the chain.

In most cases, expectations are imposed by other disciplines due to sheer discrepancies in numbers. Despite substantial growth in the past decade, design teams are still only a small part of large tech companies. While the ratio of designers to engineers is going down in the industry at large, it's common to find places with one designer for fifty engineers or one design researcher for one hundred engineers. I have managed teams with similar ratios, and I can say from experience it can be tremendously daunting. In these cases, the majority determines the culture and the methodologies that are put in place. The minority disciplines must conform to the usual methods, even if it's nonsensical to do so. And this is not only the case for design. It happens with many other functions and roles, from program management to copywriting.

Take data science as an example. Many data scientists in tech companies either directly or indirectly report to a software engineer. This means they generally adopt tools, processes, and project management practices that have evolved for software development. This is detrimental to good data science. Data science is much more open-ended. It often uses trial and error to deal with exploratory data models. Software engineering tends to be more predetermined around a specific goal or set of deliverables. And there are differences not just in tools and procedures but also in evaluating individual performance, which, despite role differences, will follow the targets and quantitative metrics of the principal discipline. When you try to shoehorn all functions into one way of doing things, it is not just counterproductive, but it can instill uniformity and conformity.

When you have only a hammer, every problem resembles a nail. Software engineering has a large influence in decision making and exercises veiled control over many other disciplines. This means it ends up imposing the management structure, reasoning, and processes of its own discipline, even in the face of better alternatives. This one-size-fits-all approach also dictates how technology itself evolves. As Meredith Broussard explains: "AI is tied up with games—not because there's anything innate about the connection between games and intelligence, but because computer scientists tend to like certain kinds of games and puzzles."[11] One can only imagine what the result would be if the people at the helm of AI teams were as passionate about history, fashion, or ecology as they are about Dungeons & Dragons. We need more diversity and representation in the tech industry, not just in terms of gender, ethnicity, and background but in thought, interest, and aptitude—not just to fill quotas but to develop better and more comprehensive tools for all of us humans.

Being a minority discipline increases your desire to be accepted, fit in, and obtain a much-desired seat at the table. This means you might develop in-group favoritism, unrealistic optimism, and positive illusions regarding your peers' behaviors and subsequent consequences. It also means there's a propensity to follow them and turn a blind eye to institutionalized practices, even when these are unethical, as in the case of dark patterns. This is a broad human tendency, also known as *herd mentality* or *conformity bias*. In situations like these, people are likely to withhold their own independent judgments for fear of causing conflict, being sidelined, or even, as it often happens, getting fired. Yes, the fear of retaliation is real and not completely unfounded. But it's important for designers not to succumb to these tendencies in order to be accepted. There are many jobs out there. You just have to look for the right one.

2. Moral disengagement

Conformity bias is our innate tendency to behave like others around us—to conform to the norm and succumb to peer pressure. It can also be the catalyst for another pernicious behavior, which psychologists call *moral disengagement*. This happens when you convince yourself that moral or ethical principles do not apply to you. It's a mechanism we adopt to protect ourselves from self-punishment and to grant ourselves permission to pursue various inhumane and immoral acts without being blamed for them. One form of moral disengagement is *ethical fading*, which happens when you are so focused on a target, such as sales, that ethics are simply brushed away. This happened when Volkswagen installed "defeat devices" in its diesel engines to avoid federal emissions standards, as discussed in chapter 5. A similar moral disengagement was a key factor in major financial ethical lapses in recent decades, from Enron's scandal in 2001, which led to its demise and the dissolution of the powerful accountancy firm Arthur Andersen, to the global financial crisis of 2007–2008, which resulted in the bankruptcy of Lehman Brothers and a loss of more than $2 trillion from the global economy.

Moral disengagement is a pervasive human trait. You might have witnessed it in a bullying or situational aggression incident, perhaps even in a large corporation where you worked in the past. It's hard to say why companies are so prone to moral disengagement. Perhaps employees see their job as a mere transaction and, for that reason, check their morality at the door. It is someone else's responsibility. The bigger the paycheck the stronger the incentive to turn a blind eye. Maybe they are so frustrated and detached from their insipid job that they simply stop caring. A monotonous routine can do that to you. Progressively, you start losing your peripheral vision and the ability to notice things around you, particularly when they go wrong. Maybe people see virtue as a one-dimensional pursuit dissociated from their workplace. They would rather find a virtuous route elsewhere, through religion, charity, education, selflessness, care, and compassion. Perhaps they simply feel powerless. It is hard for people to renounce their unethical behavior, unless they understand how detrimental it is. It is even harder to renounce when it is motivated by an overriding desire.

What is the most common element responsible when we shrug off the ethical aspects of a decision? The answer is clear—profit. Design is plainly an expedient pawn for growth. Design's viability today has become a synonym for profitability. Forget about social responsibility or environmental sustainability. What matters is financial gain. Try looking online for "design failure," and all you will find are instances of how a given product failed a business by failing to sell and make a profit. Rarely will you find examples of where design failed the environment or society by causing harm and long-lasting consequences. The cofounder of Mule Design Studio, Erika Hall, mentions in this context that "most of what operates under the label of 'design' right now is styling business models. It's not actually design, because you're not making meaningful choices. The choices have been made. They're outside your purview and designers are chasing after it, coloring in the boxes."[12] As Hall points out, the business model has become design's new grid.

To see how this is playing out, we can look at the evolution of Instagram. In 2020, Instagram made an important change to its bottom navigation bar—the easily reachable strip of icons that generally promotes the most popular features or sections of a mobile application. To use the 80/20 rule as a reference, the bottom navigation bar contains the 20 percent of features that drive 80 percent of the traffic. After several years, Instagram suddenly replaced its popular Activity icon (where users normally checked for updates such as likes, comments, and follows) with a new Shop icon (where users can search for various articles for sale and filter them by brand and product category). The change also came with a new Checkout icon, where Instagram would charge a fee to selected businesses. This diversified Instagram's revenue model and radically changed the primary focus of the bottom navigation bar.

These changes are a classic case of optimizing for income while deteriorating the experience for real users. Instagram's users were indignant, but their protests were not enough to persuade the company to restore the old icons. Eventually, people adapted to the new reality, and every confused user who accidentally landed on Shop was welcomed by the system. It was a clear case of dark pattern manipulation and one that concealed a bigger plan. As designers Dan Benoni and Louis-Xavier Lavallee noted in a case study on this Instagram move, the company started with a well-intended mission of "sharing your world through beautiful photos," but over time, the veneer came off, and the real motive was evident to everyone. Instagram was slowly becoming a "shopping mall." The business model is an ever-changing tyrant that cares only about its success, whatever the cost. As Benoni and Lavallee further explain, "if we keep optimizing products for profits over humans . . . your life could soon become an endless advertisement."[13]

But don't worry, some would say. With time, these companies can self-regulate and find their own ethical ground. Wishing for this outcome is laughable. When has it ever worked? Grading your own homework brings the worst type of self-serving biases imaginable. The organization rarely has any interest in pursuing a direction that deviates from the business model, even if it's the most principled path. Just ask prominent AI researcher Timnit Gebru, who was fired by Google in November 2020 over the release of a research paper that highlighted the risks of the large language models used to train AI systems, a research method central to Google's business.[14] Or ask Margaret Mitchell, who was fired four months later. The story takes a surprising turn when you realize that Gebru and Mitchell led Google's ethical AI team, which was meant to review the ethical implications of AI. When they started digging deeply into AI ethics, the company decided to push them out. Even deliberate attempts to provide an outside perspective don't always go so well, as happened with Google's first AI ethical board, comprised of different external experts from academia and industry. The board was established in late March 2019 with the goal of overseeing the responsible deployment of AI systems and was dismembered a few days after, following a series of controversies and ethical debates between board members.

The race to solve technology's harmful side-effects, including dark patterns, is a race against time, and we cannot expect tech companies to regulate themselves. Nor can we rely on the market to do so. It's too common for people to look at competitors as a barometer of moral behavior and then take an action that is more or less acceptable depending on who is doing it. This is what social psychologists call *advantageous comparison*. When the actions of your competitor are deeply unethical, your own behavior will appear less bad in contrast. When you are surrounded by bad practices, as in the case of the tech industry, you might look at yourself in a more forgiving light. After all, everyone else is doing it or worse. Compared to your unscrupulous competitor—and believe me, there's always one—you're not doing that bad, really. So in the meantime, let's get a few more clicks and increase that adoption curve. Canadian American psychologist Albert Bandura considers advantageous comparison one of the most effective means to distance yourself from morality. As he mentions in a seminal paper from 1999, "What was once morally condemnable becomes a source of self-valuation."[15]

So strong is the drive to put the business model above all else and to have design continue conforming to business's whims and deceits that recently a new design practice has emerged in the already wide array of design specialties. It's called *growth designer*. If there's a role that truly embodies Erika Hall's portrayal of the business model as design's new grid, this is it. And don't think that this role will be able to infuse the business model with a human-centered design approach or guide it in a different direction. Advocates of the new discipline might use terms such as "growth-driven," "strategic contributor," and "bridging the gap." But we know better. Those euphemistic labels are another form of moral disengagement that is used to conceal reprehensible behavior. After all, is there any better "growth-driven" pattern than a dark pattern?

3. Too big to notice

The Manhattan Project was enormous. Between 1942 and 1946, the World War II research initiative that led to the development of the first nuclear bomb employed more than 120,000 people and cost nearly $2 billion. In such a large-scale operation, to what extent were scientists, engineers, designers, military personnel, and technicians aware of the ethical repercussions of their work? Were they participating in a form of moral disengagement, or were they simply unaware of the purpose of their work? The few at the top who did know about the goal were compelled by advantageous competition. This was wartime, after all, and the thought that Germany could be developing a similar weapon made their actions less questionable. In fact, the project was triggered by warnings to the US government from scientists Albert Einstein and Enrico Fermi that this was a very conceivable danger. However, most low-level personnel did not fully know about it, partly due to security concerns and the compartmentalization of classified information. For others, it was impossible to see the big picture. They were incapable of consolidating all of the project's individual parts and contributions.

In large organizations where workers have highly specialized functions and teams are distributed across multiple locations, it can be hard for information to flow vertically within a single product area and even harder across silos. Information flow certainly is a challenge for many large tech conglomerates. At the time of this writing, Amazon, Facebook, Google, and Microsoft collectively employ more than 1,200,000 people. And this is excluding short-term contractors, who do a large percentage of the work. Each company also employs thousands of designers who oversee the branding, user experience, research, and design strategy for a myriad of different products, some with billions of users. The sheer scale of these corporations is the perfect vehicle for anonymity and absence of responsibility. This is further aggravated by big tech's well-known aversion to hierarchy and centralized control.

Group ownership can be hard to implement. By decentralizing control, giving autonomy to individual multidisciplinary groups (which can be called *squads*, *pods*, *units*, or *triads*), and imposing a reward and evaluation system based on a unit's achievements, you create an environment prone to rivalry and a win-at-all-costs mindset and one that lacks accountability. When a group is in control of a feature, no one is at the helm, no one is to blame, and ownership can be contested. While good in theory, autonomous, self-driven units can be a major source of ethical fading. Another common pattern in this type of organizational context is the *diffusion of responsibility*, which tends to increase with group size and specialization. It's the oldest buck-passing strategy for safeguarding oneself. How could you be the one at fault? You are responsible for only a minor, technical, and harmless task.

The struggles of autonomous units can also bring other unintended consequences. In large product teams, decisions are much more irrational than we might think and often are driven by egos, the whims of a single executive, or blind competition between feature teams. Such unhealthy rivalry and focus on their "own" feature often come at the expense of the collective. An independent team can make a series of small decisions that benefit the team's individual feature, but when added to others, the sum can prove detrimental to the long-term success of the product. This type of myopic pursuit, also known as the *tragedy of the commons*, happens because sometimes information doesn't flow freely between groups, which means most members are unable to grasp the full picture. Others simply don't care.

For product teams, the tragedy of the commons is not merely the result of short-term selfish interests, although selfishness can certainly play a factor. Unfortunately, it can become an entrenched behavior in organizations that reward people primarily based on their individual successes or their immediate team's achievements. This can result in downplaying the needs of a partner team or disregarding the other team completely. The common good becomes an elusive, abstract concept that no team really cares about if it is not aligned with the team's own reward system. It's important not to lose sight of the overall product direction and acknowledge that each team is always part of a larger group of people. In the end, the product can suffer, but so can the brand, public perception, valuation, and even employees.

I started this section by mentioning the Manhattan Project. This is not necessarily to establish an immoral equivalent with big tech, even though Silicon Valley's toxic weapon of personal alienation, social instability, and political division has tremendous civilizational magnitude and poses a dramatic existential thread. The goal was to highlight the importance of raising your head from the crowd and seeing the direction you are going; to understand the ultimate context of your work, no matter how small of a task it appears to be; to think beyond the feature or section you are developing; to question, uninterruptedly, until you get an answer; to ask deep and uncomfortable questions. To quote the head of Foresight & Transformation Strategy at ServiceNow, Martin Ryan, "The creators and designers of technology have the right to interrogate the ethics of what they are developing. But our ethics only extend as far as our line of inquiry."[16]

4. Techno-optimism

The progress of our species and human civilization is tightly coupled with the development of increasingly advanced tools. We wouldn't be where we are today without the remarkable technologies created over thousands and thousands of years. However, when portraying the advances of technology, we're too often faced with the pattern of *misrepresenting injurious consequences*—a form of moral disengagement where we tend to minimize problems and highlight benefits. It's also a type of naiveté and tunnel vision that affects modern-day tech idealists, who believe technology is an intrinsic force for good that is paving the future for humanity and that, in the end, will solve all our problems.

Technology is amoral and never neutral. It can be used to inspire and save lives or to kill and cause harm. It's as amoral as it can be faceless. While tools used to have a tangible look and feel, new digital technologies and platforms are opaque, immensely large, and complex. Such impalpable digital abstractions can be a harbor for anonymity and, with the help of designers, deception. As Douglas Rushkoff explains in *Team Human*, "Any of these technologies could be steered toward extending our human capabilities and collective power. Instead, they are deployed in concert with the demands of a marketplace, political sphere, and power structure that depend on human isolation and predictability in order to operate."[17] They are not here to help us; they are here to exploit us.

Technology is using us in more ways than one. But don't take my word for it. Here's a list of recent technological consequences, accompanied by one or more book titles on the topic (in parentheses) that were published in the last half decade alone. Among other things, modern digital technology has accentuated and multiplied precarity (Precarity Lab, *Technoprecarious*); amplified mass surveillance (Shoshana Zuboff, *The Age of Surveillance Capitalism: The Fight for a Human Future at the New Frontier of Power*); increased distraction, addiction, and social alienation (Adam Alter, *Irresistible: The Rise of Addictive Technology and the Business of Keeping Us Hooked*; Nir Eyal, *Indistractable: How to Control Your Attention and Choose Your Life*; Adam Gazzaley, *The Distracted Mind: Ancient Brains in a High-Tech World*); fostered misinformation, conspiracy theories, and ideological echo chambers (Cailin O'Connor, *The Misinformation Age: How False Beliefs Spread*; Daniel J. Levitin, *A Field Guide to Lies: Critical Thinking in the Information Age*; Lee McIntyre, *Post-Truth*); accentuated racism and inequality (Ruha Benjamin, *Race after Technology: Abolitionist Tools for the New Jim Code*; Virginia Eubanks, *Automating Inequality: How High-Tech Tools Profile, Police, and Punish the Poor*; Safiya Umoja

Noble, *Algorithms of Oppression: How Search Engines Reenforce Racism*); invaded our personal privacy (Bruce Schneier, *Data and Goliath: The Hidden Battles to Collect Your Data and Control Your World*); boosted segregation and polarization (Cathy O'Neil, *Weapons of Math Destruction: How Big Data Increases Inequality and Threatens Democracy*); automated our dumbness (Nicholas Carr, *The Glass Cage: How Our Computers Are Changing Us*; Nicholas Carr, *The Shallows: What the Internet Is Doing to Our Brains*); and even became an issue of personal safety (Wendell Wallach, *A Dangerous Master: How to Keep Technology from Slipping Beyond Our Control*).

The first thing to keep in mind about technology is that with every new piece created, ten more problems seem to arise. Take the manipulated videos that are produced by artificial intelligence, also known as *deep fakes*. Deep fake videos are able to replicate a person's movement, speech, and behavior and are eerily real and exceedingly credible. You might wonder why this technology was developed in the first place, since the opportunity for evil is so evident. As it turns out, there are some benign applications, particularly to the film industry. Deep fakes represent the next generation of advanced computer-generated imagery (CGI) and allow studios to insert new characters in a movie, mimic unavailable or deceased actors, remix old classics, improve the dubbing of foreign films, and quickly fix scenes, scripts, or other bloopers. These goals sound reasonable enough. Now let's consider the downsides.

Citing the work of legal scholars Bobby Chesney and Danielle Citron, a report by William A. Galston for the Brookings Institution gives a gloomy view of deep fakes and argues that they can "distort democratic discourse, manipulate elections, erode trust in institutions, weaken journalism, exacerbate social divisions, undermine public safety, and inflict hard-to-repair damage on the reputation of prominent individuals, including elected officials and candidates for office."[18] This seems like an exorbitant price to pay for a bit of entertainment fun. You would expect people working with this technology to weight its moral implications accordingly: Do the benefits outweigh the costs? Am I causing more harm than good? Will this work make the world a better place?

The second important consideration about technology is that it moves faster than our ability to make sense of it. While we have an innate fear of falling from an abyss or being bitten by a spider—the subject of nightmares for many, based on thousands of years of human evolution—riding a car at 60 miles per hour does not induce the same sense of fear or anxiety even though it is more likely to be lethal. Incapable of developing an instinctive uneasiness about modern technology, we also find it hard to grasp its repercussions. AI and advanced algorithms are beyond the comprehension of most people. Perhaps this always has been the case for most new forms of advanced technology in the past. However, the difference now is that no single person can comprehend the entirety of the connected, ever-evolving system of components. If the technical personnel building these wide-ranging, abstract models don't fully understand the sum of all the moving parts of their product, imagine how hard it must be for lawmakers to fathom its reach, let alone regulate its expansion.

The third important consideration about technology is that it is as biased and fallible as its creators. We should not trust it or place our faith in it. Take facial recognition as an example—an area of research afflicted by instances of racial bias. Silicon Valley developments in computer vision have repeatedly misidentified dark-skinned people as criminals, labeled them as gorillas, or simply failed to see them altogether.[19] For some of these problems, there was a lack of diversity in the training datasets, a clear case of under-representation bias. A 2018 study by an MIT researcher found that if the subject is a white man, the software accuracy was normally close to 99 percent, whereas it made mistakes 35 percent of the time when analyzing images of dark-skinned females.[20] Because institutionalized biases can persist for a long time, we can see the historical racism shown in the redlining example in chapter 5 being perpetuated in these modern-day algorithms.

"The pursuit of seamless and frictionless technology too often covers up social frictions," writes Ruha Benjamin, Princeton University sociologist and professor of African American studies, in the foreword to *The Black Experience in Design: Identity, Expression, and Reflection* by Anne H. Berry, Kareem Collie, Penina Acayo Laker, Lesley-Ann Noel, Jennifer Rittner, and Kelly Walters. She adds, "less friction for some humans means more friction for others, not inevitably, but predictably."[21] To advocate for technology without understanding its downsides and eminent threat to the fabric of society is to be naive at best. To conceal its harm behind simple and addictive interfaces is malicious. We cannot use the ethos of good design to continue misleading people and covertly sneaking addictive and discriminatory technology onto people's laps, pockets, and wrists. We cannot allow design to continue to be a slave to technology. It is simply too dangerous. The role of design is not to make new technology easier to use and adopt, to make it more appealing and engaging, or to sell more of it. The role of designers is to question and propose better solutions, even if that means a different technology, less of it, or none of it. Technology is a means to an end, not an end in itself. We must continue to dream the future and adapt technology to our needs, not let it take over us.

Actionable Advice

Speak up and make your voice heard. Don't be swayed by peer pressure or the desire for status and validation. Do what's right. As the great British American author and humanist Christopher Hitchens once wrote, "Never be a spectator of unfairness or stupidity. Seek out argument and disputation for their own sake; the grave will supply plenty of time for silence."[22] Embrace a nonconformist attitude, like Hitchens did, and always question the *status quo* and the normal *modus operandi*. But don't assume that only others are to blame. Don't assume that you haven't turned a blind eye, even if unintentionally. Don't assume that you haven't conformed to the norm and ignored the scale of the problem or have used euphemistic language to disguise something more damaging. Do some introspection, and take a deep look at your behavior and actions. Ask yourself, "Is my work causing good or harm?"

"Always design a thing by considering it in its next larger context—a chair in a room, a room in a house, a house in an environment, an environment in a city plan."[23] This important message by Finnish American designer Eero Saarinen speaks to the critical importance of context. It is paramount. You need to understand the final setting of your individual contribution and the sum of all its independent parts. If you are creating a feature for a mobile app, don't think of it as a mere icon on the screen but as a full-time companion that is available anywhere, all the time. What kind of a partner would you like to have by your side? Should it be one that's supportive and insightful and makes you a better version of yourself, or should it be one that is addictive, attention-seeking, and selfish? Think about the full contextual scale—from the inner, smaller components that make the product, both physical and digital, to the full scale of upward implications, social and environmental; from how a single pixel is lit on screen to how a product will end up in a dumpster somewhere on our planet.

Establish your own personal mission and set of values: What do you respect? What do you care about? Where do you want to go? Be clear about your own ethical ground and job expectations. If you care deeply about a product or technology and see it going in the wrong direction, you can either leave it behind or help it steer it in the right direction. It might be that you feel powerless to change things. Yet if there's an avenue of possibility, try to change the business model so that growth and profitability are not the only viable paths. As the design of a given service, platform, or experience becomes central to the business, it has an opportunity to redefine its strategy. Design becomes the master plan. Aim at designing it with others, with empathic persuasion, infusing it with ethical and sustainability concerns. Embrace the work of other institutions that walked down that path and succeeded. Consider the United Nations' list of sustainable goals as an outline that can guide your team's shared vision and mission.

Finally, it's important to put things in perspective. There's a lot of blame going around, so it's important to take some pressure off yourself. An increasing amount of responsibility is being placed on designers, but unfortunately, in most cases, they have a very slim amount of power. A single designer can't change capitalism or the rise of the attention economy. You can, however, be smart with your choices. Yes, it's a job. Design is still a job. And you have bills to pay and kids to feed. You are likely not going to change the world in your job. But there are many jobs out there. There are many principled groups, supportive teams, compassionate managers, and exciting products out there. Don't stay in a job you don't like or in a company with a disregard for ethics and integrity. You're more than your job. You can do better.

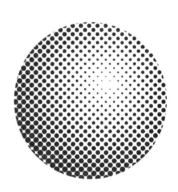

Environmental Impact

You have to demand the type of future
that you want to recognize.
—Julia Watson[1]

Civilization is revving itself into a
pathologically short attention span.
—Stewart Brand[2]

7

Design is for humans

In 1992, architect Michael Brill was commissioned with an unusual brief. He and his team had to come up with a solution that could express danger to generations thousands of years into the future. Effectively communicating with other people living six or eight thousand years from now is no small feat. What symbol or graphical representation could be used to guarantee the successful decoding of the message, particularly if no modern-day written language is likely to last that long? Is there a universal, enduring metaphor for hazard? The unusual brief came from Sandia National Laboratories, which invited artists, designers, and architects to help them communicate the location of a new underground nuclear waste facility in Carlsbad,

New Mexico. In operation since 1999, the Waste Isolation Pilot Plant (WIPP) is a deep geological repository that stores radioactive waste in a salt formation 2,150 feet (660 meters) underground. The plant is licensed to store the waste from the production of US nuclear weapons from twenty-two generator sites for up to ten thousand years. This waste can remain radioactive for at least 100,000 years.

This might be one of the most extraordinary design challenges of all time, and it has long occupied my mind, in part because of the thrill of creating a unique means of communicating with unknown future individuals, possibly even nonhuman individuals, and the monumental consequences of failure. The range of design concepts produced for the design challenge was remarkable. Out of the many ideas that didn't rely on the use of written language, such as pictograms of humans faces experiencing pain or a depiction of Edvard Munch's painting *The Scream*, was the riveting proposal by Brill and his team. Titled "Landscape of Thorns," the plan featured massive granite thorns poking up from the ground as a threatening sign to future generations that this was not a welcoming place. The fact that we all have an innate fear of sharp objects in nature and associate them with danger could work in favor of Brill's solution. Think of the thorns of a plant or the cutting edge of a rock. We have developed an instinctive aversion to them because they can really hurt us. Perhaps if future generations were to see such a frightening landscape permeated by granite thorns they will perceive it as something threatening and worth avoiding. We can only hope.

This design challenge also puts into perspective how long our stuff lasts. Not only have our cities and large structures had an undeniable impact on the planet over the past ten thousand years, but even if we stopped all that we are doing today—if we simply vanished suddenly—our stuff would still be around for thousands of years with the potential for inflicting further harm. One way of taking accountability for this is to expand our concept of the present. A similar approach has been pursued by the Long Now Foundation. Established in 1996 as a "counterpoint to today's accelerating culture,"[3] the foundation employs five-digit dates (using 01996 for a year instead of 1996) as a means of replacing the "now" with a "long now" that lasts twenty thousand years. This stretching of our historical framework is important for a couple of reasons: it expands our idea of the present and also makes the future seem closer. The next two thousand years appear to be just around the corner. Furthermore, placing humans within the "long now" enhances our sense of responsibility for what will happen within that time span. It helps us to plan and design in a long-lasting way.

The long-term effects of our presence on planet earth do not end with the end of our species. And radioactive waste is not the only thing that outlives us. Plastic can stay in the environment for up to five hundred years, and our planet is literally drowning in it. In 1950, the world produced only 1.5 million metric tons of plastic, but that figure has increased nearly 250-fold, reaching 367 million metric tons in 2020.[4] You can close your eyes and picture a line graph with a very steep line increasing dramatically in the past decade. It is estimated that 8 million tons of plastic enter our oceans every year, adding to the estimated 150 million tons already there. That's the equivalent of one five-ton truck of plastic being dumped into the ocean every minute. Unfortunately, we have been sold a myth about recycling. Chile, a country with less than 20 million people, consumes approximately 990,000 tons of plastic every year and recycles only 83,679 tons (8.5 percent).[5] This rate is consistent at a global level. Roughly 91 percent of our plastic is not being recycled. There's no monetary incentive to recycle, so we keep producing more. "It is far cheaper and more profitable to make new plastic (from oil and gas) than to recycle it. But in order to keep selling new plastic, the industry had to 'greenwash' its wasteful image by embracing recycling,"[6] writes journalist Simon Wilson in a report on an investigation by journalists at National Public Radio into the dark history of plastic manufacturing.

If plastic objects were plotted on a matrix that compared time of usage versus full lifespan, bottled water would likely be the worst ecological offender. One million water bottles are sold every minute around the world. They have a very brief single use (as long as the consumer takes to empty it) and a very long life cycle (up to five hundred years to decompose). They are the epitome of our disposable culture and a symbol of the irresponsible and gratuitous nature of most designed objects produced in recent times. To build something that is used for only a few minutes and yet stays in the environment for hundreds of years is reprehensible. Unfortunately, most of the physical objects around you will likely outlive you. Even if they are no longer operating as intended, most of their constituent parts will inhabit various dumpsters or regions of the ocean for decades and possibly centuries. The time you spend using them is a small fraction of their lifespan. As a designer, your goal should be to target the opposite quadrant of that matrix—where you can maximize the time of use and decrease the environmental impact.

"Practically everything we do today needs to change. We are still doing most things as if we own nature and have unlimited resources. We work as if waste is not a problem. We treat nature like a pantry and a toilet," says Canadian designer Bruce Mau: "We think short term, party like there's no tomorrow, and pass the check to future generations."[7] One way to mitigate this careless attitude is to stop thinking of users as the endpoint of a product's journey. We do not design for humans. Customers are only transient users of our products. We ultimately design for the environment. Your product will likely outlive your end user and inhabit the environment for much longer. We need to expand the life cycle of a design and plan for postuse. Any product journey is incomplete if it doesn't reflect this critical shift in understanding. Even digital products will continue populating a digital wasteland with no end in sight. But nature is not an unlimited resource. We cannot continue to act without acknowledging consequences. As Mau states, we need to "think forever, design for perpetuity."[8]

Our recent focus on the user has brought design to the forefront across many industries, but it has proven to be an inadequate and outdated model. "Human-centered design is great for mops and phones," writes American designer Jesse Weaver, "but it won't solve society's biggest problems."[9] In a way, human-centered design reminds me of an ancient concept called *scala naturae*, or the ladder of life, that in the Middle Ages became part of the great chain of being, which normally featured God at the top of a pyramid, followed by humans and a succession of "lower animals." It is an anthropocentric, hierarchical view of the world that led to many unintended consequences, including seeing nature as a resource to be exploited and humans as the most important element of our environment. By focusing primarily on the human part of nature, we have become blind to everything else. We have lost touch with bigger challenges that often lie outside of an individual's needs and recurring problems. We must abandon this simplistic approach. The world has moved on. To consider only the whims of a single node in a vast, interdependent web of cause and effect is shortsighted and part of the problem. It is a single solution for a single problem.

      Instead of a human-centered approach, we need to think of a life-centered or earth-centered design methodology. Humans make up approximately 0.01 percent of all life on earth.[10] Yet a vast majority of all we do as designers is done with them in mind. If we want to invest in sustainable design and reduce negative impacts on the environment, we need to stop centering on the human. We must understand the problem from the viewpoint of nature—investigate its unique needs and requirements, identify its fragilities, and embrace the immense opportunities it offers for cooperation. We need to see ourselves as part of a symbiotic, greater whole and start planning for a "long now" that looks deep into the future. This means changing the storytelling formula introduced in chapter 3 so that the main character is no longer the human but instead our planet. It means to design for the end of the customer journey, what British designer Joe Macleod calls "Endineering,"[11] but also well beyond single usage and single users. It means conceptualizing objects, structures, and systems that can be continuously adapted and modified and that can incorporate different types of unforeseeable handling. It means adopting transformation and reconfiguration as if they were features. Designing for now will not be enough.

Professor of psychology Martin E. P. Seligman and John Tierney struggle with the conventional name for our species. *Homo sapiens* or "wise man," they argue, seems "more of a boast than a description."[12] Perhaps we should use a descriptor that is unique to humans, but as we pay more attention to other species, we realize that language, tools, and cooperation are not exclusively human traits. The best distinction between us and other creatures appears to be our ability to "contemplate the future." According to the authors, "Our singular foresight created civilization and sustains society."[13] As *Homo prospectus*[14] or "prospective man," we can see the future and predict numerous consequences to our actions, both short- and long-term. Yet we continue acting on our instincts, biases, and the oldest, most reactive parts of our brain. Why are we failing to foresee what is in front of our eyes? Why are designers not doing their job? Designer Victor Papanek was sounding the alarm about social and environmental responsibility fifty years ago.[15] Why are we still not reacting in the face of an existential crisis? Why do we believe that all will be OK?

1. Grounded in the present

Close your eyes for a minute, and try to picture yourself in old age. Do you empathize with your future self? Or is that person so changed that you no longer seem to be the same person you are today? If you are like most people, your future self is a stranger to you. This is the suggestive evidence of more than a hundred functional magnetic resonance imaging (fMRI) studies. Researchers strapped the heads of study participants to a bulky, circular MRI machine and asked them various questions in order to detect patterns in brain activity. When participants were probed to think of themselves right now, an area of the brain called the medial prefrontal cortex (MPFC) lit up fully. In contrast, when they were asked to think of another person, this region of the brain grew dimmer. The less they knew about a person, the less activated that region of the brain became. And time has the same effect on self-perception: "The further out in time you try to imagine your own life, the less activation you show in the MPFC."[16] As research director of the Institute for the Future Jane McGonigal explains, "your brain acts as if your future self is someone you don't know very well and, frankly, someone you don't care about."[17]

UCLA psychologist Hal Hershfield explains how this emotional disconnect can be damaging. It can explain, for instance, "why many people don't save enough for retirement; why they continue to indulge in unhealthy behaviors, accepting the risk of incurring terrible diseases in the future; and why they make bad ethical decisions despite knowing that they might suffer consequences down the road."[18] If it is hard to contemplate our older self and come to terms with the fact we are saving money for a stranger, imagine caring for a future where we are no longer here. The founders of The Long Time Project—an initiative that fosters long-term future awareness— Beatrice Pembroke and Ella Saltmarshe argue that our failure to think long-term might be tied with the denial of our own mortality: "We've got a hunch that our inability to deal with the future of the world beyond our lifespan is wrapped up with our inability to deal with the fact that our lives will end."[19] Do we simply extend this illusion of invincibility to the remainder of our species? Do we believe that humans will always prevail regardless of what the future might hold? This would at least explain our level of comfort as we continue walking on a knife's edge that at any moment can slice through the core of our survival as a species.

It seems that we are hardwired not to care about the long-term future. We can see what lies ahead, and yet we choose not to think of it. One universal bias grounding us to the present is known as *hyperbolic discounting*. It tells us that when given two similar rewards, we prefer an immediate one over one that comes later in the future. In a widely cited 1994 study, participants were confronted with multiple options, such as getting $50 now or $100 in a year. Over and over, the most immediate reward was the one that was picked. This is a challenge we all know very well. Should I satiate myself now or save for tougher times? Should I splurge on a new outfit or build up my savings account? It appears we are in a constant battle between our present-oriented hedonistic tendencies and a faraway future filled with risk and uncertainty—not to mention a stranger you don't even recognize. And as the saying goes, out of sight, out of mind. In an online survey of 2,818 people that was titled the "American Future Gap" and was conducted by the Institute for the Future, most Americans (53 percent) admitted that they rarely think or worry about the long-term future. This present bias or "short-termism," argues BBC managing editor Richard Fisher, "may be the greatest threat our species is facing."[20]

In the face of such indifference, statements like "Leave the world better for future generations" can feel like empty demagoguery. We are already leaving it much worse than we received it for our children and their children. Perhaps Australian philosopher Roman Krznaric put it best when he compared this irresponsible behavior to the idea of colonizing the future. As he explains, "we treat the future as a distant colonial outpost where we dump ecological degradation, nuclear waste, public debt and technological risk."[21] Krznaric establishes a parallel with *terra nullius* (no one's land or unclaimed territory), a concept employed by many past colonizers to disregard the ownership rights of Indigenous populations. We are treating the future as "empty time," a nobody's land that simply ignores all future generations. Contrast this attitude with the selfless philosophy of the seventh-generation principle, which was upheld by the ancient Indigenous confederacy of the Haudenosaunee, or Iroquois, in northeast North America. According to this principle, we need to think of present decisions in a way that benefits seven generations into the future. This is the type of altruistic, long-term thinking we must adopt.

How can designers bypass our present bias and short-termism? Can we find meaningful ways to empathize with our future selves and forthcoming generations? Yes, it is possible. We have done it before. One great example is what researchers call cathedral thinking, which refers to the multigeneration, interdisciplinary effort that was needed to erect a medieval cathedral. A similar endeavor is being undertaken in Barcelona at the Basílica de la Sagrada Família. Construction started in 1882 and continues to this day. I remember visiting it in the late 1990s during a college field trip and being awestruck by the ongoing duration of the builders' effort. This effort might seem like an outlier today, yet this was the norm in the past. St. Basil's Cathedral in Moscow took 123 years to complete, St. Peter's Basilica 144, and York Minster Cathedral an impressive 252 years to build. Multiple generations saw the scaffolding and structure rising without ever seeing the result. Many of our large-scale, multinational, environmental efforts require this lengthened timespan. Earth-centered design is a long game. It requires a bold, far-reaching vision, a well-defined plan, and a "shared commitment to long-term implementation."[22] Above all, it requires us to extend our frame of reference in time and focus on the flourishing of our own descendants and the descendants of all of our fellow species. It requires an appreciation for the intrinsic value of all living creatures. In other words, it requires the adoption of deep ecology.

2. The age of numbing

In 1982, Robert Jay Lifton published a seminal paper on the psychological effects of war.[23] While paying close attention to Hiroshima survivors, Lifton portrayed people in such a state of shock that they were incapable of responding rationally to what was happening around them. They became insensitive to human death and indifferent to feelings. He called this a state of "psychic numbing" and describes it as a "diminished capacity or inclination to feel."[24] Years later, Lifton and Greg Mitchell wrote an article titled "The Age of Numbing,"[25] where they establish a parallel with today's looming existential crisis. Although we realize that at any moment we could simply vanish, either by nuclear annihilation or ecological collapse, we somehow find a way to cope with such an imminent threat. In a rural community in western Norway, sociology professor Kari Marie Norgaard found a similar defense mechanism. Local people were aware of the visible effects of climate change, but that awareness didn't affect their daily lives in a substantial way. It was as if they were living two separate lives. The underlying motive comes across in the words of a person interviewed by Norgaard, who said, "people want to protect themselves a bit."[26]

A similar coping strategy appears to be at play when it comes to managing large-scale human tragedies, such as natural disasters, mass murders, or genocides. "The more people who are suffering, the less we feel," says psychology professor Daniel Västfjäll. In a study with his colleague Paul Slovic, the two scholars uncovered a tendency to detach oneself from mass atrocities because "as numbers get larger and larger, we become insensitive; numbers fail to trigger the emotion or feeling necessary to motivate action."[27] When we are constantly bombarded by large numbers of people who are dying of poverty, hunger, or a global pandemic, we develop a type of statistical numbing where quantities don't quite add up to an equivalent human suffering. This disquieting finding means that if we become desensitized and fail to grasp the magnitude of such calamities, our capacity to support and act will inevitably be affected. And while design can play an important role in evoking awareness, introspection, and empathic action, paradoxically, it can also contribute to an increased sense of detachment.

Information design and data visualization are powerful media for bringing to light topics, events, and facts that would otherwise be left hidden. Yet they aren't always able to evoke the right type of human emotion. Charts, graphs, and diagrams are a visual abstraction of reality and inevitably create a distancing effect from the physical experience. In a chapter in Martin Engebretsen and Helen Kennedy's *Data Visualization in Society*, Norwegian scientist Jill Walker Rettberg explains that we are used to encountering situations in a spatial way. And she provides an illustrative example. Let's say you walk into someone's kitchen and open a drawer. You might see a well-organized set of knives and forks, but you also get to experience them in a multisensorial way, by grabbing and picking up some of the items. In contrast, try to picture a chart of the same drawer or even a photograph. "Once the knives and forks are transferred from spatially organized objects to a visual representation on a two-dimensional surface, our distance from them increases," says Rettberg. "We interpret them as separate from us."[28]

Seeing people as data points can be particularly dehumanizing. Instead of inducing empathy, a chart or data visualization can contribute to desensitization and number numbness and, as a result, become a form of moral disengagement. This response can be devastating when the topic is a human calamity. As Jacqueline Novogratz argues in *Manifesto for a Moral Revolution*, when we reduce people to statistics, we tell ourselves there is nothing else to be done.[29] Design's responsibility in this context is paramount. We ought to inform and relay events but also stir enough emotion in consumers to lead them to take knowledgeable, compassionate action. Too much is at stake for us to perpetuate indifference. From social breakdowns to eminent environmental collapse, we are facing critical challenges that require conscientious change and hard work. The resulting detachment from graphical abstraction is ultimately a design problem. We can help by embracing stories that complement facts and figures. These narratives can communicate the human element in the analyzed data. Alternatively, we can aim at what Italian researcher Enrico Bertini calls *anthropographics*—"visual strategies to make the connection between data and humans more direct and empathic"[30] by considering different levels of granularity, expressiveness, and realism in data portrayal.

3. Business as usual

In 2018, Starbucks launched a campaign banning plastic straws
in its North American stores as part of a long-term plan to remove
them from its 28,000 stores worldwide. While this might seem like
a praiseworthy initiative, there was a caveat: the new strawless lids
added between 0.32 and 0.88 grams of plastic to each drink.[31] In 2019,
a similar misstep was made by McDonald's when it introduced nonre-
cyclable paper straws in the UK as a replacement for recyclable plastic
ones.[32] These episodes and countless others show that companies
rarely look at sustainability in a holistic way. They see words like *green*
and *eco* as a single marketing program or product label, something
they invest in momentarily or in parallel with the "real" business,
instead of as a systemic change to their practice. Once the new quota
is filled, the job is done. It's business as usual. Unfortunately, the few
companies that do commit to ambitious proposals rarely succeed. In
2017, Bain & Company surveyed three hundred companies and found
that 98 percent of all sustainability initiatives failed to achieve their
initial expectations. According to the researchers, this happens primarily because leadership tends to "overlook the difficulties frontline
employees confront when implementing new approaches." When
forced to choose "between sustainability targets and business targets,"
they explain, "most employees choose business targets."[33]

This is not surprising. As is shown in chapter 6, when a
company focuses too much on a given metric, such as sales or profit,
ethical implications can become a peripheral worry. This type of
moral disengagement is prevalent across industries. Left to their own
devices, most corporations will focus on what they always have—
profit. This behavior is particularly appalling in companies that are
directly implicated in deforestation—a key trigger for climate change.
A July 2019 report by the environmental nonprofit CDP, entitled "The
Money Trees," found that corporate transparency on deforestation is
very low. In 2018, fifteen hundred companies that played a prominent
role in deforestation were requested by investors to reveal forest data

through CDP's platform, and 70 percent failed to do so. "The silence is deafening when it comes to the corporate response to deforestation,"[34] says Morgan Gillespy, global director of forests at CDP. The driving force for disclosing forest data to CDP is not a company's ecological conscience, though. The reasons most frequently cited by those who shared their data was that they wanted to avoid damage to their brand reputation. This reveals the true moral compass of most corporations. Having a negative impact on the environment doesn't matter much, unless it affects their own image. Sustainability is not something they do for ethical reasons but is a marketing tool to boost brand perception.

This happens, in part, because corporations have faced almost no repercussions for the environmental crimes they commit. "Our businesses use linear production models in which they are not responsible for the externalities, such as pollution, waste, or sickness,"[35] explains author and EU Commission adviser Desiree Driesenaar. Because governments frequently bear the burden of "cleaning up waste, taking care of sick people, cleaning rivers, oceans, and air,"[36] you would expect them to take a stronger stance. Yet, puzzlingly, most governments continue to support this negligent approach. In a paper that looked at more than ninety-four studies on environmental sustainability over two decades, researchers found a systemic policy implementation failure. The main factor contributing to this failure, according to the paper, was economic incentives for activities that "continue to exploit natural resources without deeper consideration of the associated damage to the environment."[37] And exploitation is the best way to describe our relationship with nature over the past centuries. For far too long, natural resources have been seen as something to exploit, tame, and control in our favor. When coupled with the idea of limitless economic growth, they make a perfect formula for ecological disaster.

Modern-day capitalism and the plundering of our natural environment as a means of production for profit soon became the approach used across all industries. And design was eventually caught by the same profiteering laissez-faire as other professions, turning a blind eye to its own ramifications. As anthropologist Daniel Miller wrote about this conundrum, "it ought to be unimaginable that a profession would spend its entire time concerned with designing the particular form of goods without seeing it as essential to attempt to know what the consequences of those particular designs would be."[38] Disturbingly eager to be respected and have a seat at the table, design today invests chiefly in business impact (increasing revenue, adoption, usage, or readership). It's a hyperlocalized bubble that is oblivious to human, societal, and environmental impacts. It is also a form of moral disengagement, as is discussed in chapter 6. It might be hard to believe, but it has not always been this way. The 1960s saw a pushback against consumerism, led by designers and architects such as Victor Papanek and Richard Buckminster Fuller. However, it was a short-lived fight.

"Socially oriented designers such as Victor Papanek who were celebrated in the 1970s were no longer regarded as interesting," write design professors Anthony Dunne and Fiona Raby: "they were seen as out of sync with design's potential to generate wealth and to provide a layer of designer gloss to every aspect of our daily lives."[39] In recent decades, design became a tool for making more money rather than a means for bringing about social change. Market forces dictated how design moves and where it should focus its attention. Any deviation from the bottom line is simply pushed aside as not being aligned with the company and therefore irrelevant. As a result, design lost its north and, with it, its ability to self-govern. We need design to refocus its attention where it is needed—not in creating things that will harm the environment for hundreds of years or in selling things we don't need in a continuous push down the sales funnel but, instead, in helping people and the planet solve real problems. Earth-centered design is compatible only with an ecologically sustainable production. Design's ultimate project is to reimagine how we produce, deliver, and consume products, physical or digital—to rethink the existing business model.

4. Digital will save us

Digital transformation is one of the many buzzwords used in the early twenty-first century. As the name implies, it is the process of using digital solutions to replace older analog tools and services, often through automated processes. Featured in countless corporate presentations and consultancy reports, this modern-day trend is built on the assumption that digital technology is an infinite and environmentally benign resource. In a way, this perception is to be expected. When faced with a new technology, we tend to overestimate its effect in the short term. According to the five-stage Gartner hype framework of technologies[40]—technology trigger, peak of inflated expectations, trough of disillusionment, slope of enlightenment, and plateau of productivity—the use of the term *digital transformation* probably appears during stage two of the cycle, the *peak of inflated expectations*, which is followed by stage three, the *trough of disillusionment*. Digital transformation is nothing new. Razorfish, a pioneering digital agency based in New York City, has used the slogan "Everything that can be digital will be" since the mid-1990s. In a way, the prediction has proven to be true. Today we see how digital technology is transforming a wide array of industries. Yet the transition from analog to digital is not always a positive outcome. It is important to appreciate its numerous benefits, but it is also critical to avoid a blind overconfidence that disregards its long-term consequences.

One important cultural downside of this transformation is what researchers call the *digital dark age*—the possibility that years from now, we will look back at the present time and be unable to read or interpret most of the digital artifacts that are being created today. This is a reality I encountered while gathering images and illustrations for my previous books. It turned out to be easier to access a diagram produced on paper five hundred years ago than a digital one created in the last two decades. The reasons for this riddle are multifold: many digital files become obsolete due to outdated or proprietary formats, plug-ins stop working or no one bothers to update the code, and there is the persistent data degradation or corruption. All of these can make it challenging to retrieve electronic documents, even ones created just ten years ago. Digital files are limited not just in their duration but also in their availability. Most digital files are stored and shared within computer networks. If you consider those networks as a shared resource, they are often limited by bandwidth. Overuse or poor management, which often happens on the internet, can deem many digital files inaccessible, either momentarily or permanently.

Now that we have looked at some of the finite qualities of the digital, let's ponder the perception of it as being environmentally benign. It is easy to see why the digital is often portrayed as an untapped rescuer of our precipitating ecosuicide. The incorporeal nature of most digital tools and platforms appears to us as something less hostile to the environment. However, pixels use electricity, lots of it. And emails, apps, and docs generate a lot of data, which is saved in large data farms, which also consume a great amount of energy. Referring to data as being stored in the cloud further reinforces the picture of something abstract that lives in the ether. Yet the cloud lives in machines that are plugged into energy sources. They also generate a lot of heat and must be frequently cooled down. As more data is generated, more machines are required to store it. The cloud is not an unlimited resource. It is estimated that data centers around the world consume as much as 2% of the world's electricity—the equivalent amount of carbon emissions of the entire airline indus-try.[41] If the internet was a country, it would be the sixth largest in terms of energy consumption, and by 2025, it is expected to become the fourth-largest pollutant in terms of carbon emissions, lagging behind only China, India, and the United States.

Some of the latest technological developments, such as artificial intelligence and cryptocurrency, are also not environ-mentally friendly. In a widely cited paper titled "Energy and Policy Considerations for Deep Learning in NLP," researchers Emma Strubell, Ananya Ganesh, and Andrew McCallum show that machine learning can have a dramatic carbon footprint. According to the authors, the number of graphics processing unit (GPU) hours and respective energy consumption required to train machine learning models has dramatically increased in recent times. While an average American is responsible for approximately 36,152 pounds of CO_2 per year, training a translation machine model using neural architecture search with several GPUs can produce 626,155 pounds of CO_2. That is roughly five times as much carbon as a car produces in its entire lifetime, from construction to junkyard, including fuel. That is a tremendously expensive process. Cryptocurrency mining is not much better. Requiring the validation of transactions across several machines, mining in cryptocurrency networks can easily translate into an enormous amount of energy consumption. By 2018, one single cryptocurrency, Bitcoin, was using as much CO_2 a year as one million transatlantic flights.[42]

The idea that the digital is a force for good for the environment needs to be demystified. We cannot continue using it as an excuse for inaction. We must be aware of its long-term implications. In the same vein, we have to demystify the notion that some designers have a higher environmental responsibility than others. When we talk about design's accountability, we normally think that industrial, product, packaging, and fashion design are the primary offenders. We think primarily of designed items that are manufactured, shipped, and sold as having a significant ecological footprint. Yet designers working on digital tools, platforms, and experiences are as accountable as any other. As such, they need to understand the ramifications of their work. Every seemingly small interaction adds to the equation. "Google estimates that a typical search using its services requires as much energy as illuminating a 60-watt light bulb for 17 seconds."[43] If you consider how many searches you do in a single day, you quickly realize how it can add up. So, think twice next time you are working on a digital feature meant to increase usage, clicks, and overall interaction. It all has a price. Awareness and transparency are vital drivers of ethical behavior. If we want to act as future agents of change, we cannot continue to fall into past traps and misconceptions. We must acknowledge our responsibility, whether we are designing physical objects or digital experiences.

Actionable Advice

Sustainability can feel like an uphill battle at times. And to make matters worse, designers who are seeking account-ability often have to argue against themselves. We all share numerous biases attaching us to the present, distancing ourselves from pain, and ignoring what lies ahead. But change is possible. And designers are particularly well suited to make changes happen. "The sustainability challenge is a design issue," says British writer John Thackara. "Eighty percent of a product, service, or system's environmental impact is determined at the design stage."[44] This means designers need to step up to the challenge. We cannot continue to be passive bystanders. After all, waste is a design flaw. One way to address this issue is by extending a product's journey to its full life cycle—to care as much about postuse as you do about the human handling of your design and to consider the environment as your ultimate user, your primary stakeholder. To put it above all else. Create a persona for it, if you need to. Uncover its needs and requirements as if it were a human. Respect doesn't stop with the end user. Be a voice for the natural world as much as you are for the user. This is a long game. You must think of products in a prolonged time span. You must consider multiple generations and adopt a "long-now" mindset.

If we truly want to decolonize the future, we need to put our environment above any exploitative, unsanction-able corporate practice. Sustainability needs to become an integral and systemic part of the business model, not just a product label or single initiative. And if that doesn't happen right away, let's aim at designing a new normal: "Design can help reverse this trend by changing the processes behind products, as well as the resources used to make them and use them. This is how a commitment to sustain-ability drives innovation."[45] In order to do this, we have to embrace a process that is more symbiotic with nature. One that upholds replenishment, reciprocity, and regeneration instead of extraction. We need to adopt a circular economy. "We must learn a lesson from the natural world," explains Bruce Mau, where "every output is an input," where "waste equals food."[46] You'll always find customers who will support you in that mission. People are geared for good. They want to do the right thing. So don't conform to the existing business model, particularly when you can see clearly through the cracks. Invent a new one.

Also, don't think you are out of the woods because you are creating digital experiences. As we saw before, digital is not particularly kind to the environment. There are many things you can do to mitigate your ecological footprint, from employing color palettes that require less energy to display to using a hosting provider that has a strong environmental policy. Don't fall back on the pretext that digital is an unlimited resource because it isn't. It is one of many myths you can help debunk. Part of your job as a designer is to inspire people—to tell them the truth, stir them into action, and motivate change. We must fight against "short-termism" and "numbness" in any way we can. We are futurists. As such, we have responsibility for that future. We have to plan it better and show others what it could be, based on what they do, buy, and support. This means not just painting a picture but creating it. "The thing is to be vocal about the type of future that you want to exist within, and the future you want your children to exist within, and your children's children to exist within,"[47] says Julia Watson. "You have to demand the type of future that you want to recognize."[48]

Stuff your head with more
different things from various fields.

—Ray Bradbury[1]

The best way to predict the future
is to invent it.

—Alan Kay[2]

8

Design is the answer

In 1842, more than five hundred women died shortly after giving birth at the Vienna General Hospital in Austria. With over three thousand births that year in the same hospital, this mortality rate was close to 16 percent. The cause of death had been known for many years, and it had killed thousands of women around the world. It went by different names, such as puerperal fever, the "black death of childbed," or "the doctor's plague." Puerperal fever killed up to 25 percent of all women giving birth in eighteen-century childbirth wards across Europe and America,[3] but it was not caused by an unknown airborne virus or a global pandemic. Physicians who were determined to understand the cause noticed that women who gave birth at home had a considerably lower probability of contracting this fever, which was a curious and vexing fact for many prestigious hospital doctors. In 1843, one year after the fatal loss of those women in the hospital in Vienna, American physician Oliver Wendell Holmes Sr. published "The Contagiousness of Puerperal Fever," an essay that identified the culprit of this plague—poor hygiene by doctors and nurses.[4]

At that time, doctors traveled from one childbirth to the next without washing their hands. And childbirth was not the only thing on the agenda. A doctor might perform an autopsy on the same day, sometimes just moments before the hazardous childbirth. Contaminated utensils, clothes, and bedding further aggravated the problem. Holmes was not the first to point out this causal relationship, but he and others before him were the targets of continuous mockery by other members of the medical profession, who couldn't come to terms with their responsibility in the matter. Their reluctance lasted for decades, resulting in the death of countless lives. A fellow American physician, renowned obstetrician Charles Delucena Meigs, best exemplified this denial of the evidence when he stated, "Doctors are gentlemen, and gentlemen's hands are clean."[5] Today, we call the "black death of childbed" simply postpartum infections. They assail a much smaller number of women, who can be treated with antibiotics and make a swift recovery in most cases.

The underlying message, according to British American author Simon Sinek, who popularized this tale in one of his talks, is quite clear: "sometimes you are the problem."[6] When it comes to eighteenth-century puerperal fever, doctors were the problem. When it comes to our modern-day culture of waste, excess, and addiction, showcased by the various cases in this book, design is the problem. While designers are eager for praise and acclaim and create an aura of ostensibly cultured and intellectual pursuit, often involving awards and accolades, design itself takes no responsibility for what happens when things go wrong. But as Sinek points out, you cannot have credit without accountability. As with the doctors who saw no wrongdoing in their own behavior, so designers today turn a blind eye at their nefarious effect on the world. The difference, however, is that the doctors' arrogance can be attributed to ignorance. After all, germ theory was just a theory back then. Hand washing didn't seem like a logical solution to the problem. Today, designers cannot claim such obliviousness. To continue ignoring the repercussions they have on society and the environment is simply negligent. We must care as much about our impact as we care about all other design elements—the creative process and craft, quality and attention to detail, user needs and empathy. We need a conscientious design that understands and prioritizes positive impact.

One reason for this shortcoming is that designers continue to be trained not to see consequences. They don't see the problem. We fetishize and worship the creation framework as if it's the only thing that matters. Frameworks are an important tool in any discipline, yet they can also condition thought. If they are simultaneously skewed and prevalent, they can have a damaging effect. In 2002, the British Design Council introduced one of the most famous depictions of the design methodology—the double diamond.[7] This diagram divides the design process into two diamonds, each with two linear phases. In the first diamond, *discover* and *define* are about identifying the problem, and in the second diamond, *develop* and *deliver* are about solution ideation and implementation. Over the past two decades, this simple model has become a universal reference for how design should operate and a symbol of the design thinking movement, influencing the corporate, nondesign world as well.

It is by no means the first attempt at visualizing the design process in an easily graspable diagram. One of the earliest models for the creative process was created by an English social psychologist and a cofounder of the London School of Economics in 1926. Graham Wallas introduced what later became known as the Wallas creativity process, a model of creativity comprised of four stages—preparation, incubation, illumination, and verification.[8] Since then, there has been a long succession of models and diagrams that have tried to bring a new perspective to the mix. In *Innovation Methods Mapping: Demystifying 80+ Years of Innovative Process Design*, GK VanPatter and Elizabeth Pastor, the cofounders of the design consultancy firm Humantific, collected and analyzed more than sixty innovation process diagrams produced between 1926 and 2014.[9] While the diagrams most often had four, six, or eight steps, underlying most was a simple, archetypal, three-stage ideation process: identify the problem, create the solution, and implement it. It is a straightforward recipe. There were a few other differences in approach, with some models showcasing a linear progression and others emphasizing ideas of iteration, repetition, and cyclicality.

One important finding in this analysis was that the creation stage appears to be the most prominent. This was the case for at least forty-eight diagrams. Most models appear holistic or balanced at first, but when looked at closely, it's clear that there's a strong weighting toward creation—toward defining and conceptualizing the solution rather than optimizing or delivering it, for instance. The overemphasis on design creation is symptomatic of a wider problem in design. It fuels the myth of the designer as the creative genius, the artist in disguise, while it downplays key design responsibilities that are covered later in this chapter. Another alarming insight from VanPatter and Pastor's research is that only a handful of methods consider human behavior, such as recommended actions, techniques, or approaches. And just one includes a mention of human values. This oversight is disquieting. If all frameworks fail to accommodate desirable human values, then ethics, integrity, and responsibility are simply irrelevant factors in a design process. We are simply locked in an unseeing production cycle.

However, the most important omission, which sits at the genesis of this book, is that all models envision the design process as ending in the last stage—invariably labeled as *delivery* or *implementation*—as if there's nothing else beyond that. This is where the work of a designer ends. And to many, so does their accountability. If we look back at the double diamond diagram, it is clearly incomplete. We are missing an equally important third diamond that comprehends the notion of effect and consequences. In the past, we shed a bright light on the first diamond and the need to understand the problem, but now we must become resourceful at deciphering an elusive third diamond on impact. We need to step out of our simplistic problem-solution narrative and ask what lies beyond: what journey extends beyond delivery? Otherwise, we risk being as compliant to the status quo as eighteenth-century doctors were, failing to see that we ourselves are the problem. We cannot afford more design solutions carelessly thrown into a vacuum of consequences.

1. Designers are generalists

The division of labor was an important driver of civilization millennia before Adam Smith highlighted it in his 1776 magnum opus *The Wealth of Nations.*[10] Today, increased specialization in the workforce is normally a sign of economic development and stability. "Much of the prosperity our world now enjoys comes from the productivity gains of dividing work into ever smaller tasks performed by ever more specialized workers,"[11] wrote American organizational theorist Thomas W. Malone with his colleagues Robert Laubacher and Tammy Johns in a *Harvard Business Review* article entitled "The Age of Hyperspecialization." We can see such mutation in almost every field we can think of, from science to commerce. Just picture any large organization, and consider all the ways it can be divided by function, process, product, service, customer, or geography. Such a multifaceted arrangement leads to a myriad of roles and responsibilities, which has intensified in today's "rise of knowledge work and communications technology."[12] Take software developers as an example. In the past two decades, the role has been fractured into a myriad of job titles that include front-end developer, back-end developer, full-stack developer, game developer, mobile developer, web developer, and DevOps (development and operations) developer, to name a few.

Design is not indifferent to specialization. Over the years, I've encountered and worked closely with designers of all types, with titles like data designers, design advocates, design specialists, design strategists, future specialists (my preferred job title), graphic designers, hardware designers, industrial designers, information designers, interaction designers, motion designers, presentation designers, print designers, product designers, trend designers, user experience (UX) designers, user interface (UI) designers, and visual designers. If, to many of us, this proliferation of design roles can seem daunting and hard to follow, imagine how confusing it must be for nondesigners. I still recall mentioning to a product manager at Nokia in London, with whom I worked closely years ago, that we had just hired a motion designer to join our team. Surprised, he asked in a tone of astonishment, "You hired an *emotion* designer?"

The major problems with hyperspecialization, however, are not how it might confuse others outside our field. One problem is that when designers are focused on a very narrow view of a problem, they lose the ability to see the big picture. They can't see where they are headed. It is a type of tunnel vision that dismisses impact and, as a result, alleviates them from their social and ecological responsibility. Another downside of specialization is that it leads people to neglect other disciplines. The American biologist Edward O. Wilson acknowledges that both the sciences and the humanities have become ever more specialized into narrower and narrower territories. "Much of the advanced technology and technical language of one discipline is at best only partially comprehensible to experts in other disciplines, even those closely related,"[13] he argues. It is as if by going down an evolutionary tree of specialization, we lose the capability to decipher each other's language, customs, and practices. We are distant cousins that have gotten so far apart that we now lack any common point.

The problem often starts at school. I'm highly critical of traditional design education for two reasons. One reason is that it continues to be associated directly or indirectly with art schools and universities. This percolates the inaccurate perception that design is an art field that is strongly inclined toward unrestricted creative expression. One solution could be for design to be taught in other schools, such as engineering or psychology, or have its own independent environment. In either scenario, we would require a deep rethinking of its pedagogy. The second reason that I'm critical of traditional design education is that schools fail to prepare students for the cross-disciplinary environment they will invariably face when they join the job market. Many design schools are echo chambers where, despite the occasional pressure of design reviews, students are in a safe monoculture of similarly minded individuals. It's the type of environment where design exclusivism flourishes and multidisciplinary goes to die. This can be a foundational problem.

Designers are generalists. We need to embrace plurality of thought, multiplicity, and multidisciplinarity. We must be curious about other domains as a source of inspiration. This can prepare us to come up with better answers to the myriad of challenges we are facing. As David Epstein mentions in *Range: Why Generalists Triumph in a Specialized World*, "A diverse group of specialists cannot fully replace the contributions of broad individuals. Even when you move on from an area of work or an entire domain, that experience is not wasted."[14] As it turns out, the combination of areas and the clash of concepts normally lead to creativity and innovation. An empty mind is unimaginative, and a mind within an echo chamber will mistake a cube for a square. You need to fill your mind with substance—ideally, from disparate domains of knowledge, from varying angles and perspectives—so you can start making relevant connections. There is never one way of looking at a problem. When you let things stir in your mind for a bit, patterns will eventually emerge. This is the primordial soup of human creativity. And frequently, you don't need new ideas. You can simply repurpose old ones.

In *Where Good Ideas Come From: The Natural History of Innovation*, American author Steven Johnson expands on the importance of exaption as a critical engine for innovation.[15] Taken from biology, exaption refers to a trait that might have evolved for a specific function in a species, only to serve another purpose afterward. In human culture, it refers to the act of repurposing existing, often unrelated parts and combining them in the creation of something new. This process has been a major drive for innovation throughout history, from Gutenberg's press, which was coopted from a wine press, to Darwin's theory of evolution. In a 1959 essay on creativity, American writer Isaac Asimov explains how Charles Darwin and Alfred Wallace were both eager to find an explanation for the mechanism of evolution, yet it was only when both read English economist Thomas Robert Malthus's book *An Essay on the Principle of Population* that the idea finally clicked for them. If they hadn't been interested in economics in the first place, they wouldn't have made the cross-connection and would have joined the legions of naturalists who failed before them. As Asimov points out, "Obviously, then, what is needed is not only people with a good background in a particular field, but also people capable of making a connection between item 1 and item 2 which might not ordinarily seem connected."[16]

This aligns strongly with the notion of combinatorial creativity described by Bulgarian-born, US-based writer and popular blogger Maria Popova. As she explains, with combinatorial creativity, "ideas are born out of the myriad pieces of stuff populating our memories, our knowledge base, our mental pool of inspiration and resources, and creativity is simply the capacity to put those together in incredible new ways."[17] For creativity and intuition to flourish, it's not just the depth of our experiences that counts but also their breadth. It's about looking elsewhere for inspiration and being open to learning from other disciplines. It's about using your whole brain and abandoning labels, preconceptions, and stereotypes. I like to say I'm a designer who doesn't buy design books, simply because I believe we can learn much more from other domains of knowledge. If you are looking in only one corner, you will likely get stuck. You must balance multiple viewpoints. And then, as musician Brian Eno said, "you should stay alert for the moment when a number of things are just ready to collide with one another."[18]

2. Design is not production

The overplay of the creation phase, as we saw earlier in the chapter, aligns well with the reality of many modern-day designers. If you ask any designer why they chose their career path, you will get a consistent variant of these two answers—to help people or to solve problems. These are commendable missions. Too often, however, designers find themselves stuck, either willingly or unwillingly, in a solution echo chamber where they are oblivious to the problem they are trying to solve and the impact they are having in the real world. The harsh reality is that many user experience designers today don't have direct access to users, which is itself a paradox. They can't talk to or interview users directly. Users are merely made-up personas who are projected on a screen during a presentation. Designers who work for small startup companies or advertising agencies probably recognize most innovation methods, even the double diamond diagram, as lavish artifacts. Inspiring materials that are read about in books and seen at conferences but rarely are put into practice at work. There's simply never enough time.

Larger design teams are not necessarily better. In many ways, they can be worse. The lack of impact awareness is particularly triggered by the way digital product designers are evaluated. The primary measure of designer effectiveness is normally the number of features they launch, which too often are shipped into a vacuum. When you launch something into the world, you ought to be curious to see if and where it lands. The feedback loop of cause and effect is important to understand. I would even argue that, when it comes to design, a launch is meaningless without an assessment of its landing. Yet many designers are still rewarded by the number of things they put out, irrespectively of whether they touch down. So what does a landing mean in the context of design? It signifies leaving a positive impression on the people using it, on the larger social group, and on the environment at large. But whereas launching is easy, deliberate touchdown can be hard. No launch has a guaranteed return. It's important to define the criteria for landing early on and then confirm that they have been met. It takes time and effort to corroborate positive landings, yet landings are what design impact is all about. As such, they are the ones worth celebrating.

The solution echo chamber can be further amplified by an excessive devotion to design tools, sometimes amounting to a fetishization. I find most discussions about tools to be a tremendous waste of energy. First, design technology is an everchanging landscape. There will always be a newer, better, shinier design tool. Also, with increased competition, different tools can become alike in more ways than one. Distinguishing among them can become more of a personal preference, and sometimes, a matter of ardent and unjustified debate. The other reason I find most discussions about tools to be unhelpful is that tools can condition your thought. They can lead you to stop imagining where you can go and instead to focus only on where the tool can take you. It becomes a limiting factor to your own creativity. Such overreliance is commonly called the *law of the instrument*. As American psychologist Abraham Maslow said, "I suppose it is tempting, if the only tool you have is a hammer, to treat everything as if it were a nail."[19] This is the type of mental conditioning that occurs in many design tools.

As if all of this was not enough, modern-day design education is further cementing the myth of design as production. Design schools can be criticized for creating too much of a soundboard and sense of elitism, failing to engage adequately with other disciplines, and even downplaying important subjects in a designer's foundation. However, most traditional institutions try to provide a good balance between theory and practice. While we accelerate design training so that it is completed within just a few weeks or months, as advertised by dozens of online programs and bootcamps, foundational theory—including the critical thinking skills that allow designers to think deeply about problems and the principles outlining the responsibilities of design professionals—tends to be brushed aside, if considered at all. Instead, programs double down on the practice—on teaching the tools and methodologies that can achieve the quickest turnaround—so that at the end of ten weeks, people leave the course feeling like they are ready to design. But they have studied design not as a strategic method for change making or innovation acceleration but as an acquiescent practice able to complete a standardized task in the shortest amount of time. Unsurprisingly, these are likely the first jobs to go with future automation.

As with specialization, an overemphasis on releases, tools, and production is problematic because it creates a distancing effect from consequences, and this obliviousness often is translated into a lack of accountability. After all, how can you be responsible for what you don't see? But many designers are not happy with this outcome and want to understand the effect they have on other people's lives. The fact that they don't can lead them to feel like they are cogs in a machine. "We're all part of the assembly line, working on increasingly smaller parts of increasingly bigger projects,"[20] says American designer Jarrett Fuller. I would argue this is also one of the many reasons for the moral failings of the tech industry. Everyone is so trapped in their low-visibility digital assembly line that they fail to see the problem. When designers see themselves as production automatons, we relinquish our ability to plan and perceive the complete roadmap. We become a simple step in a long chain of development. We don't understand how it works or how we are contributing to it. This is a dangerous mindset.

Design is not production. Being a designer is about engaging deeply in and thinking critically about a problem. It's about asking the right questions. Designers are well placed to be disruptors, shifters, and nonconformists. Fulfilling these functions should be part of our code of conduct, next to our ethical obligations. When we are looking for design breakthroughs—whether through a *paradigm shift* (a notion introduced by the American physicist and philosopher Thomas Kuhn in 1962)[21] or through *disruptive innovation* (an idea introduced by Harvard Business School professor Clayton Christensen in 1995 that helped to fuel the startup ecosystem explosion we see today)[22]—we are considering a dramatic transformation that can shake the market, change knowledge paradigms, and often reverberate through various layers of society. This is what ultimately designers should seek. We should seek to open new ground and create added value not just for business but for humans, other animals, and our environment. And we should do this not because we are necessarily better or better suited than others but simply because it is our duty. We need to unshackle ourselves from a vision-deprived production echo chamber.

3. Design is part of nature

In chapter 2, we saw how Charles Darwin's adoption of Herbert Spencer's notion of the survival of the fittest led to a series of later misconceptions that caused a tremendous amount of harm. Today, the notion of physical vigor associated with survival still underlines many capitalistic slogans about individualism and fierce competition. This is flawed thinking. As we now know, altruism and cooperation provide a much greater evolutionary advantage than selfishness and individualism. American biologist Lynn Margulis's work in advancing the notion of symbiogenesis (literally, "becoming by living together") has further cemented this notion with microbiological evidence. Twenty-five years after her seminal 1967 paper "On the Origin of Mitosing Cells,"[23] Margulis, together with her son Dorion Sagan, set forth an alternative view of evolution in *Acquiring Genomes:*

A *Theory of the Origin of Species.* "Life did not take over the globe by combat, but by networking," argue Margulis and Sagan in 1997, as their idea was starting to cement. "Life forms multiplied and complexified by co-opting others, not just by killing them."[24] In other words, species evolved by means of cooperation, interaction, and mutual dependence.

Margulis's idea can be understood as the "survival of the most symbiotic" or as the "survival of the friendliest," as anthropologist Brian Hare and writer Vanessa Woods titled their book *Survival of the Friendliest: Understanding Our Origins and Rediscovering Our Common Humanity.* Both views place a much heavier focus on altruism, cooperation, and symbiosis as vital evolutionary mechanisms. This notion is shared by other leading evolutionary biologists, such as Ernst Mayr, who in 2002 wrote, "Much advance in evolution is due to the establishment of consortia between two organisms with entirely different genomes. Ecologists have barely begun to describe these interactions."[25] This new outlook on the ecological impact of symbiosis is also fostering an important design movement that focuses on centuries-old, sustainable and nature-based practices. In her absorbing book *Lo-TEK: Design by Radical Indigenism*, Australian designer Julia Watson employs Magulis's idea of the survival of the most symbiotic as a convincing plea for a more synergetic design with nature, not by continuing our exploitative path but by understanding and embracing the traditional methods of Indigenous people.[26]

As Watson argues in *Lo-TEK*, Indigenous people have a deep understanding of their surroundings and over time have developed a set of technologies that work with, and not against, the environment. The book provides a blueprint for sustainable architecture and design, with several fascinating examples of Indigenous innovation around the world. It is also, as is discussed in chapter 10, a formidable model of decolonizing design because it gives voice to historically marginalized groups and sheds light on their unique expertise. Perhaps the most striking example exposed in the book is the Jingkieng Dieng Jri Living Root Bridges, a system of ladders and walkways created by the Khasi tribe of North India. The entire structure takes one human generation to grow and is made from of a series of living intertwined roots that are trained to grow across the river. The idea that you can mold an object as large as a bridge—which happens to be alive, growing and adapting—is astonishing and very distant from the lifeless structures that fill our urban landscapes today. This strangeness is in part due to how we have been conditioned to think of nature as being incompatible with and unfit for our synthetic necessities.

In today's modern world, where most of us live in cities, we look at nature as something outside and distant from us. Yet we are not separate from nature. Nor are we better than nature. In fact, we are nature. We are natural organisms. We should not aim at controlling it or subjugating it to our exploitative desires. Instead, we need to work together as one. Every single day, we keep layering harmful objects, materials, and infrastructures on top of our natural environment—polluting our soil, rivers, and air and overengineering an artificial system of iron, glass, plastic, and cement. "We cast nature both as a menacing force now retaliating against us, and as a forlorn figure surrendering to our saving by way of savvy technological innovation," says Watson. "By building hard infrastructures and favoring high-tech homogenous design, we are ignoring millennia-old knowledge of how to live with nature in symbiosis."[27]

How did we end up here, you may ask? Our relationship with nature has always been a twisted one. For centuries, philosophers argued about our right place within the natural environment. The most famous dichotomy has been between the seventeenth-century English philosopher Thomas Hobbes and the eighteenth-century Swiss philosopher Jean-Jacques Rousseau. While Hobbes saw nature as a dangerous, violent, and competitive place that had to be tamed, Rousseau, in clear opposition, hypothesized about a genuinely good "natural man" who lived in harmony with nature. As a key voice of the Enlightenment period, Hobbes's argument for individualism and against the chaotic state of nature had the longest-lasting effect on the environment. Emboldened by Hobbes's ideas, the Enlightenment's emphasis on human realization, at a time of imperialistic prowess, fostered an elitist mindset—a "mythology," according to Watson—that simply ignored any knowledge from Indigenous populations due to their "primitive" nature. This has been a calamitous mistake.

Part of the problem is our inevitable bias for the present. There is an idea that because we are where we are today, we somehow represent the pinnacle of human existence—the highpoint of human knowledge and technology—and that because we have reached the pinnacle, everything in the past should stay in the past. We call traditional practices primitive, archaic, pseudo, or ineffective. And while we might seem aware of the negative impact of our actions on the environment, we continue doing things the same way. We design in a solution echo chamber and expect that somehow, something will change, even if we are not changing. We have distanced ourselves from nature and other disciplines for far too long. We need to go back to our roots and rethink what we are doing and how we are doing it. We need to develop a deep appreciation for sustainable systems, structures, and artifacts. We need a more symbiotic story for design. This means we must inevitably learn from the past. "We are now at a crossroads where we can either continue a narrow view of technology, informed by our distance from nature, or we can acknowledge that this is just one way and not the only way for humans to live."[28]

4. Designers are futurists

In a not-so-hypothetical scenario, with close to 50 percent of the global population living in coastal cities, rising sea levels, and global warming, the ocean is under threat due to "unfettered coastal urbanization," where "many simply pour sand into the ocean to create new land."[29] This grim outline is the motivation behind an ambitious project to build sustainable cities that float on water. Created by Copenhagen-based architecture studio BIG and aligned to UN's Sustainable Development Goals, Oceanix is a speculative vision for a floating community living on seventy-five hectares distributed across various neighborhoods around a central harbor. Its circular layout means it can grow and expand organically, accommodating from a few hundred residents up to ten thousand. The modular structure is meant to provide a self-sustaining and negative carbon footprint lifestyle, filled with communal farming, solar panels, and locally sourced materials for construction. It might seem like a scene from a science fiction movie, but projects like this often do. Ultimately, the bold vision of Oceanix shows the importance of stretching the boundaries of our current reality and asking the question, "What if?"

Our present has become an embarrassing dump of ill-devised solutions. For design to be an answer, we need to be humble enough to rediscover sustainable practices from the past and to dream a better future. In a *Washington Post* article, Harvard Kennedy School fellow J. Peter Scoblic describes the importance of imagining future catastrophes in order to prevent them. "Even in calmer times, the future rarely holds still for our plans," explains Scoblic, and he continues, "in a dynamic environment, there is every chance that unimagined problems will arise, that our current challenges will have unexpected effects and that our solutions will have unintended consequences."[30] In this context, Scoblic argues, the best tool is strategic foresight, something that involves "envisioning alternative futures to better sense, shape and adapt to the one that is emerging." By exploring different ideas of what the future might hold, as well as predicting challenges and opportunities, we can start acting now. If we don't adopt this type of thinking, we will be left with hasty reactions to mitigate the magnitude of the impact.

Most design operates in the future. Designers are always creating something that will be implemented, launched, or produced tomorrow. As such, we frequently must anticipate needs that might not be completely clear, validated, or safe. There is always risk in what might be forthcoming. Yet a good amount of design is simply reactive. We respond to what our competitors are doing, how the market is changing, and what our clients are asking. There is nothing particularly wrong with this approach. Most designers, like most companies, have within them an ability to work on reactive or proactive innovations. However, adopting a reactive, wait-and-see approach is shortsighted. We can look at only a very slim slice of the near future and, as a result, rely mostly on short-term preparedness. While this can work with some products and experiences, it won't work with most of the large challenges we are facing as a species. With global warming, pandemics, waste and ecosystem management, it will take years before we can observe the effects of any design measures we implement today. With such a long feedback loop, the frame of action must be expanded beyond today or tomorrow.

Speculative design is a design methodology and mindset that aims at addressing large societal and environmental problems by contemplating far into the imaginary future. It's about considering disruptive innovation and boundary-pushing systems as a primary instrument of creation. Yes, sometimes speculative design projects might seem a bit farfetched, and that is to be expected. When you are considering alternative ways of being and living on this planet, you are meant to clash with the mundane. In order to dream the impossible, you must leave the current reality. As for the value of speculative design, perhaps it is better expressed in the words of one of its strongest advocates, Carnegie Mellon University professor and design futurist Stuart Candy. "Design has by now become an indispensable companion to foresight, and foresight is becoming an essential aspect of how designers think and work, too," says Candy. "Part of what design does is render otherwise abstract possible futures in a form concrete enough to help us think and feel them through more effectively. The promise there is to enable better collective choices, so that we can shape our society in wiser ways."[31]

Even though it might seem implausible at times, speculative design is still grounded in some elements of reality. Inspired by a diagram of potential futures by physicist and futurist Joseph Voros,[32] which was itself based on a taxonomy of futures by Trevor Hancock and Clement Bezold,[33] Candy showed an intriguing visual model, which has become known as "futures cone,"[34] to a design audience at the Royal College of Art in 2009.[35] It had a lasting influence on design professors Anthony Dunne and Fiona Raby, who also contributed with their own version of the diagram,[36] which provides a framework for the discipline. At its essence, the model resembles a flashlight pointing at what's to come, with three cones for different types of the future: *probable* (what is likely to happen if all things remain the same and there is no major catastrophe), *plausible* (what could happen—the realm of foresight), and *possible* (what might happen—opens the door to imagination, stretching the boundaries of science, technology, and design). While the probable is the realm in which most designers operate, a plausible future is one where BIG's Oceanix becomes a reality or even the norm. The *possible*, on the other hand, is the most speculative of the three scenarios. After all, how confident are you that something won't happen? Anything is possible, really. It's also arguably the most important. Dunne and Raby quote American professor David Kirby in their book *Speculative Everything: Design, Fiction, and Social Dreaming*: "the role of the expert is often, not to prevent the impossible but to make it acceptable."[37]

According to Dunne and Raby, "By speculating more, at all levels of society, and exploring alternative scenarios, reality will become more malleable. And although the future cannot be predicted, we can help set in place today factors that will increase the probability of more desirable futures happening."[38] By targeting a need far out into future, speculative design has also the ability to extend the life cycle of a given design solution, so that it doesn't just follow a particular short-term trend but, instead, creates something long-lasting that will still be relevant many years from now. If we want to be ambitious about the role of design in the future of our planet, we must consider a much more elongated timespan. We need to start projecting and foreseeing opportunities way ahead of time. We must be better at dreaming the impossible and fighting for the future we want to see. This shouldn't be a problem. Remember, we designers are futurists. "When we spend more time asking, What if?," says Scoblic, "we can spend less time asking, What now?"[39]

Actionable Advice

Finding the right balance between being a generalist and a specialist will likely be a lifelong pursuit. It is normal to oscillate between the two if you don't lose sight of the greater goal—feeling fulfilled as a designer while having a positive impact in the world. Remember, it is not about the scale of the impact but about its very nature. If you find yourself locked in a specialized corner or in a solution echo chamber, try to step out and see the big picture. Take a pause. Assess your environment. How are you contributing to the overall delivery and output? What tangible effect is the solution having in the real world? Yes, it might require some work and effort to get those answers, but laziness cannot be an excuse for negligence. Don't abdicate your responsibility to grasp the repercussions of your work, even if it takes a bit of investigation. Sometimes the metrics do exist, and you might have to dig for them yourself. Ask your fellow engineers, managers, leads, and peers. Be proactive by making sure your features and solutions are well instrumentalized and are being tracked in a meaningful way. If you encounter opaqueness in this search, take it as a red flag.

Don't lose too much time arguing about tools or becoming an expert in one. Tools change all the time. If you make that your goal, you'll spend your life adjusting to the latest, shinier instrument. Invest in yourself—in building knowledge, expertise, and problem-solving skills that can be applied in any challenge. Also look for insights well beyond the confines of the design community. You can learn an immense amount from other disciplines, practices, and cultures. If you are not able to meet some of the Indigenous communities Watson mentions in her book, perhaps you can travel somewhere closer to your current location. Everyone has something to teach you. Talk to your elderly family members, and learn about the resourceful ways problems were solved in the past. Their realities can often feel like a parallel universe. Dig deep into the plethora of existing historical, anthropological, and evolutionary research. Look for recurring patterns, universal behaviors and approaches, as well as singular viewpoints. Evaluate how you can combine approaches in your own exaptation idea. Finally, practice a culture of attentiveness and inquisitiveness. Curiosity can be your most powerful tool.

Anticipating what is yet to come must be part of your role as a designer. This means flying in the face of contemporary reality in order to dream the impossible and imagine the unimaginable. You can pay close attention to the work of design studios doing groundbreaking work in the domain of design fiction, such as Superflux and The Near Future Laboratory, to understand some of the methods and practices involved. Speculative design can still be a daring and challenging experience. If you are unable to work on foresight frequently, allow yourself, your team, or your organization to focus on occasional experimental projects. One way to do this is to look at existing fringe technologies, products, or trends and hypothesize how they will evolve in the future. It can provide a series of meaningful scenarios that can be discussed and evaluated as a group. It can be a great exercise to do with your peers. We need that level of abstraction and open-endedness to develop our problem-solving skills. Ask the team to imagine there were no business or technological constraints and that they could simply start from scratch. What would they do differently? Start by asking, "What if?" This can be a liberating and energizing routine, and you might run into a speculative idea worth pursuing.

Design is not a single
object or dimension.
Design is messy and complex.
—Natasha Jen[1]

The Earth has become
a design space.
—Brad Allenby[2]

9

Design is local

In the book of Leviticus, written more than 2,500 years ago, a tale is told of two goats—one that is sacrificed and one that carries all the sins and iniquities of the community about to be released into the wilderness by the prophet Aaron. This practice, known today as *scapegoating*, is based on a ritual that scholars have traced to the twenty-fourth century BCE in the early Syrian kingdom of Ebla. It is also deeply rooted in the human psyche. It's not hard to imagine why. How convenient would it be to assign the burden of our own sins on someone else as we go back to our daily life, relieved of any concern? This ultimate form of moral disengagement might seem like wishful thinking, but for many industries and governments around the world, it is part of their day-to-day business practices. Either by buying someone else's carbon quota or dumping their waste in a neighbor's landfill, humans are very creative when it comes to offloading their own responsibility. Instead of confronting the challenge head on, we prefer to make it someone else's problem. Perhaps Bruce Mau expressed this best when he wrote, "We dump problems we can't solve into places we can't see."[3] Out of sight, out of mind.

A visible example of this conundrum is the looming ecological disaster facing the West African country of Ghana, known as the "dumping ground" of the fast fashion industry. In Ghana's capital Accra, at Kamanto market alone, "around 15 million items of used clothing from Western countries arrive every week,"[4] which is highly disproportionate to the country's population of around 30 million. Moreover, an "estimated 40 per cent are of such poor quality they are deemed worthless on arrival and end up dumped in landfill."[5] These mountains of abandoned clothes seem like they are part of a dystopian science fiction movie where our waste ends up consuming us. Roberta Annan, the founder of the African Fashion Foundation and a United Nations Environment Program (UNEP) goodwill ambassador, appears in a 2021 BBC documentary that expresses the gravity of this ecological tragedy as the camera pans out across overflowing landfills. As she has written, "As fashion brands continue to overproduce to meet demands, countries in West Africa are drowning under the weight of waste shipped to our stores."[6]

And Annan is right. The overproduction by the fashion industry today is staggering. "While people bought 60% more garments in 2014 than in 2000, they only kept the clothes for half as long," says a *Business Insider* report. This is in part due to the fast fashion phenomenon, where many brands went from an "average offering of two collections per year in 2000 to five in 2011."[7] Zara and H&M put out dozens a year in a continuous cycle of production, inflated desire, and surplus. According to the World Economic Forum, it is estimated that 85 percent of all textiles go to the dump every year. Globally, that's the equivalent of one garbage truck of textiles being burned or going into landfill every second."[8] It gets worse. "Less than 1% of material used to produce clothing is recycled into new textiles,"[9] and about 60 percent of the material that makes up clothes world-wide is synthetic fibers (like polyester, nylon, and acrylic),[10] which are widely used in modern-day athletic wear, stretch pants, yoga pants, skinny jeans, underwear, and socks, primarily because they are extremely cheap and adaptable compared to natural fibers like cotton, wool, and silk.

Representing 10 percent of humanity's carbon emissions, the fashion industry is a dramatic offender, but unfortunately, it is just one of many industries. Humans are morphing our planet at such a pace and scale that some researchers have called our current stage the *Anthropocene*, a new geological epoch marked by the long-lasting human effects on earth's ecosystems. The accumulated layers of waste, oil, and pollution we have left behind us will be analyzed by future generations of geologists and archeologists. Today, across the entire globe, there are only a few corners that haven't been touched by us. According to the UN's global assessment report in 2019, "75% of the Earth's ice-free land has been significantly altered by human activity, and almost 90% of global wetlands have been lost since 1700."[11] Whatever remains faces the imminent threat of deforestation, loss in biodiversity, wildlife population decline, and possible extinc-tion. Tanya Steele, chief executive at WWF, expressed her concern by saying, "We are wiping wildlife from the face of the planet."[12] This outcome also means there are no longer many spots for your scape-goat to roam freely with your sins.

You can try to offload your responsibility, but when it comes to your waste, it might come back to haunt you. You might ship your trash to some faraway land, but it might be closer than you think. The oceans have their ways. The sea covers more than 70 percent of the surface of the planet, and its complex meandering system of currents makes it the largest conveyor belt across the globe, bringing nutrients to countless ecosystems while also car-rying the despoils of human excess. It is also under great danger.

When it rains, many unsold clothes from the Kamanto market end up being washed out to nearby beaches, creating "massive, tangled webs called 'tentacles' in the sand."[13] Eventually, many of them drift into the ocean, polluting large portions of it and causing the death of marine life by ingestion and asphyxiation. However, the most dissimulated downside of such synthetic fibers is that they can leach into the environment even before being discarded. Just washing them releases roughly 500,000 tons of microfibers into the ocean each year—the equivalent of 50 billion plastic bottles.[14] This is frightening, but even more so when you realize how fast they can travel around the globe.

In January 1992, during a hellish storm, a container on its way from Hong Kong to Tacoma, Washington, tumbled into the North Pacific Ocean. Inside the container were 28,800 bath toys manufactured in China, including thousands of yellow rubber ducks. The toys immediately spread across the vast blue ocean. In the ensuing decades, these cute rubber figurines washed up in every corner of the globe, from Australia to Alaska, some traveling more than 27,000 kilometers (17,000 miles), allowing researchers to better understand the global network of ocean currents and the ways that plastic pollution might spread across the planet. The work of American oceanographer Curtis Ebbesmeyer was of particular relevance. He created multiple models, charts, and maps of ocean movements inspired by the paths of the tiny drifters.[15] What was shown is that, despite its grand scale—the sea represents about 97 percent of the earth's water—oceans are deeply connected by a dense lattice of currents, making the whole system smaller than expected. Even two antipodal points are not far from one another.

The oceans are not the only systems where things can drift for many miles. River networks have always presented some of the most effective and fastest routes for humans to travel long distances. Even today, in many hard-to-reach areas of the globe that often are isolated due to poor land travel conditions, rivers are natural water highways that carry people and goods with great efficiency. It is not hard to imagine how other material waste, large and small, can also take a ride. In the United States alone, "if fertilizer runs off a farm in southwestern Montana, it could end up traveling more than 5,500 kilometers (3,420 miles) through streams and rivers in North Dakota, South Dakota, Iowa, and Missouri, and then down the Mississippi River to the Gulf of Mexico, where it might end up contributing to a giant algae-filled dead zone."[16] And the same thing can be said about plastic trash, such as cute rubber ducks, which, as journalist Adele Peters explains, can find its way into a stream in West Virginia and travel about three thousand miles to the Gulf.[17]

The world has always been a small place, connected in limitless ways through its natural highways and ecosystems, the extent of which we haven't fully figured out. And human innovation has simply mirrored this flux, as we can tell from the multiple exchanges and appropriations of the past between communities separated by seemingly impenetrable barriers. In a way, human design has never been local. Today's intricate air transport network means that ideas, people, and inevitably viruses are much quicker to spread, as witnessed with the Covid-19 global pandemic. Advances in technology and communications are accentuating this sense of closeness, making the world even smaller. While most communication tools of the past, such as the telegraph and telephone, used the Greek prefix *tele-*, which means "over a distance" (first applied in the word *telescope* from Galileo's Italian word *telescopi*), modern-day digital tools have abandoned the prefix altogether. The time it takes for a message to leave a computer in Tokyo and arrive in New York City is roughly the same as the time it takes a message to leave your next-door neighbor's computer and arrive at yours. The difference is measured in milliseconds. Geography and physical distance have become irrelevant in the new world order. They have been overcome.

The digital realm is also changing the very nature and availability of design. Today, the same digital tool is used by billions of people in almost every corner of the globe. People in Bogotá,

Colombia, see the same icons, press the same buttons, and complete the same tasks as people—who are different from them in every way—might do in Jakarta, Indonesia, on the opposite side of the planet. Whatever the design update or new feature might be, it is updated and experienced almost simultaneously by both individuals. Design, like any good idea, has always been able to spread like wildfire, contaminate other minds, and influence behavior. Yet now, these things seem easier than ever to achieve. Design has never been so far-reaching and truly global. But being global means there are also universal consequences. As designers, we must understand that the large-scale repercussions of our work take place in the vast multisymbiotic system of our planet. We must understand that a change here, no matter how small, can have a disproportionate effect across the globe. While design can certainly align with a circular economy—a sustainable model based on ideas involving sharing, reusing, and repairing existing products and materials—that alone might not be enough. It is not just that the world is getting smaller. We also must look at some of its global problems from a different angle.

In 1948, American scientist Warren Weaver wrote an article for *American Scientist* entitled "Science and Complexity."[18] In it, Warren describes three stages of the modern understanding of science. For the most part, during the seventeenth, eighteenth, and nineteenth centuries, scientists were primarily concerned about how one variable influenced another—what Weaver considers to be *problems of simplicity*. Toward the second stage of modern science, covering the first half of the twentieth century, scientists became aware that there is a much large number of variables in our planet, yet they were thought to relate in a somehow chaotic and unorganized fashion—what Weaver calls *problems of disorganized complexity*. Weaver points out that the various systems supporting this large number of variables were not chaotic at all. In fact, they were highly interconnected and interdependent. Looking onward from 1948, Weaver says science will have to take a third great advance in the following fifty years and learn to deal with what he calls *problems of organized complexity.*

Today we know that most large problems we are facing as a species, from climate change to political turmoil, are problems of organized complexity. But design is still stuck in an eighteenth-century mindset dealing primarily with problems of simplicity—creating a single solution for a single problem; being oblivious to the fact that each solution often creates more problems; failing to grasp repercussions in a wide, evermore connected, web of interdependence; lacking the ability to think in networks and systems. We cannot solve our modern-day problems with this simplistic mindset. And this mindset is applied to more than just natural ecosystems. As Weaver points out, there is a "wide range of similar problems in the biological, medical, psychological, economic, and political sciences."[19] We cannot continue looking at problems as a one-dimensional challenge. So how can we change this mindset?

1. Think like a network

In 1992, the devastating collapse of the cod stocks in Newfoundland led to the partial closure of the region's fishing industry and quickly became a widely cited example of failed management of a natural resource. More than thirty thousand people lost their jobs, and many communities are still recovering today. Instead of pointing a finger at overfishing and despite opposition from the scientific community, the federal government announced that seals were mainly responsible for the disaster because their overconsumption of cod was preventing its natural recovery.[20] One of the immediate actions by the Canadian Department of Fisheries and Oceans (DFO) was to increase the kill quota, which led to the slaughter of thousands of seals. Between 2003 and 2005, near a million animals were killed in an effort to bring back the golden days of cod fishing.[21] However, as suggested by many studies, the indiscriminate killing of seals had an opposite effect on the ecosystem by contributing to the spread of bacteria on the ocean floor, which in turn led to hypoxia—a condition where areas of the ocean lose their dissolved oxygen and are unable to sustain any type of fish or marine life.

In an article published in 1995 entitled "Seals, Cod, Ecology and Mythology," research scientist Peter Meisenheimer exposes in great detail the failure of government procedures to fight the collapse of cod stocks.[22] Even though early humans had to face the constant thread of large predators, says Meisenheimer, "today, humans only very occasionally lose resources through direct competition with wild predators (. . .), and even less commonly are preyed upon."[23] Notwithstanding, "the belief that humans interact in a competitive way with wild predators remains widely accepted."[24] In his harsh assessment, Meisenheimer states that the use of seals as scapegoats is symptomatic of the broad mismanagement of fisheries and wildlife and, sadly, is the result of a prevalent view that sees predators as problems to be controlled and not as integral parts of a functioning ecology. Even today, many decision makers have a naive view of nature and look at food webs as simplified trees of dependencies. However, when we talk about ecosystems, we are dealing with highly challenging problems of organized complexity, where thousands of species shape an intricate mesh of interdependency.

The renowned zoologist David Lavigne has long been fighting against this misconception. To prove that seals were not the only intervening agent in the cod collapse, Lavigne produced a visual representation of the vast Northwest Atlantic cod food web, showing close to a hundred different species in a dense network of interrelation.[25] This intricate aquatic lattice shows how infantile our conceptions of natural systems—like the linear predator-prey diagrams we learned at school—have been. Lavigne's work has been essential in exposing how obsolete this ingrained simplistic mindset is. To solve some of the largest ecological problems we are facing today, we must start with a deep understanding of the underlying reciprocal webs that abound in any healthy ecosystem. We must unravel the different relationships among the largest number of agents in our wide biosphere. Through a responsible effort at mapping such structures, future simulation models can be developed that replicate variations in the ecosystem and the consequent effects in individual species. Network thinking in this context is a remarkable ally. Thinking nature is to think systemic—to think in networks.

"The current understanding suggests that sustainability is a system property and not a property of individual elements of systems," write design researchers Fabrizio Ceschin and İdil Gaziulusoy. Therefore, they argue, "achieving sustainability requires a process-based, multi-scale and systemic approach to planning for sustainability guided by a target/vision instead of traditional goal-based optimization approaches."[26] Ecosystems are not the only domain that requires a radical shift in perception. We still treat our cities, social groups, supply chains, human conflicts, and knowledge as hierarchical, rigid, and centralized structures. We tackle problems individually, expecting, somehow, that the greater whole will be better as a result. We don't understand the multiple factors at play and the degree of interdependence between them. We also fail to grasp that, like sustainability, many of these multifaceted subjects are a moving target. Not only is it difficult to untangle all intervenient actors and forces, but the entire system is constantly changing and adapting. They are dynamic, multivariate, and highly codependent organisms. To decipher such complexity through a top-down decision-making process will never work, whether you are a politician or a designer.

Design can help bring clarity and transparency to some of these convoluted domains, since it has the power to make the invisible visible. Yet information visualization and communication are just one path. Eventually, designers must change the way they think about design itself. Although confined in scope, human-centered design is not necessarily a wrong place to start—if we expand it outward to decode the myriad of interactions and dependencies between humans and other species and between different species and the entire ecology that supports them. Thinking in networks ultimately means thinking about reciprocity, causation, symbiosis, and interdependence. It also means asking big, unusual, and often uncomfortable questions. What is the connection between weather and human conflict? Between the availability of a product in Miami and a storm in Asia? Between deforestation and hunger? Between plastic production and human health? Design thinking should become synonymous with network thinking. This is the only way for us to fully understand repercussions, to design more consciously and sustainably, and to have a long-lasting, positive impact on our planet. As Bruce Mau, Jennifer Leonard, and the Institute without Boundaries write in *Massive Change*, "When everything is connected to everything else, for better or worse, everything matters."[27]

2. Design at scale

Ties van der Hoeven is an ambitious forty-year-old Dutch engineer with a grand plan. He wants to make the Sinai desert green again. Together with a group of pioneering scientists and holistic engineers, aptly named the Weather Makers, van der Hoeven is pursuing what might well be one of the most remarkable ecological regeneration projects ever pursued, one that according to the team could "change the future of the Earth and human civilization."[28] The group's initiative is to regreen the Sinai Peninsula, a small triangular bridge of land in Egypt, roughly the size of Sri Lanka, which borders the Mediterranean Sea to the north and Israel to the east. The proposal is a five-stage, decades-long transformation of a collapsed ecosystem. The five-stage plan first restores the lagoon and wetlands, then improves the soil with marine sediments, and finally, revegetates the desert with a variety of flora. The team believes this project could reduce surface temperatures, change wind speed and direction, attract moist air from the Indian Ocean and, with it, rain, and eventually restore a thriving ecosystem. As the utmost source of life, water will play a vital role, so a robust hydraulic cycle needs to be reestablished that can continue to nurture the whole area well into the future.

The Weather Makers' project is not as farfetched as you might think. In 1994, a group of Chinese researchers led by scientist Li Rui embraced a similarly ambitious restoration project targeting a barren area in western China called the Loess Plateau. Roughly the size of Texas, the plateau's rich soils once fed roughly a quarter of the Chinese population.[29] By the end of the twentieth century, due to intense human pressure on the land, the plateau was similar to Sinai—"a dry, barren, heavily eroded landscape. The soil was washing away and silting up the Yellow river. Farmers could barely grow any crops."[30] In just twenty years, however, the restoration project transformed the entire region into green valleys and productive farmland. While impressively farsighted, the project involved low-tech methods, including water retention, "planting trees on the hilltops, terracing the steep slopes, adding organic material to the soil, and controlling grazing animals."[31] As it turns out, the Loess Plateau initiative inspired van der Hoeven, who reportedly watched a 2002 documentary on the transformation multiple times.[32] Directed by environmental filmmaker John D. Liu, "Green Gold" documents several regreening projects across the planet that seem to provide a transformational path for our planet.[33]

In an interview for *The Guardian*, Tim Christophersen, head of the Nature for Climate Branch at the UN Environment Programme, is persuasive about the need to think creatively about ecological collapse. "The main challenge is the lack of human imagination," says Christophersen, "our inability to see a different future because we're staring down this dystopian path of pandemic, climate change, biodiversity loss."[34] The message from Christophersen and the Loess Plateau project is that we don't have to accept destruction and degradation. We can also reverse them. In addition to a lack of imagination, we also have prevalent boundaries that keep conditioning the way we look at problems. We might think of a degraded ecosystem as a local or regional drawback, but it is not. As plant physiology professor Legesse Negash notes, many regreening initiatives must traverse national boundaries because ecological problems often do. In reference to the Nile River, which flows from south to north across eleven African countries from Tanzania to Egypt, he asks, "how can we support life in Egypt without restoring Ethiopia's mountains?"[35] All parts of the environment—roots and organic material in the ground, water streams, air, and wind—are firmly interconnected in a tightly knit global ecosystem.

Ever since human astronauts first flew in outer space, many of them have reported that seeing our planet from afar led to an important shift in their perception about it. They experienced a sudden realization of the planet's fragility when they looked at our small pale blue dot amid the surrounding empty darkness. In 1987, writer Frank White coined this apprehension the "overview effect."[36] According to *Apollo 11* astronaut Michael Collins, who was referring to our planet: "The thing that really surprised me was that it projected an air of fragility. And why, I don't know. I don't know to this day. I had a feeling it's tiny, it's shiny, it's beautiful, it's home, and it's fragile."[37] This type of cognitive shift could help humanity address almost every major problem we are facing as a species. From space, we don't see borders, languages, cultures, and religions. We see an isolated blue bubble that is as fragile as it is finite. In such a small ecosystem, what someone does here will certainly affect what happens there. This outlook triggers an enhanced desire for protection and cooperation and also an awareness that the overall scale of our globe is indeed small, conceivable, and, ultimately, reachable.

The biggest, seemingly impossible problems we face today are contained within that delicate blue dot. But they are far from impossible. We need to be bold and imaginative in rethinking our approach to solving them. The immensely intricate and multivariate problems that we face—overpopulation, overconsumption, pollution, waste generation, global warming, terrorism, water scarcity, refugees, hunger, ecological breakdown, societal disruption, nuclear proliferation, artificial intelligence, and genetic manipulation—demand a new outlook on the world. Such extraordinary challenges will require unprecedented international cooperation. And yet, many of them are within the reach of design, and we shouldn't be shy about it. They are our ultimate design targets. We have the opportunity to influence a vast array of hidden structures and mechanisms that are deeply intertwined with our lives and the lives of other species on this planet. We have a chance to make the world even smaller. As Tim Brown of IDEO once wrote, "where you innovate, how you innovate, and what you innovate are design problems."[38]

Designers need to expand our canvases, our outlook on the world, and our plan of action. We are no longer in the business of designing only products and experiences. We need to aspire much higher if we truly want to have a positive, long-lasting effect on our planet. While designers often use the word *system*, it refers primarily to a consistency of components within a digital platform, such as a website, an application, or a piece of software. In other words, it is used on a miniscule scale. While good in principle, this usage lacks ambition. For better or worse, the earth has now become our canvas and our system. As American environmental scientist Brad Allenby has said, "the Earth has become a design space."[39] We can either continue doing a terrible job with it or try to make it better. We must adopt the "overview effect" as part of our *modus operandi* and broaden the horizon of our systemic thinking. We must reimagine and reengineer existing processes and systems that are not working well. We must start reversing the damage instead of contributing to it. The project to restore the Loess Plateau and the Weather Makers' plan to regreen the Sinai are examples of the scale and impact we should be aiming at when we think of the future of design.

3. Design the invisible

"For a long time, it felt as if the design world had lost its moral compass, turning its back on social, political and environmental issues," writes Marcus Fairs, editor-in-chief of *Dezeen* magazine. "Designers seemed instead to seek fame for its own sake and frittered their problem-solving talents on trivial or indulgent projects."[40] While Fairs's assessment feels accurate, there are some encouraging signs of change. For one, designers have realized that turning their backs on the problem makes matters worse. Some have attempted to integrate and transform traditional businesses, while many turned to shinier, newfangled tech and digital industries, in the hope, perhaps, of finding a renewed sense of integrity. Yet the disillusionment has been widespread and still percolates today. Slowly, designers have realized that in the absence of a corporate ethical and ecological conscience, they have to roll up their own sleeves. This is what happened with What Design Can Do, a community of like-minded creatives who still believe that design can transform society for the best. The group holds an annual No Waste Challenge that invites designers across the world to dream of a future where waste generation becomes an obsolete model. A nominee for its 2021 edition was Vegeme, a sustainable recyclable system that aims at reducing waste in the city of Tokyo by collecting food waste in businesses and schools across the metropolis and recycling it as fertilizer for vegetable sowing.

Vegeme doesn't look like a conventional design project. While ingenious, it might not be not top portfolio material. And to be honest, who wants it to be? Part of the new design awakening is the realization that portfolios are an outdated concept—not just because "personal portfolio sites are too static for the pace of change,"[41] as designer Rachel Berger puts it, but because the very nature of what we design today has changed. While some of the products and experiences we design are everchanging, we are also increasingly designing invisible systems and processes that don't conform to the requirements of a traditional portfolio. There is also a misguided focus on the outer layer—the fit-and-finish—and visual aesthetics instead of the underlying method and thinking. As we transition from designing tangible, static artifacts to designing invisible, dynamic systems, we must change how we talk about our work and how we derive value from it. In a piece aptly titled "The Death of Design Portfolios," Berger includes a testament from Bryan Ku, a visual designer at Google Search, who explains this change in his own words: "We design interfaces and components that aim to be intuitive, functional, and nearly invisible. Although invisible, the fulfillment of the work comes from the number of people that directly benefit from my effort."

Designing the invisible goes well beyond digital interfaces or even voice-activated virtual assistants. It takes us to an area of study that has grown considerably in the past two decades and that is hard to include in a portfolio—service design. This comes across in the subtitle of one of the seminal books on this topic, *An Introduction to Service Design: Designing the Invisible* by design educator Lara Penin. "Services are the soft infrastructure of society,"[42] says Penin, so improving their quality through design seems like a worthwhile pursuit. This approach can be applied to any system or journey you might think off, from a patient care service to an urban recycling system like Vegeme. It is a powerful mindset that does not consider solely individual touchpoints but instead develops a holistic, systemic view of the problem. Although recent, service design is here to stay. The transition from material to immaterial might, in fact, become an inevitable path for the future of design. In a short period of time, either by templatization or automation, much of the user interface components and patterns that Ku mentions above will likely not be carefully laid out by a designer. And perhaps that is not a bad thing. It will force design to think broader and dream bigger—to reinvent itself past checkboxes and pulldowns on a screen.

Service design offers a bright future for our discipline. It is as a valuable, transdisciplinary approach to problems that allows us to flex our creative muscles and address larger and more intricate problems. Unfortunately, and similarly to user experience, it still promotes the human- or customer-centric mindset that got us to this point in the first place. Whether it is a physical process (such as shipping) or a digital process (such as communications), service design normally implies a value exchange between parties, therefore perpetuating the "business as usual" mindset discussed in chapter 7. While we might have done away with some of the veneer commonly featured in a design portfolio, traditional business imperatives still restrain the true potential of service design. If we continue to focus exclusively on profit and the needs of a paying customer, we will miss out on an opportunity for real change—an opportunity to broaden the scope of the discipline, to rethink the various hidden forces that affect design, and to reimagine the entire system of resources, materials, supply chains, production, packaging, transportation, energy consumption, human interaction, waste management, and ecological impact.

By unshackling service design from a transactional, cost-benefit mindset, we have a chance to create a truly systemic practice that embraces network thinking in redefining existing structures and in dreaming unforeseeable ones. This can be done not just in critical waste renewal systems like Vegeme or large natural systems like the project to regreen the Sinai. We can design organizations, societies, communities, and networks of change. We can ultimately design a new mindset, a new mode of thinking based on unity and cooperation, because if we have any chance of improving things, we must do it together. At a time when our differences are evermore accentuated, design has an opportunity to bring us closer and to create enablers of understanding, dialogue, public discourse, and activism. Systems that can engage citizens in democratic decision making and public discussion, not by duplicating the ad-driven, social media echo chambers of today but by upholding openness, empathy, and participation. Tools like Pol.is, a faceless AI-driven online discourse platform that is used by governments and citizen assemblies to generate civil discussion and consensus. Such tools can be centered on what unites us as a species, our human universals. If we do this right, design can appeal to the better angels of our nature. It can become an invisible force for good.

Actionable Advice

Network thinking is design thinking. This is the only viable path for the future. We cannot continue looking at individual problems as if they emerge in isolation. We must embrace a systemic problem-solving capability that becomes synonymous with design. This means coming up with multifaceted solutions that often don't appear in a portfolio. It is important to change the notion of design as something to be showed, admired, and contemplated. As we enter an increasingly immaterial and invisible stage, we must come to terms with what this means for the practice. You also must manage your expectations. If you want to do work that matters, it likely won't have a face as we know it. And that is not a bad thing. Design is not solely about products, surface, and materiality. Design is also about the deeply integrated systems and services that power our daily lives. Many of these things are hidden from sight, yet their impact can be much greater that any product or poster ever made. But a cool app or kiosk that improves the check-in process is not service design. These are only single touch points. You must consider all levers, tools, people, animals, and experiences that improve the overall system, not just an individual part.

If you think you are designing at a small scale, you probably are. If you feel a series of templatized components could do your job better, they probably will. It is time to move on to something more fulfilling. Don't lose your time, talent, and creativity tackling those problems, even if they are called by the misleading label of *systems thinking*. Not every system matters equally. If you are locked in a small-scale procedure, try to think broadly, beyond its confines. Aim higher, dream bigger. The interesting thing about systems is that they tend to be part of a larger one, like nesting Russian dolls. Navigate up the chain, and target the next greater system. This will inevitably take you beyond a single experience or local service and perhaps will include a whole community, neighborhood, city, continent, and global network of interdependence. These are all scales where design should have a voice and where you should have a voice. And we shouldn't be shy about it. Remember, the earth has ultimately become a design space.

"The future is already here—it's just not very evenly distributed,"[43] said American Canadian science fiction author William Gibson in an NPR interview in 1993. Some designers are already leading the way for the future of the discipline—by embracing change and systemic thinking, leaving behind constraining practices and outdated models, investing in large-scale network analysis, considering vast systems of reciprocity, and relinquishing old desires of a material showcase in the form of a personal portfolio. These designers are already here. It is up to you to decide whether you will join them. You must choose how you pursue your interests and direct your professional career. You can either continue perpetuating an obsolete design framework, or you can align your job prospects in a different direction. I know this can be frightening. The forefront of design can be an intimidating, mysterious place. But as is noted in chapter 1, life is too short to limit ourselves by fear. If you want to do anything meaningful in life, you must be uncomfortable, and you must be vulnerable.

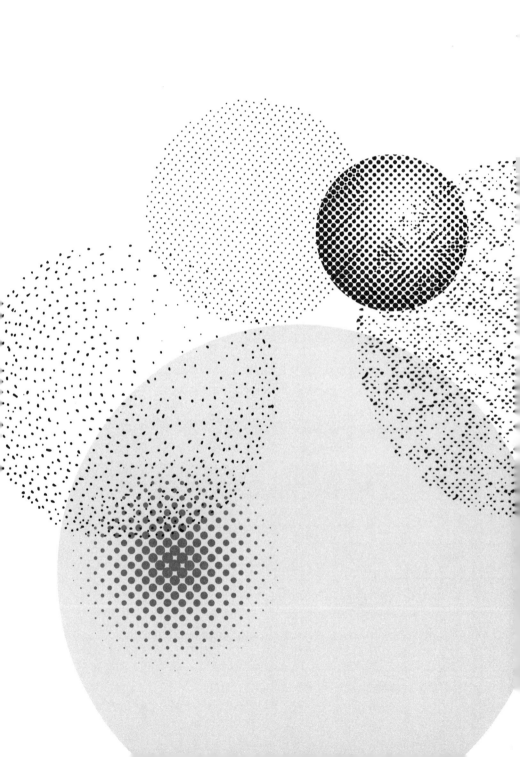

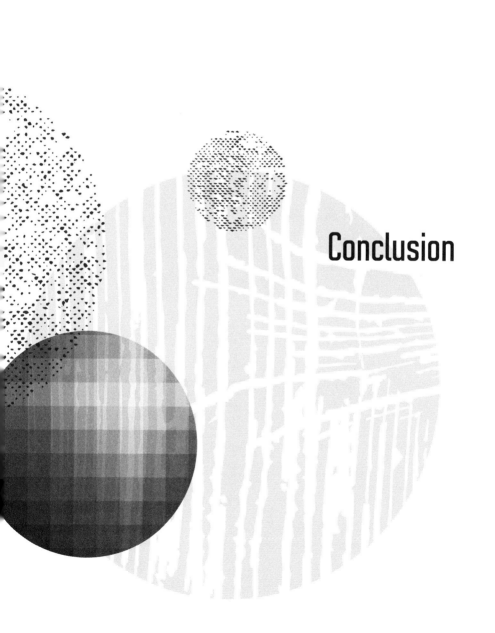

Conclusion

You can't design in an ivory tower.
—Emory Douglas[1]

Design creates culture.
Culture shapes values.
Values determine the future.
—Robert L. Peters[2]

10

Designer of the future

The designer of the future is a mix of psychologist and anthropologist, sociologist and ecologist, system theorist and futurist, activist and reformer. The designer of the future has a deep understanding of the human mind and the interdependent social fabric it inhabits, as well as the inherent complexities of ecosystems, both natural and artificial, that support our planet. The designer of the future can connect past, sustainable traditions with the prospect of radical, future change. Able to lift others from poverty and reject systemic structures of oppression, the designer of the future aims at decolonizing design while also decolonizing the future. Able to dream the impossible and show us where we could be going, the designer of the future is both a realist and an optimist who is able to display perseverance in the face of disaster as well as conviction in a better outcome. In the process, thoughtful and respectful design can be established based on inclusion, codependence, and interdisciplinarity. This is the first brick in building an ethical practice. And, as with all meaningful transformation, it starts from within—with yourself.

1. Ethics is personal

Ethics is ultimately a personal choice. It is yours to make, not something you inherit from someone or an ideology you can follow. It starts with you. Every decision you make is political and has a set of repercussions. Design, like technology, is never neutral. As American social scientist Herbert A. Simon stated so acutely: "Everyone designs who devises courses of action aimed at changing existing situations into preferred ones. The intellectual activity that produces material artifacts is no different fundamentally from the one that prescribes remedies for a sick patient or the one that devises a new sales plan for a company or a social welfare policy for a state."[3] Design is very much about making decisions that affect individuals as well as large groups of people. And if design has always been political, as we venture into larger and more ambitious projects, like the ones discussed in the previous chapter, understanding the social and ecological impact of your work is paramount. Ultimately, your design is instilled with its own set of principles and ethics. "A design cannot be disconnected from the values and assumptions in which it was created, from the ideologies behind it," says Ruben Pater, "Acknowledging that communication is not neutral puts everything in perspective."[4]

You might think there is no harm in creating an enticing burger ad for a large food chain, or even for a small neighborhood restaurant. You are just helping a business by doing what you do best. It probably wouldn't take too much effort to find out that "it takes about 15,000 liters of fresh water to produce one kilogram of beef, compared to 287 liters needed to produce a kilogram of potatoes."[5] Every choice matters and should not be taken lightly. Should you use your design skills to promote burger consumption or instead, employ it in elevating sustainable sources of food? Should you create a captivating interface that causes sleep deprivation or instead one that promotes a user's well-being? At some point, during my advertising days, there was a general agreement on where many designers would draw an ethical line: oil and tobacco industries. Funnily enough, that line has not moved, despite all the technological disruption that poses an equal, if not larger, threat to society and our planet. Perhaps because, as we explored in chapter 6, it's often obfuscated by techno-optimism. While Facebook might say "our technology connects people, what they do after that is up to them,"[6] this is in the end "an abnegation of responsibility for the impacts of technology. It is an ideology that places the onus of right action on 'users' rather than on designers."[7] This is grounded in the wrong idea that technology, like design, can be neutral.

While this book offers a counterview to design convention that can guide you along the way, the journey is yours to make. The first step is the realization that you are the primary agent of change. You have your own agency. The biggest myths worth deconstructing are the ones holding you back from reaching your true potential. Frequent mental traps can block your ability to see the big picture and affect the positive change you wish to see in the world. So before you start dismantling ingrained cultural behaviors, social inadequacies, and environmental recklessness, you must look inward first. You must become a mindful designer and pay attention to the broad range of factors covered in chapters 1 to 3. You must understand the importance of failure, imperfection, humility, and persuasion, as well as the value of cooperation and a multidisciplinary approach. The designer of the future cannot continue to be shackled by such constraints, nor be overly infatuated by design tools, processes, and standardization. In order to become a humanist, a social innovator, an environmentalist, and an ethical designer, you must put on your own mask first and learn how to breathe.

Putting on your own mask begins with self-awareness. This means questioning yourself, but also understanding how your family background, upbringing, education, and life experience might have conditioned your way of looking at the world. It means understanding how you might be susceptible to unconscious biases that affect your judgment, your design solutions, and the progressive outcomes you want to see around you. Putting on your own mask next turns to education. While we explore later in this chapter how design schools have a critical role to play here, you cannot expect large, academic institutions to change overnight. You must educate yourself and actively seek out knowledge outside the design walled garden. If you want to seek change, you cannot let yourself drown in a monoculture. You must step out and expand your horizon. Dig deep into history, philosophy, anthropology, sociology, psychology, cultural studies, biology, evolution, ecology, and network science. Create your own parallel curriculum in order to become an informed, conscientious, and pluralist creative professional. Through a combination of all these streams of knowledge and experience, you will be able to establish your own ethical design framework.

One form of moral disengagement is thinking that ethics stops at the front door of your office or, in modern times, at the screen of your corporate computer—or worse, that it belongs only to a specialized role. When Google's senior software engineer Blake Lemoine was put on leave in June 2022, following the publication of a conversational exchange between himself and the company's LaMDA (language model for dialogue applications) chatbot development system, which Lemoine claimed had become sentient, the most shocking development, aside from the discussion of whether the system showed signs of intelligence or sentience, was Google's public statement on the matter. While a breach of confidential policy appears to have occurred by publishing those conversations, Google's claim on ethics being reserved to a handful of people was incredible. In a statement shared with *The Guardian*, Google said that Lemoine "was employed as a software engineer, not an ethicist."[8] In other words, if you are a software engineer, designer, or program manager, you need to leave your ethics at the door. Ethics is apparently a skill reserved for a few. Everyone else should just be quiet and do their job.

Ethics, of course, is not tied to a role. It is personal and belongs to everyone. Each one of us. At times, for different reasons, we might feel disconnected from our ethical commitment. Perhaps our workspace doesn't feel like a safe environment to raise concerns, or we might delegate that responsibility to someone else—say an ethicist. We might lack positive examples coming from the top, be too pressured to hit a certain metric, or simply, we would rather find a virtuous route elsewhere, through religion, a charity, or recycling. While it is true that moral disengagement is often instilled by corporate culture, designers can't succumb to such tempting detachment. There is simply too much on the line. We can no longer quietly follow the stream of numbing and desensitization. Ethics must become embedded within the design practice. We can no longer compartmentalize it as though it is something separate from our job and must commit to a new principled paradigm. Because despite all our inherent human inadequacies and an occasional sense of power-lessness, designers are still well suited to be critical agents of change. Not leveraging this opportunity is detrimental to themselves, to their extended social community, and to the ecosystems that regulate our planet. As Italian architect Toraldo di Francia said 50 years ago, "it is the designer who must attempt to re-evaluate his role in the night-mare he has helped to conceive."[9]

2. Decolonizing design

In chapters 4 to 6, we examined multiple factors underlying design's recent moral failings toward society—falling into recurring cognitive dissonance patterns (such as ethical fading, moral disengagement, and automation bias), treating humans as data points, and aiming for an exclusive, idealized standard that belongs to no one. But there's another prevalent, yet unspoken, theme affecting design's societal impact: a repeated focusing on a small slice of the population while ostracizing a large majority. More and more designers understand that their beloved discipline is built on top of a system that is prone to social injustice and exploration, where instead of lifting the poor and oppressed, we continue to contribute to their disenfranchisement. As associate professor of strategic design and management at Parsons School of Design Mariana Amatullo says in *Design for Social Innovation: Case Studies from around the World*, such awareness is not exclusive to design schools and eager-for-change, young design minds: "Practitioners and students alike are aware that many of our popular design and social change narratives remain riddled with problematic asymmetries of power, class, race, gender, and geography."[10]

As a Portuguese American, I've witnessed up close, in two separate cultures, the easy dismissal of imperialism—and all its contemptable consequences—as something deeply buried in the past and therefore not worth revisiting. However, as is shown in chapters 5 and 6, the effects of that seemingly long-gone prejudice are still entrenched in our day-to-day lives in the ways we plan our cities or engineer new technology. During our human history, cultures have constantly dominated and assimilated others, going back to the ancient cultures of Mesopotamia, Egypt, China, Greece, Rome, and Mexico. But between the seventeenth and twentieth centuries, Western European culture declared itself superior in order to justify inhumane acts—such as slavery, colonization, genocide, and land appropriation—against other groups deemed inferior and less developed. Culture was seen as evolutionary, similar to the moral hierarchy known as the great chain of being, discussed in chapter 7. And even though, as designer Ruben Pater explains in *The Politics of Design: A (Not So) Global Design Manual for Visual Communication*, "ideas of the evolution of culture have largely been abandoned," "centuries of cultural dominance and colonization have left their trace, making white culture the reference point for art, ideas, science, and language."[11]

Designers Ansari Ahmed, Danah Abdulla, Ece Canli, and other funding members of an online design research platform explain in their editorial statement what this influence means for design. "To date, mainstream design discourse has been dominated by a focus on Anglocentric/Eurocentric ways of seeing, knowing, and acting in the world," they write, "with little attention being paid to alternative and marginalized discourses from the non-Anglo-European sphere, or the nature and consequences of design-as-politics today."[12] We can see this pattern in modern-day design aesthetics. Western designers tend to fetishize the "aesthetic finesse of companies like Braun or Apple"[13] and the clean graphical compositions of mid-twentieth-century European design. As an example, take the frequent pedantry around typefaces. Some fonts, such as Helvetica, are elevated based on an illusion of neutrality and universality, while others are deemed ornamental, exotic, or ethnic. Such a conception of aesthetics tends to overpower all others. Alternative approaches to Western conventions are simply ignored or deemed unessential. The designer of the future needs to put aside biased snobbery and develop a deeper understanding of the full picture. This means extending the notion of design tradition and progress well beyond twentieth-century Europe and United States. We must, as Ansari and his colleagues emphasize so clearly, aim at *decolonizing design*.

Broadening the range of Western aesthetics should not translate into the appropriation of cultural elements from marginalized cultures. This is what countless brands have done over the years, leading to justified indignation from members of those cultures. An example was the 2009 launch of an Urban Outfitters clothing collection titled "Navajo," which showcased patterns inspired by Indigenous textiles. The company did not seek approval from the Native American tribe for this use of its textile patterns and did not attempt to share profits from the sale of this clothing with tribe members.[14] Another faux pas might seem more accidental, but it stems from the same narrow world view. In 1997, Nike released a range of Nike Air shoes with a flaming logo that resembled the word *Allah* in Arabic. Following a series of complaints from the Muslim community, Nike recalled 800,000 shoes and issued the following apology: "We have, through this process, developed a deeper understanding of Islamic concerns and Islamic issues. . . . As our brand continues to expand, we have to deepen our awareness of other world communities."[15] Societies are becoming more culturally diverse. This means that designers "can no longer assume that their audience shares the same visual language and values."[16] We can mitigate this by having more diverse design teams, as discussed in chapter 4, but even better, we can codesign with people from local communities or support local designers to do the work themselves. Design can be used to challenge structural inequalities, persistent biases, and stereotypes.

But the question of who gets to decide is still the biggest moral question. Design educators Mariana Amatullo, Bryan Boyer, Jennifer May, and Andrew Shea expose a range of questions worth asking in this context: "How does power play out in problem-definition, problem-solving, and in the narrative of the project and solution? Who is given credit in a project and whose voices are lifted up? What shapes the directional flows of power, including education, perceived or promoted expertise, tools and resources?"[17] Instead of continuing to design on top of such deep-rooted biases, we should aim at dismantling those systemic injustices and prejudice. If our practice continues to be an elitist monoculture, we will never see problems differently. We will continue looking at challenges from a single, outdated angle. We will never change anything if we don't change. But decolonizing design is not just about the present. It also means decolonizing the past. Passivity will only help to continue perpetuating these biases. What we can do is revisit and retell stories, while giving voice to misrepresented groups in history, just as Briar Levit did in the book *Baseline Shift: Untold Stories of Women in Graphic Design History,*[18] Bahia Shehab and Haytham Nawar in *A History of Arab Graphic Design,*[19] and Anne H. Berry and colleagues in *The Black Experience in Design: Identity, Expression & Reflection.*[20]

The need for reshaping design history is not new. In 1994, design historian Martha Scotford tried to sidestep the ingrained conventions of design theory by introducing a new way of looking at the past. "Neat history is conventional history: a focus on the mainstream activities and work of individual, usually male, designers," she writes. In opposition, Scotford introduces the notion of "messy history," which "seeks to discover, study and include the variety of alternative approaches and activities that are often part of women designers' professional lives."[21] Accounting for a diversity of angles, viewpoints, and contributions, the notion of messy history is more inclusive, more varied, and closer to reality. But it shouldn't stop there. As Ruha Benjamin mentions in the foreword to *The Black Experience in Design*, "The imperative, as I see it, is to not only approach design from the perspectives of those who are routinely written out of Humanity—those who are typecast or get no speaking parts—but to draw on their insights, imagination, and expertise from the very beginning."[22] This is why the work of authors such as Julia Watson and Azra Aksamija is so critical.[23] They shed light on the experience, expertise, and ingenuity of commonly forgotten groups—Indigenous people, in the case of Watson, and displaced refugees, in the case of Aksamija in her riveting portrait, *Design to Live: Everyday Inventions from a Refugee Camp.*

3. Decolonizing the future

In chapter 7, we learned from philosopher Roman Krznaric that our irresponsible behavior can be compared to the idea of colonizing the future, since we are treating the future as a faraway colonial settlement. As he explains, "we treat the future as a distant colonial outpost where we dump ecological degradation, nuclear waste, public debt and technological risk."[24] So how can we go about decolonizing the future? As it turns out, the recipe for decolonizing the future is the same as the one for decolonizing design and decolonizing the present. It's about symbiosis and coexistence instead of prejudice and domination. As the authors of an insightful Wellbeing Economy Alliance report note, "We need to move away from an economic system which says that Amazon Inc. is worth 1 trillion USD, while the Amazon Rainforest is worth nothing, until its trees are cut down and sold as timber, despite being the 'lungs of the earth.'"[25] Instead of a cost-benefit approach, the authors propose a cobeneficial model, which "recognizes the intrinsic interconnections between our social and ecological systems as the basis for a just and sustainable economy, with health as the great connector."[26]

Changing the basis of our entire economic system is not easy but is not impossible. One way to start decolonizing the future is to reject several design myths, some of which have been explored in previous chapters. Perhaps one of the biggest myth worth debunking is the notion that digital technology is a benign force. To view a website as environmentally costless is at best naive. It fails to consider the widespread effects of the entire industry—the tremendous energy expenditure of data centers and cryptocurrency, the mining of rare minerals to power an increasingly number of short-term digital devices and smart objects, the cost of storing and transferring large volumes of data, and the proliferation of poorly managed software applications. As designer and futurist Cennydd Bowles says, "Sustainable software results from high-quality engineering, thorough testing, and commitment to proper post-release maintenance. Handled properly, software can be a material that gets better with age; wood that bears the contours of use, not brittle plastic."[27] Performance is therefore conservation, according to Bowles. Digital designers are not excluded from this responsibility. In fact, they should be leading the way to a true ecological digital renovation.

Another important myth worth debunking is the notion of infinite growth in a finite planet, when instead, we should adopt the idea of degrowth, where we reduce energy and resource consumption in order to attain a sustainable balance with the natural world. However, if sustainability and ecology are to work, they must become part of culture and entrenched in societal practices and costumes. You certainly see this in many Indigenous cultures, as noted by Julia Watson in her fascinating book *Lo-TEK: Design by Radical Indigenism*, which is covered in detail in chapter 8. For us to get there, we must expand the idea of what design is and what it ought to be. While design is irrevocably associated with building, making, and manufacturing, and therefore growth, it is not our only tool. In fact, one can argue this predisposition for creating material goods is part of the problem that got us where we are. But design is not production. It is about designing immaterial things—such as digital experiences, environments, and services—but also much more. We can design communities, groups, societies, and voices of change. Action and impact are not always translated into something physical and tactile. Most transformational shifts in culture and society were caused by exchanging aspirations and demanding a better future. We must go beyond our immediate response to build a tool to solve a problem.

In the view of Mariana Amatullo and her colleagues, the trap of design "solutionism" in many design programs has become synonymous with human-centered design, when instead we should aim at design "idealism," and in place of seeking "easy answers" designers ought to become "reflective practitioners and principled citizens."[28] These expectations seem to lie in the academic institutions that each year send thousands of designers into the job market without providing them with guidance on how to decolonize design and decolonize the future. We must demand such changes in our educational system. The fundamentals of ecology, systems theory, environmental science, ethics, and circular economics are still absent from most design degree requirements around the world. We keep focusing on the "solutionism" model as a cure for all maladies, which then becomes a self-reinforcing feedback loop, an incapacitating echo chamber. A similar educational gap also exists regarding the need to decolonize design. Courses in history, anthropology, sociology, cultural studies, African studies, as well as the study of other minorities are still absent from most design schools. This is a shame. If these changes don't happen in academia, designers risk becoming ill-informed, myopic automatons with a single action in mind.

In *Designing in Dark Times: An Arendtian Lexicon*, design professors Eduardo Staszowski and Virginia Tassinari write that one way for us to reverse the negative patterns threatening the planet today is for design to broaden its influence by rethinking the meaning of *action*. They mention the work of political philosopher and Holocaust survivor Hannah Arendt, who found a path to action in situations of despair. Dark times are, according to Arendt, precious moments for developing an "activity of thought."[29] This is not mere passive contemplation but, instead, an activity that can open new courses of action with a deeply transformative and political potential: "To think, where thought is a political activity, orientated to change, is something one must do with others, in dialogue with others. This is not an intellectually abstract activity but, rather, one that must inevitably lead to action, more specifically, a process that leads to action in the public realm."[30] Design is therefore about developing a reflective practice in dialogue with others. This is how ideas become entrenched in culture. This is how we affect real change. This is how we start decolonizing the future.

At the end, we must be positive, hopeful, and confident about the future. We must develop confidence in a successful outcome, particularly at a time of crisis. "When things look hopeless, positive visions become totems around which to organize, and important prompts for moral, technological, and political discussion,"[31] writes Bowles in *Future Ethics*. The designers of the future must be courageous at heart. We have no other choice. This is the only world we know. Taking no stance or distancing ourselves from the problems won't work anymore. Neutrality is an overrated myth that designers have been preaching for too long. There are no neutral designs, and design should never aspire to be neutral. It can be invisible and often political, but never neutral. Therefore, we must be conscientious about our decisions and informed about their implications. We must be tactical and rational as we slowly debunk many engrained design myths and take a bold stance in embracing change. We must transform and reshape, with open arms and an optimistic attitude about what design is.

4. Where to start?

The sheer magnitude of the problems around us might seem overwhelming at times. You want to help, but how? Associated professor of integrated design Otto Von Busch in *Making Trouble: Design and Material Activism* explains how a clear path is not always obvious in the face of urgency. "As the physical and political effects of design become explicit in social injustices, geopolitical struggles, and climate change, there is simultaneously confusion about which agency really matters in which context."[32] What could you do as a designer to yield the biggest positive change? What tool, service, or mindset could you instill to change the status quo? Is there low-hanging fruit? While productive, this type of reasoning is still grounded in the one-solution-to-one-problem design mindset of the past. As is shown multiple times throughout this book, all of the major problems we face as a species are permeated by deep layers of interdependent factors. There is no miracle solution or ultimate recipe. The issues are deeply systemic. And yet we must start somewhere and tackle such nebulous problems from multiple angles and from various starting points. Establishing a positive design impact in the world starts with us. We cannot be fearful or paralyzed by its complexity. We just have to begin.

Here is a list of ten high-level principles and considerations that can help you embrace change and develop a thriving, conscientious, and ethical design practice:

1. Develop the right tools and processes to better understand and evaluate the impact of a product, a service, or an experience on our society and environment. Launching or delivering a solution should never be enough. We must step out of a simplistic problem-solution echo chamber and assess its long-term effect. And sometimes not launching or not producing more is the best thing we can do.

2. Design is not always about design. You can affect change through discourse and activity of thought. Your voice is your agency. Embrace that power. You can contaminate others with alternative ideas and resolutions. You can take it to the streets, engage in a dialogue with people, and, as a result, contribute to the cultural shift you wish to see. Everything matters, and so does your voice.

3. Make problems discernible. Visualize the magnitude and gravity of large-scale problems, and yet at the same time, be aware of numerical numbing. Create human stories that evoke empathy and the desire to help and make things better. Don't just communicate. Remember: design is political and never neutral. Aim to stir compassion and informed action. Let your designs be themselves agents of change.

4. Be cautious of an overreliance on data and automated systems for decision making, particularly if it affects your life and the lives of others. Technology and algorithms are as prone to glitches and biases as we are. Do not collect data for data's sake, particularly if it relies on existing systems of oppression and control. Trust your intuition and experience. Designers are mirrors of society.

5. Avoid looking at customers as numbers, clicks, views, and data points on a funnel. Embrace their full humanity with all its unique circumstances and idiosyncrasies. Respect all fellow humans, regardless of their background or social status. Don't exploit their minds for profit or addict them to a tool or technology. Respect their time, privacy, and dignity. You are their ultimate guardian.

6. Design products, tools, services, and experiences that support the self-determination of the impaired, inexperienced, and excluded. Don't design for an idealized, skewed standard or norm. Be inclusive and respectful of different skills and capabilities. Aim at lifting people from their condition by investing in their agency and human potential. Think of constraints as a catalyst for innovation.

7. Do not use your design knowledge and expertise to aggravate the disadvantages created by historic patterns of racism, classism, able-ism, sexism, homophobia, xenophobia, transphobia, religious intolerance, and other forms of oppression.[33] Ask yourself who makes the final decision on a given design solution or technology, who benefits from it, and who is hurt in the process.

8. Be cautious, conscious, and diligent in utilizing resources and materials, if you are an industrial designer or if you are a digital designer. Data, code, images, and symbols are resources just like plastic, glass, and iron. They have a life cycle of their own and can translate into considerable expenditure and energy consumption. Embrace environmental frugality. Avoid material and energy waste.

9. Question the design practice, and be humble about the fact that institutionalized design is not always the answer, particularly when it's projected from a Western ivory tower. Learn from unconventional practices and from

marginalized and Indigenous communities. Give voice to more compassionate and symbiotic approaches and to alternative ideas based on replenishment, reciprocity, and regeneration.

10. Focus on the requirements of the planet as your ultimate stakeholder. Consider environmental needs as well as human ones. Rewrite your stories and journey maps to include all stages of your product's life cycle. Spoiler alert: A life cycle doesn't end with human usage, consumption, or interaction. Earth-centered design requires a change of paradigm that you can help foster in every project.

Notes

Preface

1. Munari, *Design as Art*, 25.

Chapter 1

1. Scher, "Paula Scher on Failure."
2. Avison, "Get Up and Go with These Motivational Books."
3. Seneca, *Epistulae Morales ad Lucilium* (Moral Letters to Lucilius).
4. Saint-Exupéry, *Wind, Sand and Stars*, 143.
5. Hustwit, "A Rare Interview with Graphic Design Legend Massimo Vignelli."
6. Kwun, "Frame by Frame."
7. Moore, *Contemporary Global Perspectives on Gender Economics*, 251.
8. Levanier, "22 Famous Graphic Design Quotes to Inspire You."
9. de Botton, *Status Anxiety*, 71.
10. Brown, "Listening to Shame."
11. Smith at al., "The Perniciousness of Perfectionism."
12. Enns, Cox, and Clara, "Adaptive and Maladaptive Perfectionism."
13. Swider, Harari, Breidenthal, and Steed, "The Pros and Cons of Perfectionism."
14. Novogratz, *Manifesto for a Moral Revolution*, xx.
15. Rober, "The Super Mario Effect."
16. Johnson, and Radosh, *Shoot, Edit, Share*, 135.
17. Johnson, *Where Good Ideas Come From*, 137.
18. Dweck, "Teaching a Growth Mindset."
19. Schulz, *Being Wrong*, 199.
20. Epstein, *Range*, 290.
21. Grant, *Originals*, 37.

22. Isaacson, *Einstein*, 565.

23. Douglas, *928 Maya Angelou Quotes*, 34.

24. "Most Prolific Painter."

25. Livermore, *Artists and Aesthetics in Spain*, 154.

26. Grant, "Why I Taught Myself to Procrastinate."

27. Grant, *Originals*, 96.

28. van Wyhe, "Mind the Gap: Did Darwin Avoid Publishing His Theory for Many Years?"

29. Grant, "Why I Taught Myself to Procrastinate."

30. Popova, "Combinatorial Creativity and the Myth of Originality."

31. Duignan, "Dunning–Kruger Effect."

32. Bain, *A Parent's Guide to Powerful Teaching*, 36.

33. Kurbursky, "Vulnerability in Design."

34. Kurbursky, "Vulnerability in Design."

35. Puccio, Cabra, and Schwagler. *Organizational Creativity*, 149.

36. Hofstadter, and Kuhns, *Philosophies of Art and Beauty*, 96.

37. Lewis, and Moroney, *iPhone and iPad Apps for Absolute Beginners*, xix.

38. May, *The Laws of Subtraction*, 5.

39. Meyvis and Yoon, "Adding Is Favoured over Subtracting in Problem Solving."

40. Spool, "Consistency in Design Is the Wrong Approach,"

41. Gethin, *The Foundations of Buddhism*, 74.

42. Powell, *Wabi Sabi Simple*.

43. Kumar, *Dictionary of Quotations*, 193.

Chapter 2

1. "Teamwork Quotes to Inspire Collaboration and Creativity."

2. Marsh, *Public Relations, Cooperation, and Justice*, 254.

3. Malone, "Infinite Loop."

4. Malone, "Infinite Loop."

5. Malone, "Infinite Loop."

6. Bryant, "How Many Startups Fail and Why?"

7. Efthimiou and Franco, "Heroic Intelligence," 36.

8. Malone, "Infinite Loop."

9. Malone, "Infinite Loop."

10. Miller, *Consumption*, 1.

11. Gilbert, "Your Elusive Creative Genius."

12. Curran and Hill, "Perfectionism Is Increasing over Time."

13. Santos, Varnum, and Grossmann. "Global Increases in Individualism."

14. Riggio, "Are We All Becoming More Self-Centered?"

15. Spencer, *The Principles of Biology*, 444.

16. Crosby, *The Measure of Reality*, ix.

17. Eubanks, *Automating Inequality*, 188.

18. Rosenberg and Arp, *Philosophy of Biology*, 110.

19. Hare and Woods, *Survival of the Friendliest*, xvi.

20. Hare and Woods, *Survival of the Friendliest*, xvii.

21. Ekman, "Darwin's Compassionate View of Human Nature."

22. Constable et al., "Demographic Noise Can Reverse the Direction of Deterministic Selection."

23. Welch, "The iPhone's Camera Is So Good Because 800 People Are Working on It."

24. Bacon, *The Art of Community*, 38.

25. Groysberg, Nanda, and Nohria, "The Risky Business of Hiring Stars," 86.

26. Groysberg, Nanda, and Nohria, "The Risky Business of Hiring Stars," 87.

27. Groysberg, *Chasing Stars*, 16.

28. Davies, "Is Jeff Koons Having a Laugh?"

29. Powers, "I Was Jeff Koons's Studio Serf."

30. Lalinde, "How to Make a Koons."

31. Owens, Johnson, and Mitchell, "Expressed Humility in Organizations."

32. Owens, Johnson, and Mitchell, "Expressed Humility in Organizations," 1519.

33. Owens, "The Best Leaders Are Humble with Bradley Owens."

34. McLeod, "2 Wilds Guides Took Loss of Shuttle Especially Hard."

35. Kanengieter, John, and Aparna Rajagopal-Durbin, "Wilderness Leadership—on the Job."

36. Sherry, Mackinnon, and Gautreau, "Perfectionists Do Not Play Nicely with Others," 237–278.

37. Newheiser, Barreto, and Tiemersma, "People Like Me Don't Belong Here."

Chapter 3

1. Power, "Samantha Power to Grads."

2. "Lorinda Mamo."

3. Kane, "The Story of SAMO©, Basquiat's First Art Project."

4. Barabási, *The Formula*, 55.

5. Barabási, *The Formula*, 56.

6. Dawkins, *The Selfish Gene*, 249.

7. Berger, *Contagious*, 4.

8. The invisible nature of design is discussed in chapter 9.

9. This topic is further examined in chapter 8.

10. Platz, *Design Beyond Devices*.

11. Gottschall, *The Storytelling Animal*, 186.

12. Booker, *The Seven Basic Plots*, 282.

13. The limitations of user empathy are explored in chapter 3.

14. Feinberg and Willer, "From Gulf to Bridge."

15. McGuffin, "Empathy Is Key to Political Persuasion."

16. Berger, *The Catalyst*, 7.

17. Berger, *The Catalyst*, 8.

Chapter 4

1. Novogratz, *Manifesto for a Moral Revolution*, 190.

2. Godin, "All the Same."

3. "My Gaming Addiction Stops Me from Having Relationships."

4. "Addictive Behaviours."

5. "How My Son Went from Gamer to Compulsive Gambler."

6. Kelly and Rheingold, "The Dragon Ate My Homework."

7. Alter, *Irresistible*, 26.

8. Osuch and Turner, "Addiction to Modern Technology."

9. Argyriou, Davison, and Lee, "Response Inhibition and Internet Gaming Disorder."

10. Harari, *21 Lessons for the 21st Century*, 108.

11. Madsbjerg and Rasmussen, "The Power of 'Thick' Data."

12. Gladwell, *Talking to Strangers*, 12.

13. Harari, *21 Lessons for the 21st Century*, 109.

14. Bellinger, "How Bach's Anatomy May Have Handed Him Greatness."

15. Perez, *Invisible Women*, 158.

16. Perez, *Invisible Women*, 157.

17. Bedrossian, "Recognizing Exclusion Is the Key to Inclusive Design."

18. "Does Design Have a Diversity Issue?"

19. Carroll, "Diversity and Inclusion in Design."

20. Zöllner, "Anthropomorphism," 49, 61.

21. Le Corbusier, *The Modulor and Modulor 2*, 56.

22. Hendren, *What Can a Body Do?*, 11.

23. Hendren, *What Can a Body Do?*, 11.
24. Lupton et al., *Extra Bold*, 9.
25. "Inclusive Design."
26. "Inclusive Design."
27. Ariely, *Predictably Irrational*.
28. Madsbjerg and Rasmussen, "The Power of 'Thick' Data."
29. Fogg, *Persuasive Technology*, 6.
30. "Stanford Behavior Design Lab."
31. Busby, "Social Media Copies Gambling Methods 'to Create Psychological Cravings.'"
32. Busby, "Social Media Copies Gambling Methods 'to Create Psychological Cravings.'"
33. Busby, "Social Media Copies Gambling Methods 'to Create Psychological Cravings.'"
34. Fussell, "How an Attempt at Correcting Bias in Tech Goes Wrong."
35. Rushkoff, "Douglas Rushkoff: 2019 National Book Festival."
36. Wiener, *The Human Use of Human Beings*, 162.
37. Harari, *21 Lessons for the 21st Century*, 108.
38. Manzini, *Design, When Everybody Designs*, 67.

Chapter 5

1. Cameron, *Informal Sociology*, 13.
2. Strathern, "'Improving ratings,'" 308.
3. Crosby, *The Measure of Reality*, 126.
4. Pitt, *Doing Philosophy of Technology*, 62.
5. Crosby, *The Measure of Reality*, 14.
6. Kierkegaard, *The Concept of Anxiety*, 188.
7. Blair, *Too Much to Know*, xx.
8. Blair, *Too Much to Know*, 70.
9. van Dijck, "Datafication, Dataism, and Datavcillancc."
10. Bowman, "Goodbye, Google," 198.
11. Best, "Using Design to Drive Innovation."
12. Muller, *The Tyranny of Metrics*, 20.
13. Segura and Braun, *An Eponymous Dictionary of Economics*, 92.
14. Campbell, "Assessing the Impact of Planned Social Change."
15. Mansouri, "A Case Study of Volkswagen Unethical Practice in Diesel Emission Test."

16. Barrett et al., "Impact of the Volkswagen Emissions Control Defeat Device on US Public Health."

17. Brooks, *The Social Animal*, 21.

18. *The Annual Register*, 216.

19. Scher, "Artist Series: Paula Scher."

20. Haidt, *The Happiness Hypothesis*, 13.

21. Canales, "China's 'Social Credit' System Ranks Citizens and Punishes Them."

22. Hill and White, "Designed to Deceive."

23. Rushkoff, *Team Human*, 7.

24. Hitchens, *God Is Not Great*, 91.

25. Hill and White, "Designed to Deceive."

26. O'Neil, "Weapons of Math Destruction."

27. Ferguson, "What Went Wrong with America's $44 Million Vaccine Data System?"

28. Badger, "How Redlining's Racist Effects Lasted for Decades."

29. Nagel, "Society Centered Systems Thinking."

30. Eubanks, *Automating Inequality*, 190.

31. This was the expression used by *The Guardian* in a book review of Alter's *Irresistible*. See Bhutto, "*Irresistible* by Adam Alter Review."

32. Madsbjerg and Rasmussen, "The Power of 'Thick' Data."

33. Watson, *Lo-TEK*, 399.

34. Haidt, *The Happiness Hypothesis*, 13.

Chapter 6

1. Berry et al., *The Black Experience in Design*, v.

2. O'Keefe and O Brien, Ethical Data and Information Management, 68.

3. Raff, "The Book-of-the-Month Club."

4. Raff, "The Book-of-the-Month Club."

5. Mathur et al., "Dark Patterns at Scale."

6. Smith, "Corporations' Political Reckoning Began with a Newsletter."

7. Campbell-Dollaghan, "The Year Dark Patterns Won."

8. "Deceptive Experiences to Online Users Reduction Act."

9. Shobhit, "Google, Facebook Face $8.8B GDPR Suits on Day One."

10. Gray, "What the Antitrust Lawsuits against Big Tech Companies Could Mean for Tech Leaders."

11. Broussard, *Artificial Unintelligence*, 33.

12. Hall, "The Business Model Is the New Grid, and Other Mindbombs."

13. Benoni and Lavallee, "The Scary Future of Instagram."

14. Lyons, "Timnit Gebru's Actual Paper May Explain Why Google Ejected Her."

15. Bandura, "Moral Disengagement in the Perpetration of Inhumanities."

16. "Make Stewardship the New Normal."

17. Rushkoff, *Team Human*, 5.

18. Galston, "Is Seeing Still Believing?"

19. Fussell. "How an Attempt at Correcting Bias in Tech Goes Wrong."

20. Lohr, "Facial Recognition Is Accurate, If You're a White Guy."

21. Berry et al., *The Black Experience in Design*, v.

22. Quoted in Morinelli, *Reason and Doctrine*, 140.

23. Schekkerman, *How to Survive in the Jungle of Enterprise Architecture Frameworks*, 16.

Chapter 7

1. Watson, "Julia Watson: 'Survival of the Most Symbiotic.'"

2. Brand, "About Long Now."

3. Brand, "About Long Now."

4. Tiseo, "Annual Production of Plastics Worldwide from 1950 to 2020."

5. "New Plastics Economy."

6. Wilson, "Why It's Not Worth Recycling Plastic."

7. Mau, "MC24—How to Change Everything."

8. Gessler, "*Urbis* Long Read: Bruce Mau."

9. Weaver, "Design Won't Save the World."

10. Ritchie, "Humans Make Up Just 0.01% of Earth's Life."

11. Macleod, *Endineering*.

12. Seligman and Tierney, "We Aren't Built to Live in the Moment."

13. Seligman and Tierney, "We Aren't Built to Live in the Moment."

14. Seligman et al., *Homo Prospectus*.

15. Papanek, *Design for the Real World*, x.

16. McGonigal, "Our Puny Human Brains Are Terrible at Thinking about the Future."

17. McGonigal, "Our Puny Human Brains Are Terrible at Thinking about the Future."

18. Lee, "The Stranger Within."

19. Pembroke and Saltmarshe, "The Long Time."

20. Fisher, "The Perils of Short-Termism."

21. Fisher, "The Perils of Short-Termism."

22. "What Is Cathedral Thinking."

23. Lifton, "Beyond Psychic Numbing."

24. Lifton, "Beyond Psychic Numbing."

25. Lifton and Mitchell, "The Age of Numbing."

26. Norgaard, "Climate Change in the Age of Numbing."

27. Slovic and Västfjäll, "The More Who Die, the Less We Care."

28. Rettberg, "Ways of Knowing with Data Visualization," 37.

29. Novogratz, *Manifesto for a Moral Revolution*, 190.

30. Bertini, "Can Visualization Elicit Empathy?"

31. Halina, "Why Companies Are Failing at Being Truly Sustainable."

32. "McDonald's Paper Straws Cannot Be Recycled."

33. Davis-Peccoud, Stone, and Tovey, "Achieving Breakthrough Results in Sustainability."

34. "70% of Companies Fail to Disclose Impact on World's Forests."

35. Driesenaar, "How Descartes Landed Us in a Mess and Femininity Will Get Us Out."

36. Driesenaar, "How Descartes Landed Us in a Mess and Femininity Will Get Us Out."

37. Howes et al., "Environmental Sustainability."

38. Miller, *Consumption*, 1.

39. Dunne and Raby, *Speculative Everything*, 7.

40. "Gartner Hype Cycle."

41. Pearce, "Energy Hogs."

42. Hern, "Bitcoin's Energy Usage Is Huge—We Can't Afford to Ignore It."

43. Pearce, "Energy Hogs."

44. Thackara, *In the Bubble*, 17.

45. Thackara, *In the Bubble*, 17.

46. Mau, *Mau: MC 24*.

47. Watson, "Julia Watson: 'Survival of the Most Symbiotic.'"

48. Watson, "Julia Watson: 'Survival of the Most Symbiotic.'"

Chapter 8

1. Bradbury, "Telling the Truth."

2. "Alan Kay."

3. Loudon, "Deaths in Childbed from the Eighteenth Century to 1935."

4. Shaikh, "'The Contagiousness of Puerperal Fever.'"

5. Meigs, *On the Nature, Signs, and Treatment of Childbed Fevers*, 104.

6. Sinek, "Sometimes You Are the Problem."

7. "Framework for Innovation: Design Council's Evolved Double Diamond."

8. Sadler-Smith, "Wallas' Four-Stage Model of the Creative Process."

9. VanPatter and Pastor, *Innovation Methods Mapping*, 28.

10. See "Division of Labour," in *Encyclopedia Britannica*.

11. Malone, Laubacher, and Johns, "The Big Idea."

12. Malone, Laubacher, and Johns, "The Big Idea."

13. Wilson, *The Origins of Creativity*, 193.

14. Epstein, *Range*, 290.

15. Johnson, *Where Good Ideas Come From*, 174.

16. Asimov, "How Do People Get New Ideas?"

17. Popova, "Paula Scher on Combinatorial Creativity."

18. Tamm, *Brian Eno*, 74.

19. Maslow, *The Psychology of Science*, 15.

20. Fuller, "When Did Design Stop Being Multidisciplinary?"

21. Kuhn, *The Structure of Scientific Revolutions*, 54.

22. Bower and Christensen, "Disruptive Technologies," 45.

23. Sagan, "On the Origin of Mitosing Cells."

24. Margulis and Sagan, *Microcosmos*, 29.

25. Margulis and Sagan, *Acquiring Genomes*, foreword.

26. Watson, *Lo-TEK*, 20.

27. Watson, *Lo-TEK*, 397.

28. Watson, *Lo-TEK*, 397.

29. "Oceanix: Media."

30. Scoblic, "We Can't Prevent Tomorrow's Catastrophes Unless We Imagine Them Today."

31. "Professor Stuart Candy Publishes Design and Futures."

32. Candy, "davidbenque @tobias_revell I helped infect designers with it."

33. Hancock and Bezold, "Possible Futures," 25.

34. Voros, "The Futures Cone, Use and History."

35. Dunne and Raby, *Speculative Everything*, 3.

36. Dunne and Raby, *Speculative Everything*, 5.

37. Dunne and Raby, *Speculative Everything*, 4.

38. Dunne and Raby, *Speculative Everything*, 6.

39. Scoblic, "We Can't Prevent Tomorrow's Catastrophes Unless We Imagine Them Today."

Chapter 9

1. "Definitions of Design."
2. Allenby, "The Anthropocene."
3. Mau, "MC24—How to Change Everything."
4. "Fast Fashion in the U.S. Is Fueling an Environmental Disaster in Ghana."
5. Besser, "Dead White Man's Clothes."
6. Annan, Twitter post.
7. McFall-Johnsen, "The Fashion Industry Emits More Carbon Than International Flights and Maritime Shipping Combined."
8. Besser, "Dead White Man's Clothes."
9. Cook, "Solving the Earth's Problems through Design."
10. Resnick, "More Than Ever, Our Clothes Are Made of Plastic."
11. Greenfield, "Humans Exploiting and Destroying Nature on Unprecedented Scale."
12. Greenfield, "Humans Exploiting and Destroying Nature on Unprecedented Scale."
13. "Fast Fashion in the U.S. Is Fueling an Environmental Disaster in Ghana."
14. McFall-Johnsen, "The Fashion Industry Emits More Carbon Than International Flights and Maritime Shipping Combined."
15. Ebbesmeyer and Scigliano, "How 61,000 Floating Nikes Helped an Oceanographer Find His Calling."
16. Peters, "This Map Lets You Fly along the Path of a Drop of Water from Any Place in the U.S."
17. Peters, "This Map Lets You Fly along the Path of a Drop of Water from Any Place in the U.S."
18. Weaver, "Science and Complexity."
19. Weaver, "Science and Complexity," 540.
20. Watson, *Seal Wars*, 214.
21. Duignan, "The Canadian Seal Hunt Resumes."
22. Meisenheimer, "Seals, Cod, Ecology and Mythology."
23. Meisenheimer, "Seals, Cod, Ecology and Mythology."
24. Meisenheimer, "Seals, Cod, Ecology and Mythology."
25. Gales, Hindell, and Kirkwood, *Marine Mammals*, 40.
26. Ceschin and Gaziulusoy, "Evolution of Design for Sustainability."
27. Mau and Leonard, *Massive Change*.
28. "What If We Would Regreen the Sinai?"
29. Blaustein, "Turning Desert to Fertile Farmland on the Loess Plateau."

30. Rose, "Our Biggest Challenge?"

31. Rose, "Our Biggest Challenge?"

32. Rose, "Our Biggest Challenge?"

33. Liu, "Green Gold."

34. Rose, "Our Biggest Challenge?"

35. Liu, "Green Gold."

36. White, *The Overview Effect*.

37. Chang, "For Apollo 11 He Wasn't on the Moon."

38. Brown, "Strategy by Design."

39. Allenby, "The Anthropocene."

40. Fairs, "Can Designers Save the World?"

41. Berger, "The Death of Design Portfolios."

42. Penin, *An Introduction to Service Design*, 21.

43. Gibson, "The Science in Science Fiction."

Chapter 10

1. Berry et al., *The Black Experience in Design*, ii.

2. Peters, "'Quotable Quotes' . . . (Gone Rogue)."

3. Simon, *The Sciences of the Artificial*, 55.

4. Pater, *The Politics of Design*, 3.

5. Harari, *21 Lessons for the 21st Century*, 141.

6. Wu, "The Facebook Trap."

7. "Technology Is Not Values Neutral."

8. Luscombe, "Google Engineer Put on Leave after Saying AI Chatbot Has Become Sentient."

9. Glancey, "Anti-Matter."

10. Amatullo et al., *Design for Social Innovation*, 13.

11. Pater, *The Politics of Design*, 123.

12. Ansari et al., "Editorial Statement."

13. Bowles, *Future Ethics*, 166.

14. Pater, *The Politics of Design*, 126.

15. Pater, *The Politics of Design*, 60.

16. Pater, *The Politics of Design*, 99.

17. Amatullo et al., *Design for Social Innovation*, 17.

18. Levit, *Baseline Shift*.

19. Shehab and Nawar, *A History of Arab Graphic Design*.

20. Berry et al., *The Black Experience in Design*.

21. Levit, *Baseline Shift*, 7.

22. Berry et al., *The Black Experience in Design*, v.

23. Watson, *Lo-TEK*; Aksamija, Majzoub, and Philippou, *Design to Live*.

24. Pater, *The Politics of Design*, 123.

25. Laurent et al., "Five Pathways toward Health-Environment Policy in a Wellbeing Economy," 4.

26. Laurent et al., "Five Pathways toward Health-Environment Policy in a Wellbeing Economy," 4.

27. Bowles, *Future Ethics*, 162.

28. Amatullo et al., *Design for Social Innovation*, 13.

29. Staszowski and Tassinari, *Designing in Dark Times*, 3.

30. Staszowski and Tassinari, *Designing in Dark Times*, 3.

31. Bowles, *Future Ethics*, 169.

32. Von Busch, *Making Trouble*, xvii.

33. Inspired by Virginia Eubanks's "Oath of Non-Harm for an Age of Big Data," included in Eubanks, *Automating Inequality*, 212.

Bibliography

"About the Canadian Seal Hunt." The Humane Society of the United States, accessed July 11, 2022. https://www.humanesociety.org/resources/about-canadian-seal-hunt.

"About Long Now." Long Now Foundation, accessed March 29, 2021. https://longnow.org/about.

Adams, Gabrielle S., Benjamin A. Converse, Andrew H. Hales, and Leidy E. Klotz. "People Systematically Overlook Subtractive Changes." *Nature* 592 (April 8, 2021): 258–261. https://doi.org/10.1038/s41586-021-03380-y.

"Addictive Behaviours: Gaming Disorder." World Health Organization, October 22, 2020, https://www.who.int/news-room/questions-and-answers/item/addictive-behaviours-gaming-disorder.

Aksamija, Azra, Raafat Majzoub, and Melina Philippou. *Design to Live: Everyday Inventions from a Refugee Camp.* Cambridge, MA: MIT Press, 2021.

"Alan Kay." *TED*, accessed July 8, 2022, https://www.ted.com/speakers/alan_kay.

Allenby, Brad. "The Anthropocene: Great Marketing, Wrong Product." *Slate*, February 8, 2016. https://slate.com/technology/2016/02/some-say-climate-change-marks-the-anthropocene-a-new-geological-age-theyre-wrong.html.

Alter, Adam. *Irresistible: The Rise of Addictive Technology and the Business of Keeping Us Hooked.* New York: Penguin, 2017.

Amatullo, Mariana, Bryan Boyer, Jennifer May, and Andrew Shea, eds. *Design for Social Innovation: Case Studies from around the World.* Milton Park, UK: Routledge, 2021.

Annan, Roberta (@RobertaAnnan). "As fashion brands continue to overproduce to meet demands, countries in West Africa are drowning under the weight of waste shipped to our stores. I spoke to the @BBCWorld team on its implications and the way forward. Thank you Thomas Naadi." Twitter, October 14, 2021, 9:55 a.m. https://twitter.com/robertaannan/status/1448573052002910213.

Annual Register, The: A Review of Public Events at Home and Abroad for the Year 1878, Part II, Remarkable Trials: Whistler v. Ruskin. London: Rivingtons, 1879.

Ansari, Ahmed, Danah Abdulla, Ece Canli, Mahmoud Keshavarz, Matthew Kienn, Pedro Oliveira, Luiza Prado, and Tristan Schultz. "Editorial Statement." Decolonising Design, June 27, 2016, accessed March 8, 2022. http://www.decolonisingdesign.com/statements/2016/editorial.

Antony, Martin M. *When Perfect Isn't Good Enough: Strategies for Coping with Perfectionism.* Oakland, CA: New Harbinger Publications, 2009.

Argyriou, Evangelia, Christopher B. Davison, and Tayla T. C. Lee. "Response Inhibition and Internet Gaming Disorder: A Meta-analysis." *Addictive Behavior* 71 (August 2017): 54–60. https://doi.org/10.1016/j.addbeh.2017.02.026.

Ariely, Dan. *Predictably Irrational: The Hidden Forces That Shape Our Decisions.* London: HarperCollins, 2009.

Asimov, Isaac. "How Do People Get New Ideas?" *MIT Technology Review*, October 20, 2014. http://www.technologyreview.com/2014/10/20/169899/isaac-asimov-asks-how-do-people-get-new-ideas/amp.

Avison, Phoebe. "Get Up and Go with These Motivational Books." *Bustle*, September 23, 2015, https://www.bustle.com/articles/109528-8-books-that-will-motivate-you-because-sometimes-we-all-need-a-little-inspiration.

Ayali-Darshan, Noga. "The Scapegoat Ritual and Its Ancient Near Eastern Parallels." *The Torah*, 2020. https://www.thetorah.com/article/the-scapegoat-ritual-and-its-ancient-near-eastern-parallels.

Bacon, Jono. *The Art of Community: Building the New Age of Participation.* Newton, MA: O'Reilly Media, 2012.

Badash, Lawrence, J. O. Hirschfelder, and H. P. Broida. *Reminiscences of Los Alamos 1943–1945.* Berlin: Springer Science & Business Media, 1980.

Badger, Emily. "How Redlining's Racist Effects Lasted for Decades." *New York Times*, August 24, 2017. https://www.nytimes.com/2017/08/24/upshot/how-redlinings-racist-effects-lasted-for-decades.html.

Baeyer, Hans Christian von. *Information: The New Language of Science.* Cambridge: Harvard University Press, 2005.

Bain, Patrice. *A Parent's Guide to Powerful Teaching.* Woodbridge, UK: John Catt Educational, 2020.

Bandura, Albert. "Moral Disengagement in the Perpetration of Inhumanities." *Personality and Social Psychology Review* 3, no. 3 (August 1, 1999). https://doi.org/10.1207/s15327957pspr0303_3.

Baker, Stephen. *The Numerati.* New York: Houghton Mifflin, 2008.

Barabási, Albert-László. *The Formula: The Universal Laws of Success*. Boston: Little, Brown, 2018.

Barrett, Steven, Raymond Speth, Sebastian Eastham, Irene Dedoussi, Akshay Ashok, Robert Malina, and David Keith. "Impact of the Volkswagen Emissions Control Defeat Device on US Public Health." *Environmental Research Letters* 10, no. 11 (October 2015).

Bedrossian, Rebecca. "Recognizing Exclusion Is the Key to Inclusive Design: In Conversation with Kat Holmes." *Campaign*, July 25, 2018. https://www .campaignlive.com/article/recognizing-exclusion-key-inclusive-design -conversation-kat-holmes/1488872.

"Beauty." *Stanford Encyclopedia of Philosophy*, accessed Jun 29, 2022, https:// plato.stanford.edu/entries/beauty.

Bellinger, Ines. "How Bach's Anatomy May Have Handed Him Greatness." *National Geographic*. https://www.nationalgeographic.com/culture/article/ bachs-anatomy-may-have-handed-him-greatness.

Benjamin, Ruha. *Race after Technology: Abolitionist Tools for the New Jim Code*. Cambridge: Polity, 2019.

Benoni, Dan, and Louis-Xavier Lavallee. "The Scary Future of Instagram." *Growth.Design*, January 25, 2021. https://growth.design/case-studies/ instagram-monetization.

Berger, John. *Ways of Seeing*. London: Penguin Books, 1990.

Berger, Jonah. *The Catalyst: How to Change Anyone's Mind*. New York: Simon & Schuster, 2020.

Berger, Jonah. *Contagious: Why Things Catch On*. New York: Simon & Schuster, 2016.

Berger, Rachel. "The Death of Design Portfolios." Modus, August 26, 2019. https://modus.medium.com/the-death-of-design-portfolios-218bcbc11080.

Berry, Anne H., Kareem Collie, Penina Acayo Laker, Lesley-Ann Noel, Jennifer Rittner, and Kelly Walters. *The Black Experience in Design: Identity, Expression & Reflection*. New York: Allworth, 2022.

Bertini, Enrico. "Can Visualization Elicit Empathy? Our Experiments with 'Anthropographics.'" Medium, June 15, 2017. https://medium.com/@FILWD /can-visualization-elicit-empathy-our-experiments-with-anthropographics -7e13590be204.

Besser, Linton. "Dead White Man's Clothes." ABC News, August 11, 2021. https://www.abc.net.au/news/2021-08-12/fast-fashion-turning-parts -ghana-into-toxic-landfill/100358702.

Best, Phil. "Using Design to Drive Innovation." *Bloomberg*, June 29, 2009, https://www.bloomberg.com/news/articles/2009-06-29/using-design-to-drive-innovation#xj4y7vzkg.

Bhutto, Fatima. "*Irresistible* by Adam Alter Review: An Entertaining Look at Technology Addiction," *The Guardian*, April 21, 2017, https://www.theguardian.com/books/2017/apr/21/irresistible-by-adam-alter-review-technology-addiction.

Blair, Ann M. *Too Much to Know: Managing Scholarly Information before the Modern Age*. New Haven, CT: Yale University Press, 2011.

Blaustein, Richard. "Turning Desert to Fertile Farmland on the Loess Plateau." Re.Think, April 5, 2018. https://rethink.earth/turning-desert-to-fertile-farmland-on-the-loess-plateau.

Boetzkes, Amanda. *Plastic Capitalism: Contemporary Art and the Drive to Waste*. Cambridge, MA: MIT Press, 2019.

Booker, Christopher. *The Seven Basic Plots: Why We Tell Stories*. London: Bloomsbury, 2005.

Bower, Joseph L., and Clayton M. Christensen. "Disruptive Technologies: Catching the Wave." *Harvard Business Review* 73, no. 1 (January–February 1995): 43–53.

Bowles, Cennydd. *Future Ethics*. London: NowNext Press, 2018.

Bowman, Douglas. "Goodbye, Google." Stop Design, March 20, 2009. https://stopdesign.com/archive/2009/03/20/goodbye-google.html.

Boyle, Rhonda, Robin Boyle, and Erica Booker. "Pianist Hand Spans: Gender and Ethnic Differences and Implications for Piano Playing." Paper presented at the Australasian Piano Pedagogy Conference, Melbourne, July 2015.

Bradbury, Ray. "Telling the Truth." Keynote address of The Sixth Annual Writer's Symposium by the Sea, sponsored by Point Loma Nazarene University, 2001. Posted by University of California Television (UCTV). https://www.youtube.com/watch?v=_W-r7ABrMYU.

Brand, Stewart. "About Long Now." *The Long Now Foundation*, accessed July 8, 2022, https://longnow.org/about.

Bridle, James. *New Dark Age: Technology and the End of the Future*. London: Verso, 2018.

Brooks, David. *The Social Animal: The Hidden Sources of Love, Character, and Achievement*. New York: Random House, 2012.

Broussard, Meredith. *Artificial Unintelligence: How Computers Misunderstand the World*. Cambridge, MA: MIT Press, 2019.

Brown, Brené. *The Gifts of Imperfection: Let Go of Who You Think You're Supposed to Be and Embrace Who You Are*. Center City, MN: Hazelden, 2010.

Brown, Brené. "Listening to Shame." TED2012, March 2012, Long Beach, CA, video. https://www.ted.com/talks/brene_brown_listening_to_shame.

Brown, Tim. "Strategy by Design." *Fast Company*, June 1, 2005. https://www.fastcompany.com/52795/strategy-design.

Bryant, Sean. "How Many Startups Fail and Why?" Investopedia, November 9, 2020. https://www.investopedia.com/articles/personal-finance/040915/how-many-startups-fail-and-why.asp.

Busby, Mattha. "Social Media Copies Gambling Methods 'to Create Psychological Cravings.'" *The Guardian*, May 8, 2018. https://www.theguardian.com/technology/2018/may/08/social-media-copies-gambling-methods-to-create-psychological-cravings.

Butler, Jill, Kritina Holden, and Will Lidwell. *Universal Principles of Design: 100 Ways to Enhance Usability, Influence Perception, Increase Appeal, Make Better Design Decisions, and Teach through Design*. Beverly, MA: Rockport, 2007.

Campbell, Donald T. "Assessing the Impact of Planned Social Change." *Evaluation and Program Planning* 2, no. 1 (1979): 67–90. https://doi.org/10.1016/0149-7189(79)90048-X.

Campbell-Dollaghan, Kelsey. "The Year Dark Patterns Won." *Fast Company*, December 21, 2016. https://www.fastcompany.com/3066586/the-year-dark-patterns-won.

Cameron, William Bruce. *Informal Sociology, a Casual Introduction to Sociological Thinking*. New York: Random House, 1963.

Campt, Tina M. *A Black Gaze: Artists Changing How We See*. Cambridge, MA: MIT Press, 2021.

Canales, Katie, "China's 'Social Credit' System Ranks Citizens and Punishes Them with Throttled Internet Speeds and Flight Bans If the Communist Party Deems Them Untrustworthy." *Business Insider*, December 24, 2021. https://www.businessinsider.com/china-social-credit-system-punishments-and-rewards-explained-2018-4.

Candy, Stuart [futuryst]. "@davidbenque @tobias_revell I helped infect designers with it via @DI__RCA in 2009, using Voros (2003) after Hancock & Bezold (1993)." Twitter, October 22, 2013. https://twitter.com/futuryst/status/392451752860983296.

Candy, Stuart, and Cher Potter, eds. *Design and Futures*. New Taipei City, Taiwan: Tamkang University Press, 2019.

Carr, Nicholas. *The Glass Cage: How Our Computers Are Changing Us*. New York: W. W. Norton, 2015.

Carr, Nicholas. *The Shallows: What the Internet Is Doing to Our Brains*. New York: W. W. Norton, 2011.

Carroll, Antionette. "Diversity & Inclusion in Design: Why Do They Matter?" *AIGA*, July 1, 2014. https://www.aiga.org/diversity-and-inclusion-in-design-why-do-they-matter.

Catmull, Ed. "How Pixar Fosters Collective Creativity." *Harvard Business Review*, September 2008. https://hbr.org/amp/2008/09/how-pixar-fosters-collective-creativity.

Ceschin, Fabrizio, and İdil Gaziulusoy. "Evolution of Design for Sustainability: From Product Design to Design for System Innovations and Transitions." *Design Studies* 47 (November 2016): 118–163. https://doi.org/10.1016/j.destud.2016.09.002.

Chang, Kenneth. "For Apollo 11 He Wasn't on the Moon. But His Coffee Was Warm." *New York Times*, July 16, 2019. https://www.nytimes.com/2019/07/16/science/michael-collins-apollo-11.html.

Chesney, Bobby, and Danielle Citron. "Deep Fakes: A Looming Challenge for Privacy, Democracy, and National Security." *California Law Review* 107, no. 6 (December 2019).

Constable, George W. A., Tim Rogers, Alan J. McKane, and Corina E. Tarnita. "Demographic Noise Can Reverse the Direction of Deterministic Selection." *Proceedings of the National Academy of Sciences* 113, no. 32 (August 2016): E4745–E4754. https://doi.org/10.1073/pnas.160369311.

Cook, Stacey. "Solving the Earth's Problems through Design." *National Geographic*, September, 2019. https://www.nationalgeographic.com/environment/2019/09/partner-content-solving-earths-problems-through-design.

Costanza-Chock, Sasha. *Design Justice: Community-Led Practices to Build the Worlds We Need*. Cambridge, MA: MIT Press, 2020.

"Country That Became Fast Fashion's Dumping Ground, The," BBC News, October 14, 2021. https://www.bbc.com/portuguese/media-58911546.

Coyle, Daniel. *The Culture Code: The Secrets of Highly Successful Groups*. New York: Bantam Books, 2018.

Crosby, Alfred W. *The Measure of Reality: Quantification in Western Europe, 1250–1600*. Cambridge: Cambridge University Press, 1997.

Curran, Thomas, and Andrew Hill. "Perfectionism Is Increasing over Time: A Meta-analysis of Birth Cohort Differences from 1989 to 2016." *Psychological Bulletin* 145, no. 4 (2019): 410–429. https://doi.org/10.1037/bul0000138.

Dahlström, Anna. *Storytelling in Design: Defining, Designing, and Selling Multidevice Products*. Newton, MA: O'Reilly Media, 2019.

Darwin, Charles. *The Descent of Man*. London: Penguin, 2004.

"Data Centers Generate the Same Amount of Carbon Emissions as Global Airlines." The Next Web, February 15, 2020. https://thenextweb.com/news/data-centers-generate-the-same-amount-of-carbon-emissions-as-global-airlines.

Davies, Lucy. "Is Jeff Koons Having a Laugh?" *Daily Telegraph*, June 18, 2012. https://www.telegraph.co.uk/culture/art/art-features/9329136/Is-Jeff-Koons-having-a-laugh.html.

Davis-Peccoud, Jenny, Paul Stone and Clare Tovey. "Achieving Breakthrough Results in Sustainability." Bain & Company, November 17, 2016. https://www.bain.com/insights/achieving-breakthrough-results-in-sustainability.

Dawkins, Richard. *The Selfish Gene*. Oxford: Oxford University Press, 1976.

De Botton, Alain. *Status Anxiety*. New York: Vintage Books, 2005.

"Deceptive Experiences to Online Users Reduction Act." Congress.gov, accessed January 28, 2021. https://www.congress.gov/bill/116th-congress/senate-bill/1084/all-info.

"Definitions of Design." NSEAD (National Society for Education in Art and Design), accessed July 11, 2022, https://www.nsead.org/resources/design/defining-design-in-the-context-of-art-design.

D'Ignazio, Catherine, and Lauren F. Klein. *Data Feminism*. Cambridge, MA: MIT Press, 2020.

"Division of Labour." *Encyclopedia Britannica*, February 10, 2017. https://www.britannica.com/topic/division-of-labour.

"Does Design Have a Diversity Issue?" Design Council, accessed February 22, 2021. https://www.designcouncil.org.uk/news-opinion/does-design-have-diversity-issue.

Douglas, Arthur Austen. *928 Maya Angelou Quotes*. Roosevelt, UT: UB Tech, 2019.

Driesenaar, Desiree. "How Descartes Landed Us in a Mess and Femininity Will Get Us Out." The Apeiron Blog, April 29, 2021. https://theapeiron.co.uk/how-descartes-landed-us-in-a-mess-and-femininity-will-get-us-out-f599742eb4da.

Duignan, Brian. "The Canadian Seal Hunt Resumes." *Encyclopædia Britannica*, accessed July 11, 2022. https://www.britannica.com/explore/savingearth/the-canadian-blood-festival-resumes.

Duignan, Brian. "Dunning-Kruger Effect." *Encyclopædia Britannica*, accessed June 29, 2022. https://www.britannica.com/science/Dunning-Kruger-effect.

Dunne, Anthony, and Fiona Raby. *Speculative Everything: Design, Fiction, and Social Dreaming*. Cambridge, MA: MIT Press, 2013.

Dutton, Denis. *The Art Instinct: Beauty, Pleasure, and Human Evolution*. London: Bloomsbury Press, 2010.

Dweck, Carol. "Teaching a Growth Mindset: Carol Dweck." Stanford University, November 3, 2015. Video, 1:45. https://www.youtube.com/watch?v=isHM1rEd3GE.

Ebbesmeyer, Curtis, and Eric Scigliano. "How 61,000 Floating Nikes Helped an Oceanographer Find His Calling." *University of Washington Magazine*, March 2009. https://magazine.washington.edu/feature/how-61000-floating-nikes-helped-an-oceanographer-find-his-calling.

Efthimiou, Olivia, and Zeno Franco. "Heroic Intelligence: The Hero's Journey as an Evolutionary Blueprint." *Journal of Genius and Eminence* 2, no. 2 (2017): 32–43. https://doi.org/10.18536/jge.2017.02.2.2.04.

Ekman, Paul. "Darwin's Compassionate View of Human Nature." *JAMA: The Journal of the American Medical Association* 303, no. 6 (February 2010): 557–558. https://doi.org/10.1001/jama.2010.101.

Engebretsen, Martin, and Helen Kennedy. *Data Visualization in Society*. Amsterdam: Amsterdam University Press, 2020.

Enns, Murray W., Brian J. Cox, and Ian Clara. "Adaptive and Maladaptive Perfectionism: Developmental Origins and Association with Depression Proneness." *Personality and Individual Differences* 33, no. 6 (October 19, 2002): 921–935. https://doi.org/10.1016/S0191-8869(01)00202-1.

Epictetus. *The Enchiridion of Epictetus*. Radford, VA: Wilder Publications, SMK Books, 2012.

Epstein, David. *Range: Why Generalists Triumph in a Specialized World*. New York: Riverhead Books, 2019.

Eubanks, Virginia. *Automating Inequality: How High-Tech Tools Profile, Police, and Punish the Poor*. New York: St. Martin's Press, 2018.

Eyal, Nir. *Hooked: How to Build Habit-Forming Products*. London: Penguin Books, 2014.

Eyal, Nir. *Indistractable: How to Control Your Attention and Choose Your Life*. Dallas, TX: BenBella Books, 2019.

Fairs, Marcus. "Can Designers Save the World?" *Dezeen*, October 2, 2017. https://www.dezeen.com/2017/10/02/marcus-fairs-dutch-design-week-opinion-good-design-bad-world.

Falbe, Trine, Martin Michael Frederiksen, and Kim Andersen. *The Ethical Design Handbook*. Freiburg, Germany: Smashing Media AG, 2020.

"Fast Fashion in the U.S. Is Fueling an Environmental Disaster in Ghana." CBS News, September 16, 2021. https://www.cbsnews.com/news/ghana-fast-fashion-environmental-disaster/.

Feinberg, Matthew, and Robb Willer. "From Gulf to Bridge: When Do Moral Arguments Facilitate Political Influence?" *Personality and Social Psychology Bulletin* 41, no. 12 (October 2015): 1–17. https://doi.org/10.1177/014616721560784.

Ferguson, Cat. "What Went Wrong with America's $44 Million Vaccine Data System?" *MIT Technology Review*, January 30, 2021. https://www.technologyreview.com/2021/01/30/1017086/cdc-44-million-vaccine-data-vams-problems/.

Fine, Peter Claver. *The Design of Race: How Visual Culture Shapes America*. London: Bloomsbury, 2021.

Fisher, Richard. "The Perils of Short-Termism: Civilisation's Greatest Threat." BBC, January 10, 2019. https://www.bbc.com/future/article/20190109-the-perils-of-short-termism-civilisations-greatest-threat.

Fogg, Brian Jeffrey. *Persuasive Technology: Using Computers to Change What We Think and Do*. San Francisco: Morgan Kaufmann, 2002.

"Framework for Innovation: Design Council's Evolved Double Diamond." Design Council, accessed July 10, 2022. https://www.designcouncil.org.uk/our-work/skills-learning/tools-frameworks/framework-for-innovation-design-councils-evolved-double-diamond.

Frank, Robert H. *Success and Luck: Good Fortune and the Myth of Meritocracy*. New York: Princeton University Press, 2016.

Fuller, Jarrett. "When Did Design Stop Being Multidisciplinary?" *AIGA Eye on Design*, October 19, 2020. https://eyeondesign.aiga.org/when-did-design-stop-being-multidisciplinary.

Fussell, Sidney. "How an Attempt at Correcting Bias in Tech Goes Wrong." *The Atlantic*, October 9, 2019. https://www.theatlantic.com/technology/archive/2019/10/google-allegedly-used-homeless-train-pixel-phone/599668.

Gales, Nicholas, Mark Hindell, and Roger Kirkwood. *Marine Mammals: Fisheries, Tourism and Management Issues*. Clayton, Australia: Csiro Publishing, 2003.

Galston, William A. "Is Seeing Still Believing? The Deepfake Challenge to Truth in Politics." Brookings Institution, January 8, 2020. https://www.brookings.edu/research/is-seeing-still-believing-the-deepfake-challenge-to-truth-in-politics.

"Gambling Addiction Clinic to Help Addicts Aged 13 to 25." BBC News, June 24, 2019. https://www.bbc.com/news/health-48723482.

"Gartner Hype Cycle." *Gartner*, accessed July 8, 2022. https://www.gartner .com/en/research/methodologies/gartner-hype-cycle.

Gazzaley, Adam, and Larry D. Rosen. *The Distracted Mind: Ancient Brains in a High-Tech World.* Cambridge, MA: MIT Press, 2016.

Gessler, Julia. "*Urbis* Long Read: Bruce Mau." *urbis*, August 7, 2019. https:// urbismagazine.com/articles/bruce-mau.

Gethin, Rupert. *The Foundations of Buddhism.* Oxford: Oxford University Press, 1998.

Gibson, William. "The Science in Science Fiction." Interview with Brooke Gladstone. *Talk of the Nation*, NPR, October 22, 2018. Audio. https://www .npr.org/2018/10/22/1067220/the-science-in-science-fiction.

Gilbert, Elizabeth. "Your Elusive Creative Genius." TED2009, February 2009, Long Beach, CA. Video. https://www.ted.com/talks/elizabeth_gilbert _your_elusive_creative_genius.

Gilbert, Regine M. *Inclusive Design for a Digital World: Designing with Accessibility in Mind.* New York: Apress, 2019.

Gladwell, Malcolm. *The Tipping Point: How Little Things Can Make a Big Difference.* New York: Back Bay Books, 2002.

Gladwell, Malcolm. *Talking to Strangers: What We Should Know about the People We Don't Know.* Boston: Little, Brown, 2019.

Glancey, Jonathan. "Anti-Matter." *The Guardian*, March 31, 2003. https:// www.theguardian.com/artanddesign/2003/mar/31/architecture. artsfeatures.

Godin, Seth. "All the Same." Seth's Blog, April 18, 2014. https://seths.blog/ 2014/04/all-the-same.

Goodhart, Charles. "Problems of Monetary Management: The U.K. Experience." *Papers in Monetary Economics* 1 (1975): 1–20. Sydney: Reserve Bank of Australia.

Gottschall, Jonathan. *The Storytelling Animal: How Stories Make Us Human.* Boston: Mariner Books, 2013.

Gralla, Preston. "Amazon Prime and the Racist Algorithms." *Computer World*, May 11, 2016. https://www.computerworld.com/article/3068622/ amazon-prime-and-the-racist-algorithms.html.

Grant, Adam. *Originals: How Non-Conformists Move the World.* New York: Penguin Books, 2017.

Grant, Adam. *Think Again: The Power of Knowing What You Don't Know.* New York: Penguin Books, 2021.

Grant, Adam. "Why I Taught Myself to Procrastinate." *New York Times*, January 16, 2016. https://www.nytimes.com/2016/01/17/opinion/sunday/why-i-taught-myself-to-procrastinate.html.

Grauer, Yael. "Dark Patterns Are Designed to Trick You (and They're All over the Web)." Ars Technica, July 28, 2016. https://arstechnica.com/information-technology/2016/07/dark-patterns-are-designed-to-trick-you-and-theyre-all-over-the-web/.

Gray, Patrick. "What the Antitrust Lawsuits against Big Tech Companies Could Mean for Tech Leaders." *Tech Republic*, December 21, 2020. https://www.techrepublic.com/article/what-the-antitrust-lawsuits-against-big-tech-companies-could-mean-for-tech-leaders.

Green, Leonard, Astrid F. Fry, and Joel Myerson. "Discounting of Delayed Rewards: A Life Span Comparison." *Psychological Science* 5, no. 1 (January 1994): 33–36. https://www.jstor.org/stable/40062338.

Greenfield, Patrick. "Humans Exploiting and Destroying Nature on Unprecedented Scale: Report." *The Guardian*, September 10, 2020. https://www.theguardian.com/environment/2020/sep/10/humans-exploiting-and-destroying-nature-on-unprecedented-scale-report-aoe.

Greenwood, Tom. *Sustainable Wed Design*. New York: A Book Apart, 2021.

Groysberg, Boris. *Chasing Stars: The Myth of Talent and the Portability of Performance*. Princeton, NJ: Princeton University Press, 2012.

Groysberg, Boris, Ashish Nanda, and Nitin Nohria. "The Risky Business of Hiring Stars." *Harvard Business Review* 82, no. 5 (June 2004): 92–100.

Haidt, Jonathan. *The Happiness Hypothesis: Finding Modern Truth in Ancient Wisdom*. New York: Basic Books, 2006.

Halina, Victoria. "Why Companies Are Failing at Being Truly Sustainable." Medium, July 10, 2019. https://victoriahalina.medium.com/why-companies-are-failing-at-being-truly-sustainable-17f4aa08fd9.

Hall, Erika. "The Business Model Is the New Grid, and Other Mindbombs (ft. Erika Hall)." Interview with Peter Merholz and Jesse James Garrett. Finding Our Way, October 27, 2020. https://findingourway.design/2020/10/27/20-the-business-model-is-the-new-grid-and-other-mindbombs-ft-erika-hall.

Hancock, Trevor, and Clement Bezold. "Possible Futures, Preferable Futures." *The Healthcare Forum Journal* 37, no. 2 (March 1994): 23–29.

Harari, Yuval Noah. *21 Lessons for the 21st Century*. New York: Random House, 2018.

Hare, Brian, and Vanessa Woods. *Survival of the Friendliest: Understanding Our Origins and Rediscovering Our Common Humanity*. New York: Random House, 2020.

Hendren, Sara. *What Can a Body Do? How We Meet the Built World*. New York: Riverhead Books, 2020.

Hern, Alex. "Bitcoin's Energy Usage Is Huge: We Can't Afford to Ignore It." *The Guardian*, January 17, 2018. https://www.theguardian.com/technology/2018/ jan/17/bitcoin-electricity-usage-huge-climate-cryptocurrency.

Hill, Kashmir, and Jeremy White, "Designed to Deceive: Do These People Look Real to You?" *New York Times*, November 21, 2020. https://www .nytimes.com/interactive/2020/11/21/science/artificial-intelligence-fake -people-faces.html.

Hitchens, Christopher. *God Is Not Great: How Religion Poisons Everything*. New York: Twelve, 2009.

Hoffman, Sarah. "The Hero's Journey: A Postmodern Incarnation of the Monomyth." *University of Southern Mississippi—Honors Theses* 39 (2012). https://aquila.usm.edu/honors_theses/39.

Hofstadter, Albert, and Richard Kuhns. *Philosophies of Art and Beauty: Selected Readings in Aesthetics from Plato to Heidegger*. Chicago: University of Chicago Press, 1976.

Holmes, Kat. *Mismatch: How Inclusion Shapes Design*. Cambridge, MA: MIT Press, 2018.

Howarth, Dan. "'Design and Technology Are Changing the Way We Live' Says Justin Trudeau." *Dezeen*, October 5, 2017. https://www.dezeen.com /2017/10/05/justin-trudeau-design-technology-changing-the-way-we-live -edit-festival-toronto.

Howes, Michael, Liana Wortley, Ruth Potts, Aysin Dedekorkut-Howes, Silvia Serrao-Neumann, Julie Davidson, Timothy Smith, and Patrick Nunn. "Environmental Sustainability: A Case of Policy Implementation Failure?" *Sustainability* 9, no. 2 (January 24, 2017): 165. https://doi.org/10.3390/ su9020165.

"How My Son Went from Gamer to Compulsive Gambler." BBC News, October 8, 2019. https://www.bbc.com/news/stories-49941610.

Hustwit, Gary. "A Rare Interview with Graphic Design Legend Massimo Vignelli." *Fast Company*, March 24, 2015. https://www.fastcompany.com /3044133/a-rare-interview-with-graphic-design-legend-massimo-vignelli.

"Inclusive Design." Microsoft Design, accessed July 7, 2022. https://www .microsoft.com/design/inclusive.

Isaacson, Walter. *Einstein: His Life and Universe*. New York: Simon & Schuster, 2008.

Jacobs, Jane. *The Death and Life of Great American Cities*. New York: Vintage Books, 1992.

Jacobs, Margaret D. *After One Hundred Winters: In Search of Reconciliation on America's Stolen Lands*. New York: Princeton Architectural Press, 2021.

Johnson, Kirsten, and Jodi Radosh. *Shoot, Edit, Share: Video Production for Mass Media, Marketing, Advertising, and Public Relations*. London: Routledge, 2016.

Johnson, Steven. *Where Good Ideas Come From: The Natural History of Innovation*. New York: Riverhead Books, 2011.

Kane, Ashleigh. "The Story of SAMO©, Basquiat's First Art Project." Dazed, September 6, 2017. https://www.dazeddigital.com/art-photography/article/37058/1/al-diaz-on-samo-and-basquiat.

Kanengieter, John, and Aparna Rajagopal-Durbin. "Wilderness Leadership—on the Job." *Harvard Business Review*, April 2012. https://hbr.org/2012/04/wilderness-leadership-on-the-job.

Kelly, Kevin, and Howard Rheingold. "The Dragon Ate My Homework. *Wired*, March 1, 1993. https://www.wired.com/1993/03/muds-2.

Kierkegaard, Søren. *The Concept of Anxiety: A Simple Psychologically Oriented Deliberation in View of the Dogmatic Problem of Hereditary Sin*. New York: Liveright Publishing Corporation, 2015.

Knight, Will. "Military Artificial Intelligence Can Be Easily and Dangerously Fooled." *MIT Technology Review*, October 21, 2019. https://www.technologyreview.com/2019/10/21/132277/military-artificial-intelligence-can-be-easily-and-dangerously-fooled/amp/.

Koren, Leonard. *Wabi-sabi for Artists, Designers, Poets & Philosophers*. Point Reyes, CA: Imperfect Publishing, 2008.

Kubrak, Anastasia. "Nuclear Culture Roundtable: Design for the Deep Future. Report." Matter, accessed April 20, 2021. https://matter.hetnieuweinstituut.nl/en/nuclear-culture-roundtable-design-deep-future-report.

Kuhn, Thomas S. *The Structure of Scientific Revolutions*. Chicago: University of Chicago Press, 1996. First published 1962.

Kumar, Manoranjan. *Dictionary of Quotations*. New Delhi: APH Publishing, 2008.

Kurbursky, Lindsay. "Vulnerability in Design." UX Collective, March 20, 2020. https://uxdesign.cc/vulnerability-in-design-fa5b72f6b3e3.

Kwun, Aileen. "Frame by Frame: The Legacy of Mid-century Masters Charles and Ray Eames Is as Much about Their Films as Their Furniture." WHY Magazine, Herman Miller. https://www.hermanmiller.com/stories/why-magazine/frame-by-frame.

Lalinde, Jaime. "How to Make a Koons." *Vanity Fair*, June 16, 2014. https://www.vanityfair.com/culture/2014/06/how-to-make-a-koons-liberty-bell.

Lambert, Léopold. "Architectural Theories: A Subversive Approach to the Ideal Normatized Body." The Funambulist, April 2012. https://thefunambulist.net/architecture/architectural-theories-a-subversive-approach-to-the-ideal-normatized-body.

Laurent, Éloi, Fabio Battaglia, Giorgia Dalla Libera Marchiori, Alessandro Galli, Amanda Janoo, Raluca Munteanu, and Claire Sommer. "Five Pathways toward Health-Environment Policy in a Wellbeing Economy." Wellbeing Economy Alliance, May 2021. https://wellbeingeconomy.org/wp-content/uploads/WEAll-POLICY-PAPER-Health-and-Environment_May2021_Final.pdf.

Le Corbusier. *The Modulor and Modulor 2*. Basel, Switzerland: Birkhäuser Verlag, 2004.

Lee, Cynthia. "The Stranger Within: Connecting with Our Future Selves." UCLA Newsroom, April 9, 2015. https://newsroom.ucla.edu/stories/the-stranger-within-connecting-with-our-future-selves.

Leslie, Ian. "The Scientists Who Make Apps Addictive." 1843. *The Economist*, October–November 2016. https://www.economist.com/1843/2016/10/20/the-scientists-who-make-apps-addictive.

Levanier, Johnny. "22 Famous Graphic Design Quotes to Inspire You." *99Designs*, 2013. https://en.99designs.pt/blog/creative-inspiration/10-famous-design-quotes.

Levit, Briar. *Baseline Shift: Untold Stories of Women in Graphic Design History*. New York: Princeton Architectural Press, 2021.

Levitin, Daniel J. *A Field Guide to Lies: Critical Thinking in the Information Age*. New York: Dutton, 2017.

Lewis, Rory, and Laurence Moroney. *iPhone and iPad Apps for Absolute Beginners*. New York: Apress, 2014.

Lifton, Robert Jay. "Beyond Psychic Numbing: A Call to Awareness." *American Journal of Orthopsychiatry* 52, no. 4 (October 1982): 619–629. https://doi.org/10.1111/j.1939-0025.1982.tb01451.x.

Lifton, Robert Jay, and Greg Mitchell. "The Age of Numbing." *Technology Review*, August–September, 1995.

Liu, John D. "Green Gold." Video. Posted by Permaculture Day, July 20, 2012. http://www.youtube.com/watch?v=AJzU3NjDikY.

Livermore, Ann. *Artists and Aesthetics in Spain*. London: Tamesis, 1988.

Lohr, Steve. "Facial Recognition Is Accurate, If You're a White Guy." *New York Times*, February 9, 2018. https://www.nytimes.com/2018/02/09/technology/facial-recognition-race-artificial-intelligence.htm.

"Lorinda Mamo: Profile." LinkedIn, accessed July 15, 2022. https://www.linkedin.com/in/designchroniclestudios.

Loudon, Irvine. "Deaths in Childbed from the Eighteenth Century to 1935." *Medical History* 30, no.1 (1986): 1–41. https://doi.org/10.1017/s0025727300045014.

Lupton, Ellen, Jennifer Tobias, Josh Halstead, Leslie Xia, Kaleena Sales, Farah Kafei, and Valentina Vergara. *Extra Bold: A Feminist, Inclusive, Anti-racist, Nonbinary Field Guide for Graphic Designers*. New York: Princeton Architectural Press, 2021.

Luscombe, Richard. "Google Engineer Put on Leave after Saying AI Chatbot Has Become Sentient." *The Guardian*, June 12, 2022. https://www.theguardian.com/technology/2022/jun/12/google-engineer-ai-bot-sentient-blake-lemoine.

Lyons, Kim. "Timnit Gebru's Actual Paper May Explain Why Google Ejected Her." *The Verge*, December 5, 2020. https://www.theverge.com/2020/12/5/22155985/paper-timnit-gebru-fired-google-large-language-models-search-ai.

Macleod, Joe. *Endineering: Designing Consumption Lifecycles That End as Well as They Begin*. London: AndEnd, 2021.

Madsbjerg, Christian, and Mikkel B. Rasmussen. *The Moment of Clarity: Using the Human Sciences to Solve Your Toughest Business Problems*. Cambridge, MA: Harvard Business Review Press, 2014.

Madsbjerg, Christian, and Mikkel B. Rasmussen. "The Power of 'Thick' Data." *Wall Street Journal*, March 21, 2014. https://www.wsj.com/articles/the-power-of-thick-data-1395443491.

"Make Stewardship the New Normal." Tech Stewardship, accessed June 6, 2022. https://techstewardship.com/journey.

Malone, Michael S. "Infinite Loop: How the World's Most Insanely Great Computer Company Went Insane." *New York Times*, April 4, 1999. https://archive.nytimes.com/www.nytimes.com/books/first/m/malone-loop.html.

Malone, Thomas W., Robert Laubacher, and Tammy Johns. "The Big Idea: The Age of Hyperspecialization." *Harvard Business Review*, July–August 2011. https://hbr.org/2011/07/the-big-idea-the-age-of-hyperspecialization.

Mansouri, Nazanin. "A Case Study of Volkswagen Unethical Practice in Diesel Emission Test." *International Journal of Science and Engineering Applications* 5, no. 4 (June 2016). https://doi.org/10.7753/IJSEA0504.1004.

Manzini, Ezio. *Design, When Everybody Designs: An Introduction to Design for Social Innovation*. Cambridge, MA: MIT Press, 2015.

Margulis, Lynn, and Dorion Sagan. *Acquiring Genomes: A Theory of the Origins of Species*. New York: Basic Books, 2002.

Margulis, Lynn, and Dorion Sagan. *Microcosmos: Four Billion Years of Microbial Evolution*. Berkeley: University of California Press, 1997.

Marsh, Charles. *Public Relations, Cooperation, and Justice: From Evolutionary Biology to Ethics*. Milton Park, UK: Taylor & Francis, 2017.

Maslow, Abraham Harold. *The Psychology of Science: A Renaissance*. New York: Harper & Row, 1966.

Mathur, Arunesh, Gunes Acar, Michael J. Friedman, Elena Lucherini, Jonathan Mayer, Marshini Chetty, and Arvind Narayanan. "Dark Patterns at Scale: Findings from a Crawl of 11K Shopping Websites." *Proceedings of the ACM on Human-Computer Interaction* 3, no. 81 (November 2019). https://doi .org/10.1145/3359183.

Mau, Bruce. "MC24—How to Change Everything." *Mau: MC24*. Bruce Mau Studio, accessed May 16, 2021. https://brucemaustudio.com/mc24.

Mau, Bruce, Jennifer Leonard, and Institute without Boundaries. *Massive Change*. London: Phaidon Press, 2004.

Mau, Bruce, Jennifer Leonard, and Institute without Boundaries. *Mau: MC 24. Bruce Mau's 24 Principles for Designing Massive Change in Your Life and Work*. London: Phaidon, 2020.

May, Matthew E. *The Laws of Subtraction: 6 Simple Rules for Winning in the Age of Excess Everything*. New York: McGraw Hill, 2012.

"McDonald's Paper Straws Cannot Be Recycled." BBC, August 5, 2019. https://www.bbc.com/news/business-49234054.

McFall-Johnsen, Morgan. "The Fashion Industry Emits More Carbon Than International Flights and Maritime Shipping Combined." *Business Insider*, October 21, 2019. https://www.businessinsider.com/fast-fashion -environmental-impact-pollution-emissions-waste-water-2019-10.

McGonigal, Jane. "Our Puny Human Brains Are Terrible at Thinking about the Future." Slate, April 13, 2017. https://slate.com/technology/2017/04/ why-people-are-so-bad-at-thinking-about-the-future.htm.

McGuffin, Ken. "Empathy Is Key to Political Persuasion, New Research Says." University of Toronto, November 16, 2015. https://www.utoronto.ca/ news/empathy-key-political-persuasion-new-research-says.

McIntyre, Lee. *Post-Truth*. Cambridge, MA: MIT Press, 2018.

McLeod, Michael. "2 Wilds Guides Took Loss of Shuttle Especially Hard." *Deseret News*, February 1, 2004. https://www.deseret.com/2004/2/1/19809818/2-wilds-guides-took-loss-of-shuttle-especially-hard.

Meigs, Charles Delucena. *On the Nature, Signs, and Treatment of Childbed Fevers: In a Series of Letters Addressed to the Students of His Class.* Philadelphia: Blanchard and Lea, 1854.

Meisenheimer, Peter. "Seals, Cod, Ecology and Mythology." International Marine Mammal Association, Ontario, Canada, 1996.

Meyvis, Tom, and Heeyoung Yoon. "Adding Is Favoured over Subtracting in Problem Solving." *Nature*, April 7, 2021. https://www.nature.com/articles/d41586-021-00592-0.

Miller, Daniel. *Consumption: Disciplinary Approaches to Consumption.* London: Taylor & Francis, 2001.

Moore, Susanne. *Contemporary Global Perspectives on Gender Economics.* Hershey, PA: IGI Global, 2015.

Morinelli, Tony Devaney. *Reason and Doctrine: Simple Reason and the Fallacies of Christian Doctrines : Time for Christians to Rethink What They Believe.* New York: Algora Publishing, 2016.

"Most Prolific Painter." Guinness World Records, accessed March 5, 2021. https://www.guinnessworldrecords.com/world-records/most-prolific-painter.

Muller, Jerry Z. *The Tyranny of Metrics.* Princeton, NJ: Princeton University Press, 2019.

Munari, Bruno. *Design as Art.* New York: Penguin Classics, 2019.

Musk, Elon. "Full Elon Musk Interview at WSJ CEO Council Summit." Interview with Matt Murray. YouTube, December 8, 2020. https://www.youtube.com/watch?v=7AA-P7ccRF8.

"My Gaming Addiction Stops Me from Having Relationships." BBC News, October 9, 2019. https://www.bbc.com/news/newsbeat-49978427.

Nagel, Hana. "Society Centered Systems Thinking." YouTube, October 29, 2019, UXC'19: Conférence annuelle de la Chaire UX de HEC Montréal. https://www.youtube.com/watch?v=97lm8VLIydw.

Newheiser, Anna-Kaisa, Manuela Barreto, and Jasper Tiemersma. "People Like Me Don't Belong Here: Identity Concealment Is Associated with Negative Workplace Experiences." *Journal of Social Issues* (June 19, 2017). https://doi.org/10.1111/josi.12220.

"New Plastics Economy." Fundación Chile, accessed April 20, 2021. https://fch.cl/en/initiative/new-plastics-economy.

Noble, Safiya Umoja. *Algorithms of Oppression: How Search Engines Reinforce Racism*. New York: NYU Press, 2018.

Nodder, Chris. *Evil by Design: Interaction Design to Lead Us into Temptation*. Hoboken, NJ: Wiley, 2013.

Norgaard, Kari Marie. "Climate Change in the Age of Numbing." The MIT Press Reader, June 19, 2020. https://thereader.mitpress.mit.edu/climate-change-in-the-age-of-numbing.

Norgaard, Kari Marie. *Living in Denial: Climate Change, Emotions, and Everyday Life*. Cambridge: MIT Press, 2011.

Norman, Donald A. *Things That Make Us Smart: Defending Human Attributes in the Age of the Machine*. New York: Perseus Books, 1993.

Norman, Donald A. "Why I Don't Believe in Empathic Design." Adobe XD Ideas, May 8, 2019. https://xd.adobe.com/ideas/perspectives/leadership-insights/why-i-dont-believe-in-empathic-design-don-norman.

Novogratz, Jacqueline. *Manifesto for a Moral Revolution: Practices to Build a Better World*. New York: St. Martin's Griffin, 2021.

"Oceanix: Media." Oceanix City, accessed October 26, 2021. https://oceanixcity.com/media.

O'Connor, Cailin, and James Owen Weatherall. *The Misinformation Age: How False Beliefs Spread*. New Haven, CT: Yale University Press, 2018.

O'Keefe, Katherine, and Daragh O Brien. *Ethical Data and Information Management: Concepts, Tools and Methods*. London: Kogan Page Publishers, 2018.

O'Neil, Cathy. "Weapons of Math Destruction | Cathy O'Neil | Talks at Google." Google Talks, November 2, 2016. https://youtu.be/TQHs8SA1qpk.

O'Neil, Cathy. *Weapons of Math Destruction: How Big Data Increases Inequality and Threatens Democracy*. New York: Crown, 2017.

Osuch, Michael, and Steven Turner. "Addiction to Modern Technology: What the Science Says." Elsevier Connect, August 2, 2017. https://www.elsevier.com/connect/addiction-to-modern-technology-what-the-science-says.

Owens, Bradley. "The Best Leaders Are Humble with Bradley Owens." Interview with Amber Cazzell. YouTube, August 11, 2020. https://www.ambercazzell.com/post/msp-ep37-bradowens.

Owens, Bradley, Michael D. Johnson, and Terence R. Mitchell. "Expressed Humility in Organizations: Implications for Performance, Teams, and Leadership." *Organization Science* 24, no. 5 (February 12, 2013): 1517–1538. http://dx.doi.org/10.1287/orsc.1120.0795.

Papanek, Victor. *Design for the Real World: Human Ecology and Social Change.* Chicago: Academy Chicago Publishers, 2005.

Pater, Ruben. *The Politics of Design: A (Not So) Global Design Manual for Visual Communication.* London: Laurence King, 2016.

Pavliscak, Pamela. *Emotionally Intelligent Design: Rethinking How We Create Products.* Newton, MA: O'Reilly Media, 2018.

Pearce, Fred. "Energy Hogs: Can World's Huge Data Centers Be Made More Efficient?" *Yale Environment 360*, April 3 2018, https://e360.yale.edu/features/energy-hogs-can-huge-data-centers-be-made-more-efficient.

Pembroke, Beatrice, and Ella Saltmarshe. "The Long Time." Medium, October 29, 2018. https://medium.com/@thelongtimeinquiry/the-long-time-3383b43d42ab.

Penin, Lara. *An Introduction to Service Design: Designing the Invisible.* London: Bloomsbury Visual Arts, 2018.

Perez, Caroline Criado. *Invisible Women: Data Bias in a World Designed for Men.* New York: Abrams Books, 2019.

Peters, Adele. "This Map Lets You Fly along the Path of a Drop of Water from Any Place in the U.S." *Fast Company*, May 28, 2021. https://www.fastcompany.com/90641430/this-map-lets-you-fly-along-the-path-of-a-drop-of-water-from-any-place-in-the-u-s.

Peters, Robert L. "'Quotable Quotes' . . . (Gone Rogue)." Robert L. Peters (blog), January 3, 2019, accessed July 11, 2022. http://robertlpeters.com/news/quotable-quotes-gone-rogue.

Pitt, Joseph C. *Doing Philosophy of Technology: Essays in a Pragmatist Spirit.* Berlin: Springer, 2011.

Platz, Cheryl. *Design beyond Devices: Creating Multimodal, Cross-Device Experiences.* New York: Rosenfeld Media, 2020.

Popova, Maria. "Combinatorial Creativity and the Myth of Originality." *Smithsonian Magazine*, June 6, 2012. https://www.smithsonianmag.com/innovation/combinatorial-creativity-and-the-myth-of-originality-114843098.

Popova, Maria. "Paula Scher on Combinatorial Creativity." Brain Pickings, November 19, 2010. https://www.brainpickings.org/2010/11/19/paula-scher-on-combinatorial-creativity.

Powell, Richard R. *Wabi Sabi Simple: Create Beauty. Value Imperfection. Live Deeply.* Holbrook, MA: Adams Media, 2004.

Power, Samantha. "Samantha Power to Grads: Start Changing the World By 'Acting As If.'" *Time*, May 18, 2015. https://time.com/collection-post/3883303/samantha-power-graduation-speech-upenn.

Powers, John. "I Was Jeff Koons's Studio Serf." *New York Times*, August 17, 2012. https://www.nytimes.com/2012/08/19/magazine/i-was-jeff-koonss -studio-serf.html.

Precarity Lab, *Technoprecarious*. London: Goldsmiths Press, 2020.

"Professor Stuart Candy Publishes Design and Futures." Design, Carnegie Mellon University, January 21, 2020. https://design.cmu.edu/content/ professor-stuart-candy-publishes-design-and-futures.

Puccio, Gerard J., John F. Cabra, and Nathan Schwagler. *Organizational Creativity: A Practical Guide for Innovators & Entrepreneurs*. New York: SAGE Publications, 2017.

Raff, Daniel M. G. "The Book-of-the-Month Club: A Reconsideration." Paper presented at the Yale Economics History Workshop, November 27, 2016, revised January 2, 2017.

Resnick, Brian. "More Than Ever, Our Clothes Are Made of Plastic. Just Washing Them Can Pollute the Oceans." *Vox*, January 11, 2019. https://www .vox.com/the-goods/2018/9/19/17800654/clothes-plastic-pollution -polyester-washing-machine.

Rettberg, Jill Walker. "Ways of Knowing with Data Visualization." In *Data Visualization in Society*, edited by Martin Engebretsen and Helen W. Kennedy, 35–48. Amsterdam: Amsterdam University Press, 2020.

Riggio, Ronald E. "Are We All Becoming More Self-Centered?" *Psychology Today*, July 27, 2017. https://www.psychologytoday.com/intl/blog/ cutting-edge-leadership/201707/are-we-all-becoming-more-self-centered.

Ritchie, Hannah. "Humans Make Up Just 0.01% of Earth's Life: What's the Rest?" April 24, 2019. https://ourworldindata.org/life-on-earth.

Ritchie, Hannah, and Max Roser. "Plastic Pollution." Our World in Data, September 2018. https://ourworldindata.org/plastic-pollution.

Rober, Mark. "The Super Mario Effect—Tricking Your Brain into Learning More." TED Talk at TEDxPenn, May 31, 2018. https://www.ted.com/talks/mark _rober_the_super_mario_effect_tricking_your_brain_into_learning_more.

Rose, Steve. "'Our Biggest Challenge? Lack of Imagination': The Scientists Turning the Desert Green." *The Guardian*, March 20, 2021. https://www .theguardian.com/environment/2021/mar/20/our-biggest-challenge-lack -of-imagination-the-scientists-turning-the-desert-green.

Rosenberg, Alex, and Robert Arp. *Philosophy of Biology: An Anthology*. Hoboken, NJ: John Wiley, 2009.

Rushkoff, Douglas. "Douglas Rushkoff: 2019 National Book Festival." Discussion on Team Human, 2019 Library of Congress National Book

Festival, Washington, DC, August 31, 2019. https://www.loc.gov/item/webcast-8886.

Rushkoff, Douglas. *Team Human*. New York: Norton, 2019.

Sadler-Smith, Eugene. "Wallas' Four-Stage Model of the Creative Process: More Than Meets the Eye?" *Creativity Research Journal* 27, no.4 (November 13, 2015): 342–352. https://doi.org/10.1080/10400419.2015.1087277.

Sagan, Lynn. "On the Origin of Mitosing Cells." *Journal of Theoretical Biology* 14, no. 3 (March 1967): 225–274. https://doi.org/10.1016/0022-5193(67)90079-3.

Saint-Exupéry, Antoine de. *Wind, Sand and Stars*. Translated by Lewis Galantière. Boston: Houghton Mifflin Harcourt, 2002.

Santos, Henri Carlo, Michael E. W. Varnum, and Igor Grossmann. "Global Increases in Individualism." *Psychological Science* 28, no. 9 (July 2017): 1228–1239. https://doi.org/10.1177/0956797617700622.

Schekkerman, Jaap. *How to Survive in the Jungle of Enterprise Architecture Frameworks: Creating or Choosing an Enterprise Architecture Framework*. Bloomington, IN: Trafford Publishing, 2004.

Scher, Paula. "Artist Series: Paula Scher." Interview with Hillman Curtis, 2005. https://vimeo.com/18839878.

Scher, Paula. "Paula Scher on Failure: Interview with Jay Dixit." *Psychology Today*, May 21, 2009. https://www.psychologytoday.com/us/blog/brainstorm/200905/paula-scher-failure.

Schneier, Bruce. *Data and Goliath: The Hidden Battles to Collect Your Data and Control Your World*. New York: W. W. Norton, 2016.

Schüll, Natasha Dow. *Addiction by Design: Machine Gambling in Las Vegas*. New York: Princeton Architectural Press, 2014.

Schulz, Kathryn. *Being Wrong: Adventures in the Margin of Error*. New York: Ecco Press, 2011.

Scoblic, J. Peter. "We Can't Prevent Tomorrow's Catastrophes Unless We Imagine Them Today." *Washington Post*, March 18, 2021. https://www.washingtonpost.com/outlook/2021/03/18/future-forecasting-strategic-planning.

Segura, Julio, and Carlos Rodríguez Braun. *An Eponymous Dictionary of Economics: A Guide to Laws and Theorems Named after Economists*. Cheltenham, UK: Edward Elgar Publishing, 2004.

Seligman, Martin E. P., and John Tierney. "We Aren't Built to Live in the Moment." *New York Times*, May 19, 2017. https://www.nytimes.com/2017/05/19/opinion/sunday/why-the-future-is-always-on-your-mind.html.

Seligman, Martin E. P., Peter Railton, Roy F. Baumeister, and Chandra Sripada. *Homo Prospectus*. Oxford: Oxford University Press, 2016.

Seneca. *Epistulae Morales ad Lucilium* (Moral Letters to Lucilius). London: William Heineman, 1917.

"70% of Companies Fail to Disclose Impact on World's Forests." CDP, July 16, 2019. https://www.cdp.net/en/articles/media/70-of-companies-fail-to -disclose-impact-on-worlds-forests.

Shaikh, Safiya. "'The Contagiousness of Puerperal Fever' (1843), by Oliver Wendell Holmes." The Embryo Project Encyclopedia, July 26, 2017. https:// embryo.asu.edu/pages/contagiousness-puerperal-fever-1843-oliver -wendell-holmes.

Shehab, Bahia, and Haytham Nawar. *A History of Arab Graphic Design*. Cairo: The American University in Cairo Press, 2020.

Sherry, Simon, Sean Mackinnon, and Chantal Gautreau. "Perfectionists Do Not Play Nicely with Others: Expanding the Social Disconnection Model." *Perfectionism, Health, and Well-Being* (2016): 225–243. https://10.1007/ 978-3-319-18582-8_10.

Shobhit, Seth. "Google, Facebook Face $8.8B GDPR Suits on Day One." *Investopedia*, May 29, 2018. https://www.investopedia.com/news/google -facebook-face-88b-gdpr-suits-day-one.

Simon, Herbert A. *The Sciences of the Artificial*. 3rd ed. Cambridge, MA: MIT Press, 1996.

Sinek, Simon. "Sometimes You Are the Problem." Video, 2:10. Posted by 1 of a Kind Media, July 20, 2012. https://www.youtube.com/watch?v=dTYUekxP954.

Slovic, Paul, and Daniel Västfjäll. "The More Who Die, the Less We Care: Psychic Numbing and Genocide." In *Imagining Human Rights*, edited by Susanne Kaul and David Kim. Berlin: De Gruyter, 2015. https://doi.org /10.1515/9783110376616-005.

Smith, Gerry. "Corporations' Political Reckoning Began with a Newsletter." *Bloomberg*, January 14, 2021. https://www.bloomberg.com/news/ articles/2021-01-14/corporate-america-s-political-reckoning-began -with-a-newsletter.

Smith, Martin M., Simon B. Sherry, Samantha Chen, Donald H. Saklofske, Christopher Mushquash, Gordon L. Flett, and Paul L. Hewitt. "The Perniciousness of Perfectionism: A Meta-analytic Review of the Perfectionism-Suicide Relationship." *Journal of Personality* 86, no. 3 (September 4, 2017): 522–542. https://doi:10.1111/jopy.12333.

Spencer, Herbert. *The Principles of Biology*. London: Williams and Norgate, 1864.

Spool, Jared M. "Consistency in Design Is the Wrong Approach." Center Centre—UIE, North Andover, MA, December 12, 2018. https://articles.uie .com/consistency-in-design-is-the-wrong-approach.

"Stanford Behavior Design Lab." Stanford University, accessed February 18, 2021. https://captology.stanford.edu.

Staszowski, Eduardo, and Virginia Tassinari. *Designing in Dark Times: An Arendtian Lexicon*. London: Bloomsbury, 2020.

Strathern, Marilyn. "'Improving Ratings': Audit in the British University System." *European Review* 5, no. 3 (1997): 305–321. doi:10.1002/ (SICI)1234-981X(199707)5:3<305::AID-EURO184>3.0.CO;2-4.

Strubell, Emma, Ananya Ganesh, Andrew McCallum. "Energy and Policy Considerations for Deep Learning in NLP." *Proceedings of the 57th Annual Meeting of the Association for Computational Linguistics* (July 2019): 3645–3650. https://doi.org/10.18653/v1/P19-1355.

Swider, Brian, Dana Harari, Amy P. Breidenthal, and Laurens Bujold Steed. "The Pros and Cons of Perfectionism, According to Research." *Harvard Business Review*, December 27, 2018. https://hbr.org/2018/12/ the-pros-and-cons-of-perfectionism-according-to-research.

Tamm, Eric. *Brian Eno: His Music and the Vertical Color of Sound*. Cambridge, MA: Da Capo Press, 1995.

Tatarkiewicz, Władysław, and Christopher Kasparek. "Perfection: The Term and the Concept." *Dialectics and Humanism* 6, no. 4 (1979): 5–10.

"Teamwork Quotes to Inspire Collaboration and Creativity." *Southern Living*, accessed July 15, 2022. https://www.southernliving.com/culture/ teamwork-quotes.

"Technology Is Not Values Neutral: Ending the Reign of Nihilistic Design." *The Consilience Project*, June 26, 2022. https://consilienceproject.org/ technology-is-not-values-neutral/.

Thackara, John. *In the Bubble: Designing in a Complex World*. Cambridge, MA: MIT Press, 2006.

Tiseo, Ian. "Annual Production of Plastics Worldwide from 1950 to 2020." Statista, January 12, 2022. https://www.statista.com/statistics/282732/ global-production-of-plastics-since-1950.

van Dijck, José. "Datafication, Dataism, and Dataveillance: Big Data between Scientific Paradigm and Ideology." *Surveillance & Society* 12, no. 2 (2014): 197–208. doi:10.24908/ss.v12i2.4776.

Van Doren, Charles. *A History of Knowledge: Past, Present, and Future*. Toronto: Ballantine Books, 1992.

VanPatter, GK, and Elizabeth Pastor. *Innovation Methods Mapping: Demystifying 80+ Years of Innovative Process Design.* Scotts Valley, CA: CreateSpace Independent Publishing Platform, 2016.

van Wyhe, John. "Mind the Gap: Did Darwin Avoid Publishing His Theory for Many Years?" *Notes and Records of The Royal Society* 61, no. 2 (March 27, 2007): 177–205. https://doi.org/10.1098/rsnr.2006.0171.

Von Busch, Otto. *Making Trouble: Design and Material Activism.* London: Bloomsbury, 2022.

Voros, Joseph. "The Futures Cone, Use and History." *The Voroscope,* February 24, 2017. https://thevoroscope.com/2017/02/24/the-futures-cone -use-and-history.

Wachter-Boettcher, Sara. *Technically Wrong: Sexist Apps, Biased Algorithms, and Other Threats of Toxic Tech.* New York: Norton, 2018.

Wallach, Wendell. *A Dangerous Master: How to Keep Technology from Slipping Beyond Our Control.* New York: Basic Books, 2015.

Walters, Kelly. *Black, Brown + Latinx Design Educators: Conversations on Design and Race.* New York: Princeton Architectural Press, 2021.

Watson, Julia. "Julia Watson: 'Survival of the Most Symbiotic'—Live from IMPAKT Festival." Interview with Douglas Rushkoff, December 8, 2020. https://www.teamhuman.fm/episodes/julia-watson-survival-of-the-most -symbiotic-from-impakt-festival.

Watson, Julia. *Lo-TEK: Design by Radical Indigenism.* Cologne, Germany: Taschen, 2020.

Watson, Paul. *Seal Wars: Twenty-five Years on the Front Lines with the Harp Seals.* Richmond Hill, ON, Canada: Firefly Books, 2003.

Weaver, Jesse. "Design Won't Save the World." Medium, August 1, 2018. https://hairyelefante.medium.com/design-is-not-going-to-save-the -world-8985870471a5.

Weaver, Warren. "Science and Complexity." *American Scientist* 36, no. 4 (October 1948): 536–544. https://www.jstor.org/stable/27826254.

Welch, Chris. "The iPhone's Camera Is So Good Because 800 People Are Working on It." The Verge, December 20, 2015. https://www.theverge.com /2015/12/20/10631330/iphone-camera-team-800-people.

"What Design Can Do: Who We Are." What Design Can Do, accessed June 1, 2021. https://www.whatdesigncando.com/about-wdcd.

"What If We Would Regreen the Sinai?" Green the Sinai, accessed May 24, 2021. https://www.greenthesinai.com/home.

"What Is Cathedral Thinking?" Cathedral Thinking, accessed April 26, 2021. cathedralthinking.com.

White, Frank. *The Overview Effect: Space Exploration and Human Evolution.* Reston, VA: American Institute of Aeronautics and Astronautics, 1998.

Wiener, Norbert. *The Human Use of Human Beings: Cybernetics and Society.* Boston: Houghton Mifflin, 1950.

Wilson, Mark. "The Untold Story of the Vegetable Peeler That Changed the World." *Fast Company*, September 24, 2018. https://www.fastcompany.com/90239156/the-untold-story-of-the-vegetable-peeler-that-changed-the-world.

Wilson, Edward O. *The Origins of Creativity.* New York: Liveright, 2017.

Wilson, Simon. "Why It's Not Worth Recycling Plastic." *Money Week*, October 3, 2020. https://moneyweek.com/economy/global-economy/602081/why-its-not-worth-recycling-plastic.

Wong, Leonard, and Stephen J. Gerras. "Lying to Ourselves: Dishonesty in the Army Profession." Strategic Studies Institute, US Army War College, 2015. www.jstor.org/stable/resrep11350.

Wu, Andy. "The Facebook Trap." *Harvard Business Review*, October 19, 2021. https://hbr.org/2021/10/the-facebook-trap.

Wurman, Richard Saul, David Sume, and Loring Leifer. *Information Anxiety 2.* Indianapolis: Que, 2000.

Zöllner, Frank. "Anthropomorphism: From Vitruvius to Neufert, from Human Measurement to the Module of Fascism." In *Images of the Body in Architecture, Anthropology and Built Space*, edited by Kirsten Wagner and Jasper Cepl, 47–75. Berlin: Ernst Wasmuth Verlag, 2014.

Zuboff, Shoshana. *The Age of Surveillance Capitalism: The Fight for a Human Future at the New Frontier of Power.* New York: PublicAffairs, 2019.

Index